D1490649

THE JUROR AND THE GENERAL

M. Patricia Roth

William Morrow and Company, Inc.
New York

Library of Congress Cataloging-in-Publication Data

Roth, M. Patricia.
  The juror and the general.

  1. Westmoreland, William C. (William Childs),
1914–   —Trials, litigation, etc.   2. CBS Inc.—
Trials, litigation, etc.   3. Trials (Libel)—New York
(N.Y.)   4. Vietnamese Conflict, 1961–1975—Military
intelligence—United States.   I. Title.
KF228.W42R68   1986   345.73′0256   86-8766
ISBN 0-688-06085-4   347.305256

Printed in the United States of America

First Edition

1 2 3 4 5 6 7 8 9 10

BOOK DESIGN BY RICHARD ORIOLO

For my family, and especially for
my husband, Bob, to whom I could never explain
the daily anguish I experienced in the courtroom.

CONTENTS

Introduction   11

Definitions of Acronyms and
Abbreviations   13

The Perfect Juror   15

The First Issues Are Avoided   30

Going on Guts   52

The Observer   75

Absolutely Not!   89

A Warning Flag   133

Was There Light at the
End of the Tunnel?   161

An Impossible Decision   185

Let the Evidence Speak
for Itself   209

Less Is More   232

Artful Fillibuster   250

One Little Lie   263

THE JUROR AND THE GENERAL

INTRODUCTION

Background of the Trial

The Uncounted Enemy: A Vietnam Deception was a documentary that CBS aired in early 1982.

The program was prompted by investigations that had taken place concerning a larger enemy than had been reported, especially by Sam Adams, a former CIA analyst whose job it had been to estimate enemy strength in South Vietnam between 1966 and 1968.

In researching Sam Adams's allegations, the producers of the documentary found further evidence to support his claim; that the Tet offensive (the turning point of the Vietnam War) should not have been the military surprise that it was.

On January 23, 1982, CBS aired the program, produced by George Crile and narrated by Mike Wallace.

The documentary produced minor waves in certain circles and a few major newspapers carried editorials about the broadcast.

On January 26, 1982, General William Westmoreland, who had been commander in chief of ground forces in Vietnam at the time of the Tet offensive held a news conference denying the allegations set forth in the broadcast.

The issue seemed to be put to rest.

But then, in May 1982, *TV Guide* carried a cover story, written by Don Kowett, accusing CBS of defaming General Westmoreland with the material it had presented in its broadcast *The Uncounted Enemy*.

This reignited interest in the documentary, and CBS began an intensive internal investigation reevaluating the materials it had used.

General Westmoreland felt he had grounds for a libel suit and he approached some prestigious attorneys, who refused to take his case.

In the summer of 1982, the Capital Legal Foundation, headed by Dan Burt, approached General Westmoreland offering to handle the case at no expense to him.

CBS offered Westmoreland fifteen minutes of prime-time to air his views and refute the broadcast. Westmoreland declined the invitation and continued with litigation.

On September 13, 1982, General William Westmoreland filed a libel suit against CBS, Mike Wallace, the narrator of the broadcast, George Crile, the producer of the broadcast, and Samuel Adams, who had acted as a consultant for CBS. He initiated the litigation in Greenville, South Carolina, which was in his home state.

Cravath, Swaine & Moore was the law firm CBS hired for its defense.

Attorney David Boies, representing the firm, went to Greenville, and was successful in having the trial moved to the U.S. District Court in New York City. Judge Pierre Leval presided over the case.

On October 9, 1984, jury selection commenced for the *Westmoreland* vs. *CBS* trial.

The First Amendment was at issue.

Definitions of Acronyms and Abbreviations

CIA Central Intelligence Agency

CICV Combined Intelligence Center Vietnam

CIIED Current Intelligence and Indications Estimate Division (General Danny Graham)

CINCPAC Commander in Chief Pacific (Admiral Ulysses S. Grant Sharp)

Communication information information regarding enemy picked out from the airwaves; radio eavesdropping

Collateral information all other information: reports, documents, POW interrogation, diaries, etc.

COMUSMACV Commander of U.S. Military Assistance Command Vietnam (General William Westmoreland)

CORRAL Study of Vietcong: infrastructure, the political cadre

DIA Defense Intelligence Agency

ICEX Program program designed to eliminate the enemy

INSUM daily Intelligence Summary

KIA killed in action

MACV Military Assistance Command Vietnam

MACV J2 Military Assistance Command Vietnam Intelligence
(General Joseph McChristian
General Phillip B. Davidson)

NIE National Intelligence Estimates

NSA National Security Agency

ONE Office of National Estimates (part of CIA that published the NIE and SNIE)

PERINTREP Periodic Intelligence Report (a large document of a couple hundred pages published monthly)

Pike committee a House subcommittee headed by Otis Pike from May 1975 to February 1976. It held hearings on several issues affecting U.S. interests around the world, including the Tet offensive.

RITZ study of irregular forces

SAVA Special Assistance for Vietnam Affairs

SD Self-defense

SNIE Special National Intelligence Estimates
SSD Secret Self-defense
WIA wounded in action
WIEU Weekly Intelligence Estimate Update (weekly meeting)
14.3–67 Special National Intelligence Estimate (SNIE) report for 1967

THE PERFECT JUROR

October 1, 1984

My plans are foiled again. Just when things are running smoothly.

M. Patricia Roth is summoned for jury service October 9, 1984, at 9:00 A.M. in the United States District Court for the Southern District of New York. So says Raymond F. Burghardt, Clerk of the Court.

He must be crazy! I got his first notice last April and wrote saying there must be some mistake: I live in Putnam County, sixty miles away from Foley Square in downtown Manhattan.

Okay, so I live within his jurisdiction. But with more than seven million people living in New York City, why are they calling me?

I'm really upset. Halloween is a busy time in an elementary school art room. The children go wild with their designs. Then there's the advertising course I've just begun with the sixth grade, and my reading group is starting new material that I want to monitor closely. The art budget for the school is due in three weeks' time.

What's worse, the big real estate deal I've been negotiating is in the crucial stage. I've been relying on some big commissions to get me out of the classroom and into my own studio full-time. This has been my five-year game plan and the commission I've been working on would have shortened the plan by a year. Ah, well. The best laid plans . . .

Fortunately, Bob has had great success in creating a new career as an insurance underwriter after spending twenty years on Wall Street. Both his daughters are in college. Tracy is just starting pre-med; Leslie is a freshman. I can't figure out how many more years we'll be concerned about budgeting and such.

Oh well, jury duty is only for two weeks.

October 4, 1984

All I've done for the last few days is plan, organize, cook, and freeze meals. Thank heaven for the invention of the microwave oven.

I've also arranged new lesson plans and reviewed them with my substitute, Mrs. Jensen. I've done the first draft of the art budget for the school. I've notified my active real estate clients and referred them to colleagues at the office who I think will work well with them.

But I'm annoyed with myself for not having gotten further with my sculpture commission. I'm still having trouble planning what I want the end result to look like, and the statues are due in two months' time. Perhaps I can do some sketches while I'm performing my civic duty. I gather there are long hours of boredom involved. People have time to read books.

Got a phone call from the girls. Leslie and Tracy are coming for the weekend. Hooray.

October 7, 1984

I only had one couple to take out on Saturday, but with all the houses I'd lined up, it took all morning. They're thinking seriously about one of them.

Now that the girls are in college, weekends like this are becoming a rarity. It seems like yesterday that they were here all the time.

We all turned into ten-year-olds at the Outhouse Orchard. We each picked a big bag of apples. There was a prize for the biggest and reddest one. We ate so many while we were picking that I couldn't believe we had room for the pies when we got home. Tracy and Leslie peeled apples. Bob sliced them. I baked.

It was fun.

October 8, 1984

Bob and I have been planning the logistics of getting me to court on time.

Bob is savvy to the train commute and he says I have to leave the house at six to get to Foley Square by nine. There are two trains I wanted to take. The 6:50 out of Croton Falls will get me into Grand Central by 8:03. The 7:03 will get in at 8:24.

The subway from Grand Central to Foley Square takes thirty minutes. But depending on the day and the crowding, that time could be longer.

Bob says I'd better take the 6:17 the first day just to make sure I get to court by nine. "By the time you drive the twenty minutes from Carmel to Croton Falls, park the car, get a newspaper and coffee . . ."

At least if it gets to be too much of a hassle Bob says we can stay overnight at his father's apartment in the city. I'm thankful for that alternative, and I feel sorry for anyone else traveling this distance who doesn't have a similar back-up.

I laid out my clothes for my big day in court and got ready for bed. Bob turned on the eleven o'clock news.

The announcer said that jury selection would begin tomorrow for the libel trial of the century: *Westmoreland* vs. *CBS*. Bob got all excited.

"I knew it! I knew it!" he said. "You're going to be on that case."

"Who's Westmoreland?" I asked.

"Oh God!" he groaned. "Where were you during the Vietnam War?"

I just looked at him and shrugged my shoulders.

"Never mind," he said. "You'll find out. You'll be the perfect juror."

My heart sank. I set the alarm for 5:15 and went to bed.

October 9, 1984

Bob was right. The commute is horrible, and I may be on a big case. A lot of other people seem to think so, too. I never saw so many reporters in one place in my whole life. They seemed to be standing on each other's shoulders to see what was going on. And they were lined up two and three deep along the walls of the courtroom. I saw more people in court today than I usually see on my way to work each morning.

It had started out normally, I guess. I reported to Room 109. I had no trouble finding it because half the population of New York City seemed to be spilling out of the doors.

Forms were passed out and our names were called, one by one.

Problems were eliminated. Someone couldn't speak English. One woman had a sick mother at home; another had four unattended children. A nervous-looking man had his own business and a family to support.

A woman clerk spoke to us through a microphone from a platform up in front. She told us about mileage forms and toll receipts.

I marveled at the cross-section of people in the jury room. Everyone imaginable was represented. There were two well-dressed women knitting. A lot of people were reading newspapers; some were into paperbacks. Many were just sitting gazing at everyone else. One man was wearing a lumberjack shirt. He was big. He sat with his legs spread apart and his arms folded high over his chest. He looked mean and angry. A couple of people down from him sat a Hassid, reading a prayer book. There was a man in a three-piece suit sitting two rows behind. He was frantically working on some papers from his briefcase.

The bailiff was calling out in a booming voice. He looked perfect for the part: bald, corpulent, serious. "If there is anyone else who has a problem, raise your hand now. This is your last chance to make your appeals."

Finally, we were ushered out to the hall. We were lined up along one side, and ten of us were placed on each elevator as it came along.

We were literally crammed into a courtroom, seated in pews, just like the kind you would see in a church. People were lined up along the sides. There were elevated platforms up in front of the room. Several people sat there, and a judge sat on the top level facing us all.

Everyone around me was whispering. There's so and so—he's on Channel 5. There's . . . he's on cable—no! That one there is General Westmoreland. You know he has a suit going against CBS. I shivered.

The guy next to me was reading *Variety*. He was wearing camouflage fatigues. He told me he was going to get off. He works in a court upstate someplace. The bald man from downstairs was now standing on the platform below the judge. He was spinning a drum and calling names. Meanwhile, they had passed out questionnaires for us to answer. One had thirty-seven questions on it. It was called "Checklist for Prospective Jurors." Not one damn question applied to me. I could speak English. I'd never been in the armed forces. I didn't read *TV Guide* or follow any movies or read books on Vietnam. Nor did I care about it. I had always believed that we were in good hands in Vietnam—both in terms of our leaders in Washington, and also in the military. But as I read down the list, I felt downright embarrassed. Bob's always complaining that I don't keep up with anything but art and real estate.

One page was titled "Questions and Answers for PETIT (Trial) Jurors." The page was difficult to read. The typing was tiny, the inking irregular. Some words were dark, others so light you couldn't make them out. The lights in the courtroom were glaring and high overhead. I kept looking around the courtroom. It *was* set up like a church. Even the jury box resembled the section for the choir.

I began to read another page we'd been handed. Questions for each juror:

1. Age
2. How long have you lived in this country?
3. Occupation over last five years (unemployed)
   (retired)
   Employers
   Length of employment
   Number of jobs in last 10 years
4. Marital status
5. Occupation of spouse
6. Occupation of children
7. Level of education (details)
8. Residency over last five years
9. Residency between 1965–70

I wondered why they weren't asking for my Social Security number.

People's names were being picked out of the drum like at a lottery. With my luck this would be the drawing I'd win, when even in the school lottery I can't win two dollars.

Eighteen names were called. Some people answered that one of the thirty-seven questions applied to them; others requested secret discussions at the side bar. A court reporter with his little machine followed them everywhere. Everything would stop until the court recorder was in position. Some jurors were eliminated; new names were called from the drum. The process went on all morning.

The judge painfully went through each and every question on the list.

"Have you had any association with the military? Did you ever know anyone in the military? Are you certain? Did any of your children serve in the military?"

A woman in the back row of the jury box shot up her hand.

"You know someone in the military?" asked the judge.

"Yes, Your Honor," she answered.

"Who?" asked the judge.

"My ex-husband, and my daughter's former fiancé."

"And when did your husband serve in the military?" continued the judge.

"He was in the Second World War and I don't know what he did or what his rank was," she answered.

"And your daughter's fiancé?" he continued.

"No! He's not her fiancé anymore. But you know they were childhood sweethearts and then they got engaged, but then they didn't get along, so she dumped him."

Laughter broke out in the courtroom.

The judge answered, "Gee, you had us in suspense there. I'm glad it all worked out!"

A young woman raised her hand to another question. "You have dealings with parties or attorneys involved in this litigation?" asked the judge.

"Yes, Your Honor!"

It turned out she was affiliated with one of the law firms representing the parties.

People in the courtroom got a kick out of it, and the judge dismissed her.

One of the young attorneys up in front said laughingly, "Well, I tried." That got even more response.

The judge was now reading a long list of names—of people and of companies. I guess they were all the people and companies involved in this trial. He mentioned something to the effect that there were ninety witnesses to appear. I was certain I didn't hear that correctly, but then . . .

We were released for lunch. I called my friend Dorothy, who teaches at Pace University, just down the street. We met for lunch, a treat we've rarely been able to enjoy with me teaching up in Westchester in a rural school. Lunching in a restaurant is unheard of. Maybe being in Manhattan for a while could be fun!

When I got back into the courtroom, there was a woman around my age sitting next to me. She introduced herself and we began to chat. Cheryl pointed out various people around the courtroom. "He works for the *Daily News*." She peered up over the bulky shoulders in front of her. "And that man over there, the one with the red tie—he works for CNN."

When I found out she knew all this because she worked at the New York City Public Library, I became excited. I told her about the commission I had for the Christmas show at an art gallery. "I've been searching high and low for pictures of the Grimm Brothers. I have to make statues of them to fit into a library setting. By any chance, do you know of any pictures or photos of them?"

Not only did she know of them, she was in charge of the picture collection and she promised to look them up for me. I gave her my address. Fate works in strange ways.

The commission has been worrying me for six months. I'd sketched out ideas and had made a few feeble attempts in soft sculpture, and lately I'd been building an armature in my basement. I was in the process of covering it in chicken wire. The figures were life-size. They were due the week after Thanksgiving.

When the judge had informed us that this trial could go on for four months, I was trying hard to think of how I could tell him that I had a commission to work on. Unless he was an artist, he wouldn't understand.

My part-time real estate business would be dead. Thank God I had had that closing last week.

Two weeks out of my life. I didn't know how I could handle it. Every name the judge called from his long list was recognized by a man in the first row of the jury box. The only name I had recognized so far was Robert McNamara. I knew he was big in Washington, but I really wasn't sure of his position.

I began to chastise myself: You really must begin reading more. I buy *The New York Times* regularly, but I really just skim it. I use the ads for my art classes—I never miss the food section or the home section. I'm aware of some headlines.

Since I began with real estate four years ago, I stopped reading the Arts and Leisure and Book Review sections. I scarcely have time. It's strange. I got involved in country real estate to broaden my horizons. I'd felt so sheltered just teaching elementary school. Instead, it's probably isolated me even more. I can tell you every house on every street in a five-town area that's up for sale—why it's for sale, for how long, and why it's not selling. But in the context of the outer world, who gives a damn? I can't even recognize ten famous names on a list of over one hundred.

I began to glance through the paperback I had picked up at a newsstand across the street. Their selection was minimal, probably for jurors like myself.

The only author I had recognized was Ken Follett. I'd enjoyed a book by him on my vacation two summers ago. I thought I could escape on some spy mission to alleviate the boredom I'd heard accompanies jury duty.

Finally, the lawyers were questioning the man who knew everyone. "And how did you know Admiral Bunker?" the lawyer asked.

"Oh! I never met him, but I wrote his obituary," he answered. It turned out he worked for *The New York Times*. He was dismissed, along with four other people who'd been there since early this morning.

The procedure went on and on. I lost count of how many were replaced, but I think it was around fifty or sixty people. We were finally given a break. Everyone raced for the phones. Reporters were calling in stories. I was getting madder and madder as they monopolized the phones. I had to get through to Bob before 4:00 P.M. I finally did as they were announcing time for court to continue.

When we got back in, three more were dismissed. I was surprised at a couple of them. I didn't see anything wrong with their answers.

The court bailiff was spinning the drum. He called out M. Patricia Roth. My heart jumped into my throat. I felt this strange dull ringing in my ears. That was me! My usual confident self turned to rubber. I wondered how I could stand. I looked around for the suitcase I usually carry as a purse and realized that today I had crammed everything I own into a tidy-looking purse.

I don't know how I made it to the front of the courtroom. Every face was looking at me. I was glad I had decided not to wear one of my usual arty-type outfits, but instead opted for my real estate business image: tweed jacket, silk shirt, straight skirt, and heels I could walk in. I climbed up to the only available seat in the top row. I turned around and saw all those faces and I almost fainted.

Somewhere in the distance, I heard my name again. I was told to answer the questions on the list, please. Start with your address and your age.

How anyone could hear me I didn't know. I could hardly hear myself. My voice sounded like it was in an echo chamber. I didn't want to give my age in front of all these people. I made the mistake of stealing a glance at all the reporters sitting there, pencils in position. My God, everyone in the world will be able to read . . .

"I'm forty-two years old. I've lived in this country my whole life. I was born in Connecticut." I was actually speaking!

"I've taught art for twenty years. I'm also a real estate agent. I'm married. I have . . ." I went on and on. The reporters were feverishly writing. The court recorder was clicking away. Every eye was glued on me. My throat got very dry.

"And where were you between 1965 and 1970?" asked the judge.

"I lived in San Francisco, where I had an art gallery." Mr. Burt, the lawyer for General Westmoreland, asked me one additional question.

"Who do you most admire in politics or government?"

I simply answered, "I wish there were someone."

We were dismissed at five. By this time I had been moved up to seat number two. They were still choosing, so I wasn't sure if I would be kept on the jury.

I didn't have time to concern myself with this, for I had to be at open house for parents at the school where I teach. By the time I got out of the city, with traffic and rush hour, I only had time to grab a quick hamburger and barely got to my classroom when parents started pouring in.

I got home at eleven-fifteen. I was in bed by eleven-twenty.

October 10, 1984

The judge had impressed us with how absolutely important it was for us to be on time. Many people would be inconvenienced if one juror was late. Court would not be held if we were all not present.

We had started driving from Carmel at seven forty-five. It was a beautiful morning. Perfect weather—high sixties, promising to go into the seventies. I was anxious about my dress. I wanted to look good yet be comfortable. All my clothes had paint on them from the classroom. In the back of my closet, I found a suit I seldom wore.

I found out yesterday that all you do in court is people-watch. I wore my new silk blouse.

We made it to midtown by nine-ten and there the anxiety really began. Traffic came from every direction—Lights, honking, cabs, trucks. Everything was at a snail's pace. It took forever to get to Centre and Pearl streets.

I thought we would never get there. I finally jumped out of the car a block away and ran through Foley Square, up the steps, and arrived in the courtroom one minute late—court was already in session. The judge was at the side bar with the attorneys from both sides.

Several other people were late. A deranged person had been sitting on the subway tracks at Forty-second Street and all power was shut off. Several people later told me accounts of waiting for a half hour on a train between stations. (There was a full moon last night.)

The judge came back to the stand and announced that of all the days court would be in session, this probably was the only one in which we could proceed without everyone present. He was informed of the subway problem and was aware that these things happen, but he again lectured us on the importance of being on time.

The same procedure was followed as the day before. Someone whose name was chosen at random was called to the jury box. Some asked to speak at the side bar. Others were dismissed after questioning.

This went on until around three. We had had an hour and a quarter for lunch, which I learned was barely enough time. By the time you got the elevator and walked all the steps out of the building, you had already used fifteen minutes. Then, to find an eating establishment with no major lines and a seat was another trick, even though there were thousands of places to choose from.

Around three, the last two names were called, one of which was Cheryl's, the librarian with whom I had become acquainted yesterday. I knew she was not disposed to sitting for a trial that could possibly take four months.

Sure enough, as soon as she was called, she asked to go to the side bar. I was not surprised that they denied her request to be excused. She seemed to round out the jury. There were now eighteen of us in all—twelve jurors and six alternates. The judge stood up and announced that the jury had been selected.

From this point on, declared the judge, we in the jury would not be allowed to enter through the front of the courtroom or mingle with *anyone* having to do with the case. We were to use only the restrooms in the jury room and the only time we were allowed to leave the building or make calls was at lunchtime. At this point he called a fifteen-minute recess and had the clerk show us our way to the jury room. I felt like I had just entered prison.

The jury room was just like those you see in the movies. A long table filled the center of the room, with twenty leather chairs arranged around it. There was a long coatrack at one end and a men's room and ladies' room at the other. It was drab and depressing.

The clerk pointed out a list of rules that were typed on a sheet of paper by the door, and he dumped a package of paper cups on the table. The only thing we could use those cups for was a drink of water. The room was otherwise bare.

We were instructed that this was not a cafeteria. If we wanted to bring coffee in the morning, that was okay, but that was it.

He left us and we all looked at each other with mixed emotions. Do you realize how long we could be here? I want to get sick. Want to get out now? Should we try Trivial Pursuit? You make the turkey for Thanksgiving—and on and on.

They called us back in to the courtroom. All the other jurors had been dismissed, the press had moved to fill up all the seats in both sides now, and the alleged psychologist was gone. The rumor that had spread through the jury box was that the large white-bearded formidable-looking character who kept staring at all of us was a psychologist hired by the plaintiff to help choose a favorable jury.

It was four o'clock. The judge swore us in and then started addressing us. He read the rules, the protocol, the steps to expect. He stressed constantly the magnitude of this trial, the interest it had stirred, the national nature of the entire issue—the First Amendment was being questioned.

He emphasized what an important job had been laid on our shoulders and how we had to keep a clear head and an unbiased attitude— not allow anyone to influence us. We had to stay away from all TV, radio, and newspaper accounts, which he admitted would be difficult because of the great interest this case had stirred and the opposing viewpoints. He went on and on for an entire hour.

I was scared.

Westmoreland was there from the start. He constantly examined every face in the jury box. His table was in front of the judge; it was a long, large table and his counsel was there by his side.

Behind Westmoreland was the defense—the counsel, two young men and a young woman, and George Crile, plus someone I assumed to be Samuel Adams. (George Crile and Sam Adams were being sued along with Mike Wallace and CBS.)

The judge spent a lot of time talking about a chart. He passed out a copy to each of us. It was a four-part "uses of evidence" chart that came to be known as the X chart.

```
                    EVIDENCE RECEIVED
                           ON
                      BOTH TRUTH                            HERESAY
                          AND
                       STATE OF                               ↙
    EVIDENCE            MIND            EVIDENCE
       ON                                  ON
     TRUTH                            STATE OF MIND
     ONLY                                 ONLY
                      EVIDENCE
                    NOT RECEIVED
                         ON
                   TRUTH OR STATE
                      OF MIND
```

October 11, 1984

Court was to start at ten and since we had been dismissed late last evening, we stayed in the city. I fell asleep at ten and woke up later, looked at the clock, and was certain it was ten after six in the morning. When I came back from the bathroom, I saw Bob dead to the world. I realized it was only one-thirty. I lay down, but was so wide awake it was painful. The antique clock on the mantel donged—a rich, loud dong. I realized, at two, that it would dong again at two-thirty, and so on. I tossed and turned and didn't sleep.

Finally, at three-fifteen, I decided to get up and make some tea. I felt a cold coming on and decided my grandmother's cure would be the answer—tea with lemon and brandy.

I wrote in my diary, determined to be more conscientious. I filled in the details of the last two days.

The judge had passed out pads yesterday afternoon. He did this quite ceremoniously, telling us that previous rulings disallowed note-taking for the reason that the juror with the most notes would have had an advantage over the others. However, in this case he felt the trial would be so lengthy that we should take notes to keep a handle on what had transpired.

However, the notepads were to stay locked up in the jury room. It was even a misdemeanor to remove the pens that we were given from the courthouse.

Taking notes was difficult. I did not have a grasp of the characters involved—or the positions they held. I didn't know how to spell their names, nor did I know shorthand. We were told to listen to, but yet to ignore (in so many words), the opening statements of the attorneys. They, as the judge put it, were salesmen, fighting a defense for their interests (their clients).

The third day started off with all of us taking the back way into the jury room. We had been told that the only stairwell and elevators we could use were in the main lobby and we were *not* to mingle with anyone; we were to inform the judge if anyone attempted to discuss anything about the trial with us. We were not to acknowledge anyone from the courtroom except each other.

We sat there patiently waiting in the jury room. The clerk came in and counted us and left; they came back and counted us again and at ten-twenty we were ushered into the courtroom.

The judge gave us an eight-minute lecture on being on time and then proceeded with business. The business was the plaintiff's attorney starting his speech. An hour went by and we had a recess, at which point the jurors were up in arms at the fact that we had all been present and had been miscounted. They demanded an apology from the judge. When we were called back in, the judge began. "Boy is my face red. I was informed you were not all present. I apologize. However, let the warning sit for the real occasion."

Everyone in the courtroom laughed.

Fortunately, the judge and the parties involved appeared to have a sense of humor.

Mike Wallace was present.

Counsel for the plaintiff took up most of the day. He seemed to me young and inexperienced but well prepared. He had about thirty pages of notes, but for the most part he read them unemotionally and occasionally paused to show segments of the television show, *The Uncounted Enemy*, on TV monitors positioned in front of the jury box. He showed what had been cut, and he tried to show that the cuts distorted the issue, or the meanings, of the final product. It was hard to understand. Several of the jurors admitted when we recessed for lunch that they could hardly follow the proceedings. It was disappointing, because we knew we had a long afternoon ahead of us. We were careful not to try to influence each other, but we couldn't help but discuss some of our feelings. It also appeared that the press was having the same difficulty following the proceedings. Four of us jurors lunched together in a small restaurant, and we mostly discussed the fact that we would probably get to know each other quite well. We would be going through the holidays, and perhaps the winter, together. We arrived back at one-ten, as the judge instructed, and spent the first part of the afternoon listening to the concluding statements of the plaintiff's attorney. At three-thirty, we recessed to allow the defense attorney to ready himself.

When we arrived back in the courtroom, it was obvious this presentation would be quite difficult. Two enormous easels were placed before us. The defense attorney began. He purposefully reviewed every statement he made and made sure that we had an idea about what he was trying to say. Once he went back to refer to a statement from notes, stating he wanted to make sure he was delivering it correctly—for it was a quote. He, too, showed segments of the program at issue and gave us his point of view.

Wisely, he asked the judge if we could be dismissed by four-thirty. He knew we were already overwhelmed with statements from the previous lawyer.

We were dismissed at four forty-five.

October 12, 1984

I arrived at Foley Square about forty minutes early. I met two of the other jurors outside the courthouse by the coffee wagons that line the street.

I sensed we were fortunate in the warmth the jurors showed for each other. They all seemed overly conscientious about getting along and having everyone feel like a part of the group.

By now our environment was old hat; the slow elevators were familiar, and we greeted each other like old friends. Court was called relatively on time, and the defense attorney continued in the same manner as the previous day.

He was slow, deliberate, only referring to notes occasionally, and he continued using oversize easels to illustrate contents of various documents. I was aware that much of this was not evidence but points he felt would illustrate his case.

I couldn't help but recall the thesis I had to write for my master's degree. The same type of thought and outline had to go into his presentation: first, state the problems, then use illustrations to verify your thesis. Quotations from recognized authorities were used—all those things we had learned to build up an argument.

Fortunately, the defense attorney was a good teacher. He explained the meaning of initials. My head was spinning with MACV, CINCPAC, OB, etc.

When mentioning names, he would slowly explain the men's position in command, and he too referred to the documentary *The Uncounted Enemy*. He showed us segments that the plaintiff's attorney had showed, but continued them past the point the opposition had played.

It was tough. I really wasn't sure what the real issues were. And the lawyers weren't spelling them out so someone like me could understand them. Both were convincing. Just when you thought for sure the side you were listening to was the correct one, you would hear the opposition and be equally swayed.

The judge was correct. I must discount the opening remarks, keep an open mind, and pay attention only to the evidence. Until now we had heard none. The defense attorney informed us at one o'clock that he only had fifteen more minutes of presentation. Would the judge allow him to continue and dismiss us all for the day?

The judge ruled accordingly.

We were all delighted to be dismissed. All of us agreed we had gotten a lot more out of defense's presentation. We wished each other a good weekend and went off in all directions.

I met Bob at his dad's office, picked up noshes at Zaro's in Grand Central, and we made our way home. Life goes on.

I spent the whole next day running errands, washing clothes, cooking for the week, writing bills, returning phone calls. Everyone I knew must have called, even people I hadn't seen in years.

Monday would almost be a welcome relief.

THE FIRST ISSUES ARE AVOIDED

October 15, 1984

I rushed downtown. The fear of being late had been deeply planted. I had a horrible breakfast at McDonald's and tried to read my novel. Finally, I went to the courthouse. I was the first one in the jury room. I was fifty minutes early.

One by one, the jurors arrived. We shared weekend experiences, signed in, complained about the room. Finally we were called in to the courtroom.

Everyone was there—same seats, same characters, same reminders from the judge.

It was time for the plaintiff's attorney to call his first witness.

Mr. Burt—I finally learned the name of the plaintiff's attorney—had done a lot of homework. He seemed more relaxed. He, too, brought out an oversize easel and instructed an assistant to place on it a large felt panel showing the chain of command.

First, he introduced his witness, Dr. Walt Rostow, who had been National Security Chief under Lyndon Johnson. With his help, the chain of command was outlined on the panel for all of us to refer to.

Before all this began, Mr. Burt questioned Dr. Rostow: Where do you reside? And what's your age? What positions have you held in the past? Have you written any books? (He had—twenty-four in all.) Presently, he was a professor at the University of Austin. Previously, he had been at Oxford, Yale, Harvard. He did indeed sound like he had impressive credentials.

The judge's words rang in my ears. Do not look at the package, the salesman. Listen to the evidence.

He was questioned for well over an hour by Mr. Burt. Do you recall? In your opinion? Where were you in November '67? Do you recall a meeting that took place in Saigon? Did you have figures of Vietcong? Did you? Do you? Have you? I couldn't take notes fast enough, so I just stopped and listened.

The defense attorney, Mr. Boies (I have his name now), raised a few objections. Most were overruled. It sounded as though CBS didn't have a case.

We broke for lunch.

I could tell by the glazed look of all the other jurors that they were as confused and exhausted as I was. Could it be possible that we were to be here for four months? It seemed hard to believe. My backside was aching.

Lunch was a welcome relief. We stretched, walked, ate at a fish and chips place. I was happy that the other jurors were likable. We returned at one-ten as instructed and one of us was missing. We all groaned when the court clerk came in to count us.

At one-fifteen the other juror arrived. We all had complained about the elevators; they were terrible—slow, unreliable. Sure enough, the missing juror had been waiting for one in the lobby.

We were ushered into the court at one-twenty and all the characters were in position. Counsel for the plaintiff finished questioning Dr. Rostow, and the defense attorney took over.

Again without notes, he reestablished his edge. He questioned and requestioned, but remained quite civil.

Boies asked Dr. Rostow to repeat certain statements, and he questioned others.

All I could really ascertain was that Dr. Rostow really had no confirmed figures about the strength of the Vietcong, nor could he verify that the President had.

The main issue seemed to be this: CBS had presented a documentary called *The Uncounted Enemy*. North Vietnam had its military forces in South Vietnam that supposedly numbered around 280,000. However, they were also running a guerrilla war and thousands were involved who were not counted as soldiers. They included the SD and SSD—

self-defense and secret self-defense. The SD were the townspeople from the area that the battle was taking place in. Some of them were normal self-defense. Others, I think, were secret self-defense, those who possibly moved around from place to place. They were women, children, and old men who did not wear uniforms. Supposedly they were untrained, so our military was questioning the propriety of counting them.

However, they were armed. A gun from an untrained civilian is as capable of killing an American as a soldier's gun. Were they indeed untrained? How could an American soldier shoot a ten-year-old?

This supposedly untrained guard numbered well into the thousands, totaling perhaps 400,000. I'm not quite sure of that figure! It's huge.

It all seemed to boil down to this: Was the President aware of these staggering numbers? Did Westmoreland inform him? Did he know from other sources? Did the advisors at the top know of their numbers?

According to the CBS documentary, 25,000 infiltrators were coming into South Vietnam each month.

The figures that the advisors to the President were using was something in the neighborhood of 8,000! The real issue I had to remember was this: Did CBS purposefully and maliciously tell a falsehood? Did it tell a falsehood knowingly and with the purpose of ruining the reputation of General Westmoreland?

Mr. Boies continued to cross-examine Rostow, who refused to be pinned down to numbers. Were there 15,000 each month? I can't answer that. I had no way of knowing. There were conventional infiltration counts and the Johnson infiltration counts. Mr. Boies jumped on this—from then on it was—well, according to the conventional infiltration counts, would you estimate that there were 10,000? Still no affirmation.

It seems as though the conventional counts came from POWs and CIA counts. As Rostow admitted, these were grossly inaccurate because of the time element. Court was dismissed at five-ten. We were to meet tomorrow at ten.

Be on time.

October 16, 1984

The race began before dawn. I felt like I was on the Grand Prix, back roads, side roads, main roads—traffic at the most unexpected places!

I hit the city at about 8:40 "to the best of my recollection." (I'm beginning to think like a witness: never totally pin yourself down; never say anything definite.)

It is my belief . . . it was my belief at the time . . . to the best of my recollection . . . if I recall correctly . . . I was told . . . I don't remember.

Anyhow, I finally arrived at the courthouse—out of breath—at 9:48. Had my coffee and bran muffin in three giant gulps. The court clerk opened the door at precisely 10:00.

David was missing. We all groaned. He walked in five minutes later. Court began immediately.

The procedure was this: First, we signed a sheet, then the clerk would check the sheet, call for us, and we'd line up in the hall in seating order. We would file in to the jury box, take our seats. The judge would greet us with a good morning and immediately court would proceed.

Walt Whitman Rostow was still on the stand. We listened to more painful testimony. Dr. Rostow, it was obvious, still refused to be pinned down. He had these broad losses of memory. He was quite a likable fellow; he had the kind of looks that we immediately took to. It was obvious from his presence and from his credentials that he was a man of remarkable intelligence.

Was his memory really failing him? Was this his way of avoiding definite answers? My belief was that he wanted to avoid giving answers. But then he would go through long elaborate stories to tell a point, sounding like he was most sincerely trying to be helpful. On the other hand, he was avoiding issues both attorneys were trying to pin him down to.

It was Juror 14's birthday. I asked the foreman if we should take up a small collection to surprise her after lunch with a birthday cake. He kind of shrugged, but Juror 3 started passing a note.

I feel like I'm in grammar school. Here we are in a courtroom filled with press from the four corners of the country, with top CIA agents, generals, and judges sitting in front of us, and we're passing a note— "It's Norma's birthday, 50¢ for a cake." It's welcome comic relief.

We returned from a short recess to Robert W. Komer on the witness stand. His testimony was the exact opposite of Dr. Rostow's.

Mr. Komer was the chief civilian deputy to General Westmoreland and in charge of CORDS in Vietnam. He was definite, direct, no-nonsense. His testimony was factual and precise.

Where Dr. Rostow had a soft literary way about him, more like the philosopher, Komer was all business. (All I could think of was from whence they came.) Komer was obviously aware of just what he was allowed to say—how far he could go—and he went to the edge, it appeared. Whereas Rostow was more skittish about saying too much.

Komer concentrated on himself—what Komer said, what Komer did, what Komer thought, what Komer put into action.

He was immediately aware, he said, when he got to Vietnam that there was something wrong with the numbers that the MACV had been using. He spoke of heated debates among MACV and CIA representatives.

Komer felt that you *could not* include the SD and SSD and the home count in the figures—they were too inaccurate. There was a large gap between what had been represented and what would have to be reported—such an enormous gap that the response would be catastrophic. The issue of logging data constantly came up. The figures they were getting from official sources were several months off.

So many initials were thrown at us, "typical military lingo"— MACV, SD, SSD, CINCPAC, COMUSMACV—it was difficult to get it all straight. Who was who? Who were the good guys? The bad guys?

I felt quite inadequate. However, from what I could ascertain, Komer stated that they all—at least those in Vietnam—were well aware of a problem with the numbers of the enemy. They had a problem among themselves on how to count them.

Was the President ever made aware of these numbers? (*I* didn't find that out today.) It was obvious, though, that they had been concerned about the press finding out.

Several documents were given to us as evidence—heresay! evidence! truth! Again, my head was swimming. Could this possibly go on for four months? I found it extremely difficult to believe.

We broke for lunch—found a great inexpensive Chinese restaurant that served fast take-out food, too. Six of us lunched outside. We bought Norma a cake and clapped as she blew out the matches we used as candles.

The attorney continued with Komer; the same type of testimony continued. We broke at four-forty. Court will begin at ten sharp. You are dismissed.

October 17, 1984

I had open house last night with the fourth- to sixth-grade parents. Specifically, I had to make a presentation to the sixth-grade parents about their children's program and be prepared to talk with the parents of my reading group. It was hard to keep my mind on the task at hand.

After a day at Foley Square listening to the inner workings of the

CIA tallying numbers, to suddenly focus on eleven-year-olds was difficult, to say the least. However, it went well.

I didn't get home till 10:30 and was up at 5:40 A.M., showered, dressed, and out the door by 6:45. My Grand Prix started again.

I had to get money from the Action Banking Center in Katonah—there are none in the vicinity of Foley Square that can help me—I needed eleven dollars to give to the parking attendant when I leave my car.

Money for coffee, lunch, a subway or bus if I find too much traffic to get downtown in time. I have on the average been going through twenty dollars a day.

For the first time in twelve years I've understood why my husband, who does this every day, is so reticent to take me out to dinner. Just to work in the city costs a fortune.

When I heard that I was to get thirty dollars a day for jury duty and forty-one cents a mile one way, I felt I was robbing the bank—not really, but I felt it was fair. Actually, I'm barely breaking even.

I must hand in the money to my employer, who in turn gives me my normal salary. Anyhow, it is a sacrifice. The change is welcome for a week or so, but I can already tell that months of this will be wearing.

In any case, aside from the philosophizing and personal sacrifices, it is exciting to be involved. It is definitely hard to sit, sit, and sit and listen and concentrate. It is difficult being herded out into the jury room every time there is a deliberation.

The room is depressing—especially for a person like me, who has color around her all day. The starkness and drabness of the room are disturbing.

However, there are new people to be acquainted with (the jury), who are rather pleasant and eager to get along—and then there are newspapers and magazines.

The book I've been trying to read is difficult to get into. Not because of the content, but because of the situation. Reading a book requires concentration. That is difficult with seventeen other people in a small room. Newspapers and magazines lend themselves to this because you can stop and start.

We were all there at 9:55. At 10:00, the court clerk opened the door—"Oh, fine! Great! I'll tell the judge you are all here!!" They called us into court at 10:15.

Komer was still on the witness stand! (Had he been there all night?) Actually, throughout the day, he and the attorneys made references to long hours of deposition-taking—last night, Saturday, etc. The lawyer finally made a crack: "I'm glad my client knows the long hours I'm putting into this case."

As a matter of fact, something that disturbs me is the naïveté of the attorneys. I find it rather puzzling that a case of such supposed magnitude is to be fought by two young lawyers who seem to have little courtroom experience. They seem to be basically competent men, one with a little better speaking presence, but they both seem basically to have little courtroom experience.

I could be wrong. Have I seen too many movies with F. Lee Baileys and Melvin Bellis? And I'm encouraged to see a politeness between the parties concerned that I hadn't expected. It's almost like it's a college debate and they are going through the motions of being big-time attorneys.

Often they are called to the side bar and there are moments of levity in the courtroom. Always a welcome relief, I must admit.

It is obvious that the whole court case is basically splitting hairs on interpretation. I wish I had even read a cover story about the upcoming trial.

It is very disconcerting in one way to have not an inkling of what the issues leading up to this case have involved.

Oh, I definitely understand what is being told in the courtroom. The story is unfolding.

I haven't a clue as to what the critics—the analysts or the press—think of the whole matter. I have taken quite seriously the warnings of our good judge: "You are not to discuss this case with anyone—not even your family. You are not to listen to TV coverage or read articles in the newspapers or magazines—especially editorials!"

Having been rather apolitical is perhaps what makes me a valuable juror. On the other hand, I question my opinions—not having shared them, really, or even perhaps tested them is more like it.

I can only base my decision on what is happening in the courtroom—evidence, testimony, and gut feeling.

My feelings change with each witness and go back and forth with whichever attorney has command of the floor.

It seems CBS has an open-and-shut case. On the other hand, it appears that Westmoreland has handled his affairs on the up and up—not necessarily to the American people or the press, but in general to his immediate advisory staff. I'm still not sure about his supervisors—I think in a broad sense, yes.

I get the feeling after today's testimony and putting it into context with yesterday's that if there was any coverup or distortions of facts, it was most likely on the CIA level! Did Johnson know the figures? Hmmmm?

I get the feeling someone higher up than Westmoreland should be on trial. I think just maybe he was just doing the job he was told to do.

I could be wrong, and of course with eighty more witnesses to be called, the plot should thicken!!

Anyhow, Komer spoke again:

All day, in fact. He is rather articulate. He is a forceful, convincing speaker.

However, he doesn't shut up. My God, can he go on. He is rather self-impressed. Amazing. He is low man on the totem pole. The totem pole we are discussing, anyhow. The lower the position, the more verbal the character seems to be.

The cross-examination from the defense attorney produced much of the same. Immense ego—he (Komer) was a wonderful asset to the Vietnam entourage. Just ask him (Komer)—he'll tell you how great he was.

He, of course, produced some points to question upon cross-examination. How accurate was his testimony, really? Not necessarily how accurate, but how valid was his information? He quite frankly seemed to be in a position such that the information being asked for would simply not be available to him.

I wonder what the other jurors think. No one has discussed opinions. We have been quite careful to heed the judge's words. We discuss the case, but it's mostly to clarify terms and to tidy up questions on notes. I have been overwhelmed with the military penchant for initials—SD, SSD, MACV, COMUSMACV, J2, SNIE.

As the witnesses are talking, I am so busy trying to figure out what the hell they are talking about with these initials that I'm losing the gist of the whole conversation. I asked the foreman to ask the judge to have a list made up for us to clarify these initials.

He just about flatly refused to, claiming how can he do it? There is no such list—I'm the only one who has asked, etc., etc. I'm a little annoyed, to say the least.

My feeling is they'd be delighted to have the jury know what is going on in the court. Some of the main points that happened in the courtroom today, in my estimation, were:

An excerpt from the Pike report seemed to confirm to me that this problem of the uncounted numbers is not new. The Pike report found them irregular!! Hmmm.

The testimony of Komer, I would say, is dubious. He has come up with a few humorous comments. I wish I'd been able to write quickly enough to capture them. One was that upon reviewing the intelligence reports of SNIE, we realized that SNIE had a SNAG.

SNIE, I believe, is another word for CIA. He also talked at length about the WIEUs, which were Weekly Intelligence Estimate Updates. These WIEUs were held every Saturday, and the bigwigs from MACV reported to General Westmoreland at these meetings. The judge did remind Komer on several occasions he was to answer testimony only and not debate the counsel. Komer did like to debate!

In any case, four days, two witnesses—I guess we will be here for four months. I do hope further witnesses will be less skirting of the issue.

We were dismissed at three-fifty and told to return tomorrow at the usual time.

October 18, 1984

The weather has been nothing short of perfect up through today. It's almost too much to hope for. Though we are confined to the court and jury room and can't enjoy these last lingering days of summer weather, it does make getting to and from the courthouse rather pleasant.

Foley Square, I can see, must be brutal during inclement weather. The wind can whip through there like nobody's business.

I took the subway today. We stayed at Bob's father's apartment last night. Found a good spot on the street, so decided to leave the car there. Last night the doorman told us he chased an ornery-looking guy away from our car. Even the doorman next door reported the guy had actually come back and tried to break into the car, but he called the police and they chased him around the corner.

This has made me rather anxious about leaving the car in the city. Having had two radios stolen in two months' time leaves me very anxious, to say the least.

Court started as usual. The hellos in the jury room, exchange of stories and filing into court.

I took matters into my own hands upon the prodding of several other jurors who were also having difficulty following the military jargon.

I handed a note to the court clerk, who in turn handed it to the judge. He read it aloud to the court. It stated:

Your Honor,
Would you be so kind as to arrange to have a list made up for us of

military initials and their meanings—those that are pertinent to this case.

Though we understand SD—Self-Defense; SSD—Secret Self-Defense; MACV—etc., etc., there are several that have left us confused. It is difficult to follow who is being spoken of when we are busy trying to comprehend the meaning of these terms.

The courtroom broke into laughter. It was evident that the majority shared our confusion.

The judge directed the letter to the lawyers of the plaintiff and defense and asked if they wouldn't act upon this matter for us. It did become a bit clearer today as the testimony went on. Both attorneys stopped after each group of initials to clarify their meaning. Even one of the main witnesses, a former major general, when asked to tell what a certain group of initials stood for could not remember the entire meaning.

Komer had a bit more testimony and was dismissed after about forty-five minutes. It was mostly cross-examination and defining of terms.

He confirmed that the argument even back then was whether the SD and SSD should or should not be included in the overall figure.

He described a couple of instances where the head of MACV and SNIE almost came to blows over this fact—how to report it. He felt they were too difficult to count.

I thought to myself: was it a case that it was too difficult to count them, so therefore ignore them. Was it that they couldn't be contended with for official estimates—or that *he honestly* felt they weren't a military threat?

Colonel Caton was the next to be called to the stand. He had impressive credentials, dating back to World War II. He was elderly and most likable. He did have a touch of a hearing problem, but a very dry, solemn direct manner. He pulled no punches, told it like it is, and often broke up the courtroom with his answers—maintaining a very dry composure the whole time. He never cracked a smile. The audience really was laughing with him, not at him.

At one point he told the attorney to speak to him. "I can't hear you when you turn your back."

The attorney apologized and said, "Sir, can you hear me now?"

"Yes," he answered.

The attorney repeated his question and added, "If you can't hear me, just ask me to repeat it."

Colonel Caton answered, "I just did."

MACV INTELLIGENCE STRUCTURE

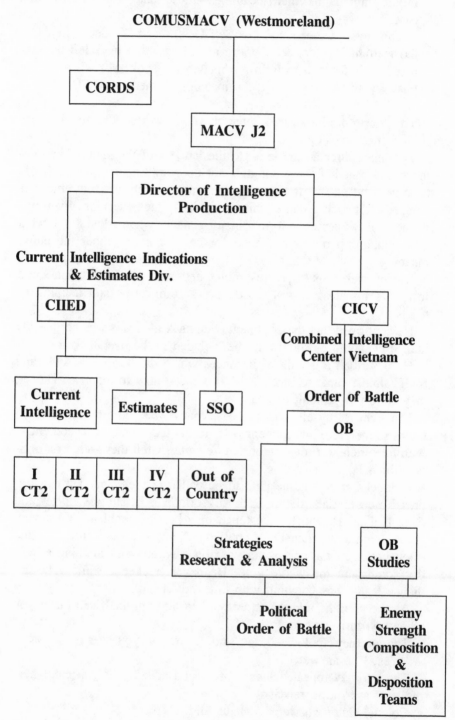

Everyone but Caton laughed. I'm sure he must have chuckled inside, but he never let on.

It seems his job was to get daily estimates from the field of the enemy's strength. He published reports every day. He established that this was no easy task because he had to not only send out the reports, but also establish their validity.

You can't always rely on what a POW will tell you. They'll tell you anything they think you want to hear. The information has to be verified.

He was a regular at the weekly WIEUs, but it seemed as though he placed himself in a lower command capacity. However, the data that crossed his path seemed to be more pertinent than what had crossed Komer's.

Caton was modest about his role, stating that those higher up looked at a broader spectrum. He, Caton, was only interested in these daily estimates. He verified the position of the guerrillas and SD and SSD. He stated, "You only counted them in relationship to the area you were concerned with. If you were going into district I, you only counted the presence of the SD and SSD in that area, whereas the regulars could move around.

He described the role the SD and SSD played. Although they did not use conventional arms, they did do a lot of damage. They made booby traps—passive booby traps, and I can't remember the names for them—but booby traps that amounted to nails and such, attached to boards that upon being activated would do considerable damage to troops."

He was cross-examined on these issues at length. His answers were very matter-of-fact. That they were definitely an entity that had to be dealt with is how I interpreted the whole thing.

I want to pause for a minute here to give some of the feelings that have bothered me.

Say we sent fifty thousand men to Vietnam. For argument's sake, forty thousand were armed soldiers, five thousand were clerical, and five thousand had assorted jobs—commanders, messengers, drivers, and the like. Do we count that we have fifty thousand men fighting or forty thousand? If we count fifty thousand, then why can't we count the entire manpower *they* have?

No one seems to have addressed this issue. Who is really counted in our OB—Order of Battle—only armed militia, or all the supporting staff. I would think that anyone who is capable of inflicting a casualty would be counted!

Back to the courtroom:

Mr. Dorsen took over for Mr. Burt today. They are the counsels for the plaintiff. Mr. Dorsen seems to be a senior in the law entourage.

At first, ten minutes or so into things, I felt aha! We have a more experienced courtroom attorney. That thought lasted ten minutes.

He was boring. He read—he'd pass out a document—put it up as evidence, and then read the entire document along with us.

If you want to read boring material, read some military documents.

Every break was long overdue. The most painful part of this duty is to try to concentrate.

By four o'clock I was consciously trying not to nod off in front of a couple of hundred people, especially when so many of them were counting on me to judge them.

Today was *painful!*

Thank God for our judge.

I'm quite impressed with him. He is competent, astute, and articulate. I can't believe how he sits there taking notes all day long. Both counsels should be thankful for him because he has several times, for both sides, stopped questioning and asked his own questions, to clarify statements.

Colonel Caton was asked if anyone had been assigned to help him gather this data. "Oh yes!" he said, "but it didn't help much. I had to dismiss him!"

"Why, sir?" asked the counsel.

"Oh, he was incompetent. He just couldn't do the job." He paused. "Hey, I didn't want to give these guys a poor report. You had them for thirty days and you had to write a review on them. I just didn't want to do it. I'd tell him, 'Go get a job you can do.'"

The counsel asked, "Did you get many people who couldn't do the job, sir?"

"Oh yes, quite a few."

"How many?"

"I can't answer that—I don't remember. You know, you have a bad experience and you just want to put it out of your mind, forget it. You don't want to remember it."

At this point the court recorder spoke up. "Sir, could you speak up, talk slower. I can't catch what you're saying."

Caton replied, "Oh! I forgot about you. Yes, sir!"

The courtroom broke up!

When Caton was asked if he had ever heard Westmoreland say "What will I tell the President?" he said, "No, he never said that. That would have been totally out of character. But I heard Wheeler say that." He was questioned further on this by the defense attorneys.

"When did you hear Wheeler say this?"

"Oh, on a couple of occasions." He went on: "Wheeler had just returned from Washington, where he gave the President a briefing on how we had crossed over the line or something to that effect. The numbers of enemy were declining, and he came back here to Vietnam and we gave him these new numbers and he was furious. 'What am I going to tell the President?' he said. I said to him, 'Well, just tell him you didn't know the figures before, and you just got them from us. It should be easy.' I realized later that it was very presumptuous of me to be telling a four-star general what to do. He wasn't too happy." (I felt this whole revelation on Wheeler was quite important.)

I'd say Edward Caton's main points were that the SD and SSD were forces to reckon with—they could indeed do damage. However, they were limited to their particular locale. Everyone was concerned about them. How do you count them? It was difficult.

After Colonel Caton was dismissed, General Peterson took the stand. His main job seemed to be to verify documents and cables that the plaintiff had as evidence. Many of them were objected to by the defendant. They seemed to verify the fact that Westmoreland had indeed passed on the information—but others were reluctant to pass it on to Washington, because they were afraid of the press getting wind of it. It seemed to me that the CIA was most reluctant to accept this information. The defense had a document that they were anxious to submit as evidence. Apparently, it had figures of movement of guerrillas and infiltration into areas like Cambodia and the DMZ. The figure of 3,000 seems to ring a bell with me.

Peterson was quite adamant about the fact that the DMZ was not an area you'd consider for infiltration; that is not the route they'd take. The DMZ was off-limits: You wouldn't count those figures; it's not on the right path to South Vietnam.

Court ended with a deadlock on this issue. I wouldn't be surprised if it was picked up on Monday, or perhaps at least in a deposition by the defense attorneys.

We were dismissed at four forty-five with the usual precautions—don't speak to anyone. We had Friday off. Back to court on Monday at ten.

I think I've forgotten to mention that we've been talking about the lawyers' clothing. The plaintiff's attorney comes in every day with a different suit; he seems to favor the sea green-blue tones.

The attorney for the defense has worn the same jacket every day. I thought I was the only one who had noticed, but the ladies began to mention it too. We all enjoyed making verbal bets each day if he'd change his navy blazer with gold buttons and navy blue weave tie.

Today he did. He had on a navy pin-striped suit with a tie in the navy family. I believe he may be consciously trying to avoid looking slick.

October 22, 1984

Peterson was on the bench when we entered the courtroom. All the same faces were there—same characters, same seats.

It was like a movie had stopped in a freeze and at ten Monday morning it was once again set into motion.

"When we left off last week," the attorney for the defense resumed his cross-examination.

Was it last week? My God, what happened to the weekend? I had to go and teach Friday—that was like walking through another lifetime. Was it only three weeks ago that I was doing that every day?

Have I been in this courtroom for only two weeks? How disrupted my life seems. I spent the weekend getting caught up. I made the foundation for my sculptures, cleaned the downstairs bathroom, acted as a go-fer for my carpenter. Did the post office, bank, recycle junk route, and entertained Louise and Greg on Sunday. No wonder Monday came so fast. I ran all weekend long.

The drive down here is treacherous. One has put in a day's work negotiating traffic. Over two hours on the road each morning and every night is not conducive to longevity. Actually, it's a pleasure to be able to sit down for these long stretches. If only it wasn't so difficult to concentrate. Concentrate on each word, sentence, new testimony, new exhibits—this is evidence, this is not evidence.

"Sir," he continued. "Let us go back to Thursday, when you mentioned that you had been at a meeting with . . ."

The cross-examination went on and on. Peterson was cautious not to give any more information than he had to, but it seemed to be his nature. He just wasn't a talker. I could picture him twenty years ago. He just did his job—didn't ask questions. If he had any, he kept them to himself and went about his own business. He might have spouted off to his wife now and then in a rare moment, but for the most part, he would have kept it all inside. If the general said to do this, he's in charge, so do it. That's it. That's the kind of person he seemed to me.

It's terrible, I can't even remember what he said today. We can take notes in the courtroom, but we must leave them there. I'm trying hard to get impressions from each day. Be able to remember key passages.

But it's hard—it's one big blank. Even the faces blend into each other. Who said what? Who was on the stand today? What did they say? What were the key issues?

Did anyone say anything relevant today? What is relevant? Truth? State of mind?

One of the most amazing things that I'm experiencing in this whole experience is "I'm looking through a window!"

A window—I'm sitting here day after day to see one small capsule of an event. We have here a general who claims he was defamed through a documentary that a big giant network produced on him. He is so angry, his ego is so crushed, his reputation is so tainted by this documentary, that he is willing to drag the network to court, suing for $120 million!

What is so awful about this documentary? The program stated that General Westmoreland had lied about the number of enemy in a war fought eighteen years ago. Actually, we are discussing the fall of 1967 and into 1968, so that makes it seventeen years ago!

He knew the number of enemy that he and his men were facing, but in order to keep the President and the American people from feeling too bad—or too pessimistic about this war—he refused to count the secret self-defense and the self-defense and maybe some of the political cadres and maybe a few guerrillas. Therefore, the numbers of the enemy didn't look so bad. They only had to fight about 294,000—instead of 420,000.

One decision that this general, with such impressive credentials, made seventeen years ago.

I guess if we had won the war anything he did would have been wonderful. All, of course, based on the same mind, the same individual, the same state of mind: the same reason for making decisions.

After all, any person in authority has a multitude of decisions to make in regard to the daily business at hand, the enormous overall picture, and then the public relations. Any person in authority has these types of concerns. It's a large picture.

He has a big responsibility to a lot of people. Then we have the press—CBS—what are its responsibilities? The general is looking at state of mind. The camera is looking for truth: What is truth? Can it be told in pictures? Statistics? Is it formed? Do they make it up for a story? Can they stretch the truth?

Anyone who has heard that I was chosen as a juror gets ecstatic— my God, the Westmoreland case! All these famous people—it must be so exciting! How does one break the bubble?

Everyone else's life is so exciting, so romantic, so wonderful.

Mike Wallace is in court most every day.

Oh, there's Mike Wallace, was my first reaction. But it's been two weeks now—so, big deal! There's Mike. I never heard of George Crile before, nor did I even know there was a living Sam Adams. However, there they are—just average men. Nice-looking, nice clothes, but here they are in the court every day, just like me.

General Westmoreland—a name every man has probably heard. Every man that follows wars—TV news coverage—until this trial—

I knew not of his existence . . . Now, if he had been Louis Morris, Van Gogh, Delacroix, Cézanne, George Segal, or Louise Nevelson—then I would have gotten excited. Art is my bag, war is not!

I closed my eyes during Vietnam. I didn't wave flags. I didn't protest. I didn't even watch the news when Vietnam went on. I sang, I painted, I had an art gallery in San Francisco while these men were making decisions about telling the American public that they really didn't know how many enemy they were really fighting.

I knew not of his existence . . . Now, if he had been Louis Morris, Van Gogh, Delacroix, Cézanne, George Segal, or Louise Nevelson—then I would have gotten excited. Art is my bag, war is not!

For the last fifteen years I've been teaching art, doing art, making art, trying to make money to just do art and closing my eyes to the world of men fighting each other on issues of government and the economy and foreign relations.

Suddenly, in the midst of my pastoral life—art and country house and country real estate and apple pie—I'm rudely awakened.

A juror for *Westmoreland* vs. *CBS*!

I'm not sure what is affecting me more—the fact that my life as an ostrich is rudely interrupted or the fact that I'm disillusioned with what I'm experiencing.

Court case—federal court—famous people involved—$120 million lawsuit—an important case—the libel trial of the century—the First Amendment is being questioned. How exciting.

Is this all there is? Is this what important people do? Sue each other for their egos? Make up stories to get a good story?

All I can ascertain after two weeks of testimony is: This whole issue about the number of enemy soldiers has been fought for more than twenty years. They didn't agree then, they don't agree now. Is this what big generals and chief justices and the CIA do all day? Argue over how to count?

But I have been called upon—quite at random—to be a judge. Thank God there are eleven others!

What are they thinking? Do they feel like me? They look intent.

They are taking notes. I am taking notes. Do I look intent? Who am I? I am a mere subject in this vast universe—randomly called upon to judge these men, who, I am told, are famous and are arguing the very First Amendment of our country.

I must pay attention—

I must listen to the evidence—

This is now my job—to judge.

Peterson leaves the stand and Charles Morris is sworn in. Charles Morris also enlisted in the Second World War. He, too, started out as a National Guardsman. Did he have his head in the sand like me and sidestep in?

He became a career man. He was called upon to serve in Vietnam. He said he wouldn't volunteer, but they got him in.

Is that how it happens?

"Sir, could you tell me when you first were stationed in Vietnam?"

"What was your position?"

"Were you there during 1967 and 1968?"

"Who was in charge?"

It was always the same, to a degree. Davidson was there. McChristian was there. When will I meet them? Will I?

Westmoreland was there. Johnson was President. The same CIA. MACV had the same ideas. The same argument.

Apparently, it had been the SNIE or the CIA versus MACV all along. They both had numbers, and each wanted to use its own.

Apparently, there was a compromise and MACV won out. All the witnesses so far seem to have worked at one time or another for MACV.

For the most part, any real evidence that has been presented from the plaintiff's side, it seems to me, the defense could use too. There is such a thin dividing line in the argument. I can't believe some of the evidence that is being brought up. It sounds like the defense should be using it.

Charles Morris had been involved in intelligence for MACV. He talked about some guy he fired. Apparently, we're going to have him as a witness for the plaintiff also.

Apparently, Parkins refused to obey an order. Morris had asked him to make up a formula that would enable us to count the enemy better. We had a formula for wounded in battle—for every 1 dead, there were 1.5 wounded. Out of every 150 wounded, 35 would die.

Anyhow, Parkins refused to carry out the order. He said it's impossible—it can't be done—I won't do it. So Morris fired him. Morris pretty much confirmed what everyone else has said. The argument over SD and SSD went on and on—CIA versus MACV figures.

MACV figures won out. There was a bit said about Hawkins, who told each group what it wanted to hear.

He reported MACV official numbers, but then said he personally thought they should be higher.

October 23, 1984

It's warm, high sixties, and overcast. We went to the South Street Seaport for lunch today. I just wanted to walk—fast and hard—my legs needed it.

It was wonderful to see some color—crafts, food, clothes, more food, cobblestone streets or, rather, brick streets. Brick walls, beautiful window displays, the sky behind.

The courtroom is austere—nice paneling, comfortable chairs, but austere. I'm afraid to wear color in there. I felt guilty about my red bead necklace. I want to look presentable. I'm sitting up in a jury stand in front of up to two hundred people a day.

The first two rows of the courtroom are filled with artists, looking at you with binoculars tied to their heads. My God, you want to look presentable!

In the classroom, all I'm concerned about is comfort—and how easily I can clean these clothes. Suddenly, I'm forced to use the half dozen garments I own for presentable occasions.

Well, if the defense attorney can wear one jacket day after day, I guess six outfits are acceptable for a juror.

Today we spent the first hour and a half watching a video on all the uncut tapes that CBS made of interviews with Colonel Gains Hawkins. After about a half hour of taking notes, I realized he was pretty much saying the same thing over and over again. The same questions in different ways—all basically leading to the number of uncounted troops and why that came to be.

Hawkins, I liked. He was a feeling person with a nice, soft yet direct way about him. That all seemed to come across in the interviews.

He had an interesting face, and the way the camera framed it in the interviews fascinated me. His face was dominated by a pair of dark-rimmed glasses. He had a delicate nose that had a line sliced thinly from its end to his thin lips, and the line continued at the top of his nose halfway up his forehead. He had two pronounced smile lines that fell down into his jowls and two identical lines falling from the corners of his mouth. With that vast forehead for lack of hair, I couldn't resist it anymore—I started sketching his face alongside my notes.

Occasionally, the video offered an interesting fact that I jotted down, but in the meantime, I had fun—I did a sketch.

I was delighted to hear the defense attorney say after the end of the tape that Colonel Gains Hawkins had been subpoenaed to be a witness and we would see him later on in the trial. I felt that was something to look forward to. After hearing a person's name mentioned so much and hearing an hour of his testimony in video, it would be nice to see him in person. At one point Hawkins told about taking the figures to General Westmoreland and his reaction. He never said to change anything—he said go back and take another look at those figures. We all knew what he meant.

When we got back from lunch, General Davidson was called to the stand. So that's what he looks like! His name had been mentioned several times already, and I had already made a mental picture.

General Davidson looked like a hawk—long neck, bald head, hard eyes, determined mouth, and glasses to accentuate the picture.

He said pretty much what most of the witnesses have said so far. It was boring to hear the same questions asked of each witness. What was your background? When did you first join the military? When did you arrive in Vietnam? What position did you hold there? What was your feeling as to the numbers being reported?

Yet it was fascinating to hear how many different ways you could say the same thing!

Each with a slight deviation. It was the deviations that you recorded in your notes.

Each one said one minor thing that became an issue to you because it was different.

Fascinating. It became an art—just like a real investigation.

Though Davidson commanded attention—looked the part and spoke with authority—he was nervous. He kept asking questions to be repeated, and he kept asking the judge if he was allowed to say this or was this confidential material. It kind of kept you awake—hoping to record something that perhaps was a slip of confidentiality. He asked to be excused early. He was tired, he said. What kind of information is classified? If it's anything like the exhibits coming out in court—cables and letters and secret documents—you can rest assured it's *boring*.

How can anyone spend his life being concerned about hiding real numbers? From the testimony we've had so far in court, all anyone did between March 1967 and January 1968 was hide numbers—lie about numbers and worry about numbers.

I was grateful to hear testimony today on the other ways they spent their day. They did have other concerns.

It was interesting to hear James Meechem on his video today—more evidence for the plaintiff! I really can't believe the plaintiff is using some of this stuff to make us favor his side.

One of the things that Meechem said is that there was an overabundance of chiefs, not enough work to go around—people were looking for things to do, in so many words.

George Crile interviewed him on the video, reading letters Meechem wrote to his wife while stationed in Vietnam. He admitted writing the letters, and he admitted that he had probably written under stress at the time. But he denied anything at this date.

He can't remember—it wasn't important—the letters were out of context—they were simply a day's account of frustration.

Meechem was nervous, anxious to get the interviews over with and obviously trying not to remember those days.

He admitted that Daniel Graham came to him to change the data base in the main computer and Meechem refused.

He admitted he felt squeamish about doing it and tried to talk Graham out of it. But seeing he was his superior, there wasn't much he could do.

Then Meechem proceeded to say that the numbers were inaccurate to begin with. So what difference did it make? Indeed, the plot is thickening!

Meechem went on to give his recollections of the account of Parkins being fired. He answered the question George Crile posed: "Was it dangerous to go in to Morris with higher figures than he wanted?"

Meechem said, "No, it was dangerous to go in and yell at Charles Morris."

There was laughter in the courtroom.

High points of the day: Any time Danny Graham's name was brought up, the witness said something to the effect that he couldn't be wrong (Danny Graham thought this of himself). It makes sense then that that kind of personality would go so far as to change figures in a computer to prove himself right.

Hawkins discussed a young analyst, Richard McCarthy, whom he described as a sensitive, honest analyst who worked his ass off.

He did a good job. He told Hawkins about a meeting he went to that he described as a bunch of rug merchants selling their wares. They were exchanging numbers like nobody's business. It was like a card game. He was shaken by the experience.

He had worked hard to compile those numbers—they were his baby—and he felt this was dishonest and false.

Hawkins said he (Hawkins) was no virgin. He tried to console McCarthy.

MACV had a meeting with Carver, who represented the CIA. Carver gave his solution to counting SD and SSD—verbally count them, put them in a footnote.

Davidson objected vehemently. Westmoreland and Carver agreed—that was it.

Morris was for himself, according to Meechem. After Tet, Westmoreland ordered all on-duty administrators to carry weapons and wear fatigues.

Meechem's letter to wife:

"Someday it may come out as to how we lied about the figures."

GOING ON GUTS

October 24, 1984

The day started out with the judge lecturing us about the witness's "state of mind." Then Davidson continued his testimony.

"After the Tet offensive, did CICV infiltration reports ever report the number of infiltration to be 25,000 North Vietnamese for the month of September?"

"No, sir."

After the Tet offensive, did CICV infiltration reports ever report the number of infiltration to be 25,000 North Vietnamese for the month of October?

"No, sir."

After the Tet offensive, did CICV infiltration . . . it went on for November, December, and January.

Interruption.

Sir, the reports came near that figure in January.

Where did you get the report from? Where did they get the report? What did you think about the report? Every question—every answer— took ten minutes. I watched the clock this morning.

Twenty-five minutes—one question was asked. Either it wasn't stated coherently or the court found bad form or the witness didn't understand or the opposing attorney objected to its form.

Twenty-five minutes on one damn question.

Davidson had the stand for most of the day. But there were long periods—thirty minutes, forty-five minutes—when the jury was excused to the jury room.

Form—procedure was the apology. Davidson was nervous—elderly and nervous. He didn't look as elderly as he acted. He didn't look as forgetful as he acted. He looked like a hawk, as I said before. Hawks don't forget! Davidson did! He couldn't remember what he said in a deposition yesterday.

Half the day was spent asking questions; the other half spent in rebuttal of his deposition last night—last year. He disagreed with what he said ten minutes ago!

He was questioned a great deal about Tet. Eighty-four thousand was the number of enemy.

How many were killed? Forty-five thousand, sir.

Is there a formula for wounded? Yes.

One-point-five wounded to every 1 killed—that brings the wounded number to—hmmm, oh, 67,500.

That brings the number to 112,500, sir. Oh, well, some people are wounded twice, and then there were 5,000 civilians killed—and, oh yes, 5,000 political cadre—

Sir, what does it—

As I said in the beginning—

You can only watch, listen, go on guts. Someone is full of shit.

Davidson reminded us it takes six months to get a clear picture. You don't get to see some infiltrators until they get out of the jungle.

Some surface five months later.

Today was a long day in the jury room. I felt sorry for Davidson. He looked like he was under a lot of stress. I was told he'd been sick.

October 25, 1984

My friend Claudia, who also works in the city, picked me up at 6:50 A.M., and we drove in together. Bob had work to do at home before he went into Manhattan. He hoped to meet me at court today if he got all his work done.

It took us a long time today. Traffic was bumper-to-bumper all the way from the Taconic and Route 6 in Mahopac till we hit our exit off the West Side Highway in Manhattan. I was beginning to wonder if I wouldn't be late.

I got to court around nine forty-five, exhausted.

Mr. Burt made opening statements.

Mr. Boies made opening statements. It's a game.

"Do you recall yesterday General Davidson said this—not what Mr. Burt just told you . . ."

Commander Heon was called to the stand. He was short, out of proportion—big head and shoulders, short arms and legs. He looked like a worker who took orders, did his job, and didn't ask questions. He looked like a fighter who respected his superiors.

Most of these witnesses are retired. It is evident these men still respect their commanders. They are reticent to disclaim them. Heon's immediate supervisor was Colonel Caton. The colonel, who I felt was a credible witness, appeared last Thursday, the eighteenth.

These men were compiling daily intelligence data, which we've already been informed needed a higher clearance than the CICV intelligence reports, which compounded monthly estimates. Heon testified that he briefed General Westmoreland every day.

He said current intelligence was not interested in the self-defense numbers. Khe-Sanh was his main concern (that was an area in Vietnam).

Current intelligence was not interested in guerrilla self-defense, SD, or SSD secret self-defense. They were only concerned with the regular armed forces of North Vietnam. They gathered their data from captured documents, CIA reports, POWs, etc.

I think I'm beginning to see the light. Each one of the people we have been listening to is only concerned with one area, one aspect. Of course! That makes sense. Each person or department reports one aspect to the general. He in turn gathers all the information. Actually, then, no one of these witnesses would really know if all the figures were being reported or not. I feel kind of foolish that it took me this long to figure that out. The military is so overstaffed that no one knows what anyone else is doing.

Heon had only praise for Danny Graham. He claimed he was concerned over erroneous Order of Battle figures. He wanted to review the OB from CICV and have his own analysts review it.

Heon said they knew of movement of enemy over borders, but not how many. He also said Adams had contacted him in 1980, saying he was writing a book. Heon was annoyed that Adams kept asking questions about Graham. Could it be that Adams's suspicions of Graham are the same as mine?

Remember, you have not heard all the evidence or seen all the witnesses. You must not allow yourselves to form any opinion until you have reviewed all the evidence. The evidence is all that counts.

A strange man appeared in the courtroom. I've noticed him before, only when certain witnesses are on the stand. He is big. He has a tough look about him. He doesn't look like an attorney or act like one. He takes no notes. However, when they go to the side bar to review certain questions, the mystery man goes to the side bar also.

I believe he may be with the CIA or some secret-service agency. I think, if I've noticed correctly, he only is there when someone is appearing from CIIED [Current Intelligence and Indications Estimate Division], where they needed a higher clearance due to data they were working with.

General George Godding takes the stand. He is a large, trim man with chiseled features and a firm jaw. He has a striking presence, and you can tell he was good looking in his youth. His stance is military. Looks like he means business.

He is questioned by Mr. Dorsen, the older attorney from the group representing the plaintiff. I'm not sure who makes a poorer appearance—Dorsen or Burt. They are unconvincing speakers; they do not talk with firmness.

It's hard not to fall asleep when they are doing the questioning.

Most of the testimony they're looking for from Godding is to verify that he took these OBs to the big meeting in Virginia in August 1967. He was to brief the higher-ups. Finally, after several trips to the side bar, certain documents were able to be used as evidence, one of which was a page of records, which Godding had taken to the briefing.

It looked acceptable. All the groups we've been hearing about seemed to be represented—the regulars, irregulars, administrative services, etc.

Then it was Mr. Boies's turn to cross-examine.

It turned out to be the most exciting afternoon so far. Boies is becoming stronger as the trial goes on. He was relentless in his cross-examination. At times you were so aware of the tension in the air it was electrifying. He put Godding in the corner on discrepancies between his testimony today and his testimony in his deposition, which Boies kept reminding him was also taken under oath.

Both men were red-faced. Godding, you were aware, was not used to being in this position. He was not the least bit happy about it. The restraint in both men's voice was ringing in the air. We all woke up. I didn't know who to look at. I studied all the faces of the actors.

One needn't have to watch Boies and Godding—their voices were telling. The lawyers for the plaintiff were stiff and still. Westmoreland is a master of disguise, but he has a habit of moving his lower lip when he is tense or uncomfortable.

George Crile's eyes were a dead giveaway. Though his face stayed motionless, his eyes blinked rapidly, as if he were saying, What am I hearing? He started to tap his pen repeatedly to let out his anger. Sam Adams's nostrils flared and his eyes turned black.

Boies didn't stop. The title general meant nothing to him. He had a witness on the stand who had said two different things under oath.

Godding denied ever giving any figures to CBS. However, it was evident from the reaction of Adams and Crile that he had.

Under more cross-examination and definition of terms, he admitted, yes, well he may have given some to Sam Adams. Adams's face relaxed. Crile was still quivering—his nostrils—darting his eyes, and tapping his pen.

Godding admitted that he "personally" felt that the SD and SSD were a military threat. He also claimed he knew of no cable with new estimates having been sent to Washington.

The jury was dismissed at four forty-five. Have a nice weekend. Be here Monday at ten. Talk to no one. Do not read any reports on this matter.

I'm dying to know what the papers will say tomorrow. How many weeks do I have to wait to find out?

October 29, 1984

Monday morning, back to the whirlwind—honking, traffic, people crammed in subways like sardines, dodging traffic, dodging pigeons, waiting in lines.

It's another planet.

I still can't get over the sensation I had standing in Grand Central Station last Thursday.

I was in the middle of the terminal, trying to make my way to my train from the information booth. All I can liken it to is the illustration we had in chemistry classes of an atom—all those things spinning around the center. People—thousands were moving past me in every direction—so fast that I actually got dizzy. For a moment I was afraid to move.

This morning I had breakfast in a nice quiet restaurant around the corner from the courthouse: good food, good prices, nice service. I've eaten here a few times now. It's a pleasant way to start the day.

I paid my check, got a coffee to go, and made my way up the

impressive steps of the courthouse, walked through the door, turned to my left to go through the metal detector. They have one just like this at airports.

I handed my coffee to the guard, put my purse on the roller, and walked through the gate. A loud beep went off. I backed up, emptied my pockets of change and pen, and walked through again. The beeping was as loud as ever.

"Oh, let her go through" said the guard.

"I can't," said the other. "It's reporting over a hundred."

"What do you have on?"

I took off my jacket. Still the beep. By now a long line of impatient people was behind me. I walked through again. Still the beep. Then my bracelet fell down from under my sleeve.

"Oh! The brass bracelet." I continued upstairs.

I was glad to see the other jurors. We all exchanged our weekend stories. They're like a new family. We do get involved in each other's lives.

How was your party?

Did you have a good time on your trip?

Is your cold getting better?

Did your sister's move go all right?

The clerk called us. Once again we lined up in the hall and filed into court.

As usual, everyone was watching—all eyes on the jurors as they filed in.

Mike Wallace was there today. He missed last Wednesday and Thursday. So were George Crile and Sam Adams and their counsel.

General Westmoreland with his counsel. All the news people. The artists and the court recorder.

General Godding was on the witness stand.

Mr. Boies continued his cross-examination. "When we left off Thursday, we were discussing the many discrepancies, General, with your testimony in court and the deposition you gave on October 27, the day we took your deposition."

"Well, I wouldn't say there were many discrepancies. You had discussed the testimony I gave before my mind was refreshed on the figures that I had brought to the NIE [National Intelligence Estimates] conference in Langley, August 1967."

"Yes, sir, and if you recall, we also were discussing . . ." Boies went on. He was not going to give an inch. Both men had cooled somewhat over the weekend. The tension of Thursday wasn't there,

but you could tell that General Godding was not pleased with the interrogation he was being subjected to.

"General Godding, wasn't there a significant difference between the
figures of the PERINTREP [Periodic Intelligence Report] and the figures that MACV had approved to be presented at the NIE conference—wasn't there a difference of 100,000?"

"Well, yes, there was a difference, but I wouldn't call it significant!"

"General Godding, do you not call 100,000 significant?"

"Well, Mr. Boies, it depends . . ."

"What does it depend on, what figure do you call significant?"

"Well, Mr. Boies, it depends . . ."

"What then does it depend on? What do *you* call significant? What
figure would you give to call it a significant difference?"

I quickly looked over at the protagonists. Adams and Crile and Wallace were smirking. Even Westmoreland couldn't disguise a smile.

Apparently, the CIA had figures it was presenting or had compiled
and MACV had figures it compiled.

In essence, they weren't that far off—if you don't consider 100,000
significant.

The problems began when you considered the so-called irregulars.

Basically, you had main forces—like in any military—trained soldiers. There wasn't too much argument over these numbers.

The South Vietnamese gave figures—they seemed to tally. The
North Vietnamese gave their figures for their armed trained soldiers.

But there was where the agreement ended. There was a group called
administrative services—they included the transporters, cooks, secre-
tarial staff and, I believe, the decision-makers.

Then there were the guerrillas. Their figures showed a great discrepancy.

And the political cadre. I have a vague grasp of what they represent,
but not enough at this point to write it on paper.

Then there were the SD and the SSD.

Here in particular was where everyone disagreed. The guerrillas—
the SD and SSD—were all dressed in black pajamas, as most witnesses have described them.

The SD were people in particular locales that were sympathetic to
the enemy's cause. They stayed in their locales. They did things like
make booby traps and homemade bombs and in general were bigger in
imagination than on military skills. However, some *were* armed.

The secret self-defense were a step more clandestine than the plain
old SD. Maybe they moved around more.

Another group was introduced in testimony today, called the assault youth. They numbered several thousand. That's how the documents recorded them.

The assault youth were too young for draft age.

The self-defense was comprised of women, children, and old men. I guess the secret self-defense were the more agile of the latter.

It seems as though hours of meetings and conferences took place about all of these groups and how to record them.

MACV's official position, if I understand correctly, was to list them separately, and incidentally.

On one page of documents, the regulars and guerrilla and some administrative services were tallied. They numbered 297,800.

So MACV's official position seemed to be the enemy numbered under 300,000.

If you tallied all of these groups together, you were talking about almost a half million enemy.

This was the figure that everyone was reticent to allow to leak out to the press. The press, and public opinion, seemed to have influenced these hardened military men a great deal.

We were even shown a cable today that said something to the effect: There are screams of protest over these figures—will not accept higher figures.

Before this cable was introduced, Godding swore press and public opinion made no difference. To him, personally, is how he retrieved his words.

Boies was ruthless today. As the courtroom scene has unfolded, he has, too. He, Boies, is relaxed. He is in his element. He is sharp, confident, and is calling the shots. His every movement has become almost purposeful. He'll ask a question and walk over and thumb through pages, not miss a step, and come back with another question: a rebuttal, "And, sir, do I understand what you said as . . ." and repeat the question and answer verbatim. It's exciting to watch this mild-mannered, conservative-looking boy flap his wings.

He knows what he's doing.

Apparently, the CIA or SNIE or NIE, or whatever they call themselves—whoever *they* were—wanted to break up this whole enemy count into two groups: military and nonmilitary.

The military were the regulars. Their numbers tallied to 291,000. The nonmilitary numbered 205,000.

MACV seemed to be opposed.

"Sir," Boies continued with Godding. "How many of the SD and

SSD in your estimation, your personal opinion, did you feel were armed?''

"Oh, about ten percent," answered Godding.

"And, sir, may I ask, how did you arrive at that figure of ten percent? Did you see any charts or studies? Or did anyone tell you this?''

"No, but from my experience in Europe, when I was stationed in Germany, we had the same type of element, and according to the . . .''

I couldn't believe what I was hearing. I'm not a military person. I have no basis on which to judge war or combat. I was an infant during World War II, and I was an ostrich during Vietnam. But even I knew that combat and people and the whole attitude of the Eastern mentality was a world apart from Western man. From anything I had read about Vietnam and anything I learned from my acquaintances who were Oriental, this war was different. We were dealing with different people, different values, a different era.

We were on their soil, a foreign one, with a foreign climate and another set of values.

I had made no judgments in my head as to whose values were right—if any. They were just different.

Was I hearing correctly? A general in charge of a lot of men and a lot of big decisions, basing his decisions on archaic experience?

Boies went on. "Did you, personally, ever see a study made of the number of armed SD and SSD?

". . . Did you ever, personally, see a study of the percentage of SD and SSD engaged in battle?

". . . Did you, yourself, personally ever see a study made or a list of figures of the number of SD and SSD engaged in battle or killed in battle?''

All had a negative answer.

"Tell me, sir, if you can—was there a problem counting bodies or casualties?

"I mean to say, sir, what I'm asking is—was there a breakdown of casualties or dead that differentiated the bodies as to regulars, SD, or SSD, or guerrillas? If you know? Can you answer that?''

"No, sir, to the best of my knowledge, I have no idea if there was a differentiation.''

"So, what you are saying is . . .'' Mr. Boies reworded the question into an answer, verified it, reasked it, asked it again in different words.

And to the best of my understanding—as a juror—the answer was: No, there was no way of separating the casualties or body count.

So many dead, so many injured, period.

"And so, then," continued Boies. "You arrived at the battle figures, and how did you solve the problem of SD and SSD involved? If there were any? To the best of *your* knowledge?"

Hmmm, of course, how do you disregard 183,000 people and then subtract their bodies from the 297,000 that you have listed as being the enemy?

They kept talking about the crossover point that supposedly was reached in April 1967—the point at which the enemy was losing more men than it could replace.

How could that number be accurate if there were almost 200,000—perhaps—engaged in combat that you refused to recognize? Whole, or in part—to the best of your knowledge, of course.

I must take special note of exhibit 246, exhibit 248, and, oh yes, the cable that was exhibit 251-A. I'm sure we will want to refer to these in deliberations.

If I recall correctly, to the best of my recollection, the CIA draft for figures was 121,000 regular forces—40,000–60,000 administrative, 60,000–100,000 guerrillas, 90,000 political, 100,000 self-defense, and 20,000 secret self-defense, assault youths, several thousand.

To the best of my abilities, taking the higher figures that totals 491,000, not including the several thousand assault youth.

Who knows what several thousand means? My God, that's over 500,000 probably, as opposed to MACV's *approved* estimate of under 300,000.

As Burt said in his rebuttal, everyone knew of these figures. They made a lot of noise.

Boies retaliated: "There you go again" (a famous quote these days!).

We know the noise was made, but to whom and—the key—with what *intent*? Was it in good faith?

Don't you want to know exactly what the enemy is comprised of? As a soldier? "Did you, yourself, personally, feel that the SD and SSD were a threat to be reckoned with?"

"Yes, sir, I did! To a degree!" Was he speaking for himself? Or did having his former boss in front of him intimidate him? His former general's wife was sitting there in the audience. Did she intimidate him too? I worried for *her*, a great deal.

All interrogations were complete. Godding was dismissed.

It never ceases to disturb me.

A witness who obviously had to interrupt a life—work, family, present matters—is interrogated, disputed, questioned, cross-examined, put on the line.

Okay, you may go.

There is no "thank you for your testimony"—for your life interruption, for your information.

Just plain, You are dismissed!

It must be a horrible feeling, climbing down from the witness chair and being thrown away.

We will not meet this Friday. We will meet next Friday. We will adjourn early on Wednesday. Election Day will be a short day. November 12 is a court holiday.

The jury is dismissed—you are to avoid discussing this case with anyone. . . .

October 30, 1984

David was late again. This is the second or third time he's been late. When he hasn't been late, he has come in at the stroke of ten. We all groaned when the court clerk opened the door. When David finally came in, we still had to wait a half hour until the judge called us in, so at least we didn't get our usual lecture. In fact, the judge apologized for the delay. He informed us that there were court procedures that had to be discussed.

The day began with another segment of the documentary in question. We have seen this section before, but of course now we were given instructions by the plaintiff's attorney to pay close attention to certain aspects.

General Westmoreland was being interviewed by Mike Wallace. The segment was not very flattering. Westmoreland contradicted himself. He seemed nervous. He has a habit of licking his lower lip. They mention Parkins being fired.

Cooley was being interviewed, and he claimed on the segment that Parkins was fired because he wanted to pass on some figures of infiltration that were much higher than any previous reports and that Colonel Morris got crazy—stating we can't accept these figures. Parkins was fired.

I wonder what the truth is. So far we've heard that Colonel Morris fired Parkins because he refused to do a study that Morris had requested. Morris told us that.

Meechem said Parkins got fired because he yelled at Morris.

Cooley said Parkins got fired because he wanted to do his job right, in so many words—pass on data of high infiltration that he had discovered.

Lo and behold, the TV monitors went off and Parkins himself appeared as the next witness.

Mr. Murry was one of the attorneys for the plaintiff who, until now, has not examined a witness or spoken to the jury.

He is a good-looking, young, well-dressed black, with a cool, polite manner.

What is your name, sir?

Everett Sam Parkins.

What is your educational background? Where do you reside? What is your military background?

He was lieutenant colonel, West Point, had eight children, worked in CICV (Combined Intelligence Center Vietnam) in September 1967. He was responsible for infiltration-of-enemy reports. He stated that it took one to six months to even a year to get accurate data on enemy infiltration.

"Why does it take that long, sir?" asked Mr. Murry.

"Because the enemy didn't want us to know," answered Parkins.

The house came down with laughter.

Finally, the attorney led him through all the necessary channels of questioning to the incident that we're all so curious about. "Did you know a Colonel Morris?"

"Yes, sir."

"What was your feeling of Colonel Morris?"

"I disliked him intensely—it was reciprocal." Parkins claimed that they had a personality conflict from the minute they met, and that everyone had told him Morris didn't like him.

His side of the story was: There was one jeep in his outfit. He wanted to use it. He had to deliver this report to another commander in Morris's section.

Morris intercepted him and read the document and started yelling. Parkins claimed he had no idea what was in the report. He was only a messenger. But he yelled back and Morris fired him.

This is not what we want to report, was one statement I recalled Morris having had said.

Boies did his usual brutal cross-examination. He pulled out a deposition that Parkins had given in August 1983.

Here we go again. Totally different testimony. Again we heard the I can't recalls and the Tet attack was seventeen years ago.

Apparently, Parkins refused to be interviewed for the documentary.

He had been interviewed by Samuel Adams in the fall of 1980. Adams was writing a book. Upon cross-examination and more digging questions from Boies, it appears that Parkins himself had prepared the

document. Yes, he vaguely remembered that it did include some infiltration figures, but that's all he could recall.

His deposition in August 1983 was more in keeping with the allegation in CBS's documentary.

That mystery man is here again today. However, today he has a
legal pad with him. I only saw him write on it once. Most of the other
time he just sat and observed, with his arms folded.

We broke for lunch and were given one hour and twenty minutes.
So Cheryl (Alternate 6), Linda (Juror 10), David (Juror 5), and I
walked briskly to the South Street Seaport.

We are having fun going to lunch. So far we've gone to a different
restaurant every day. I bet if we worked here for two years we could
hit a different restaurant every day. We've started nicknaming each
other: J1, J2, J17, and so forth. This military jargon does become
contagious—I'm J2; David is J5; Cheryl is A6; Linda is J10.

I managed to get J5's phone number and passed it out to the jurors
who live in New York City. We are going to start calling him at 7:00
A.M. to make sure he gets here on time tomorrow.

We heard some more cross-examination from Parkins and then he
was dismissed.

Next we saw another segment of the documentary, an interview with
General Daniel Graham.

So that's what Graham looks like—thick white hair, glasses, direct
manner: doesn't allow Wallace to lead him. Graham is not going to let
anyone put words in his mouth. Wallace told Graham in the interview
that Meechem and Cooley had told him that he, Graham, had changed
the data base in the computers. Graham, of course, denied this, saying:
Do you think I'm crazy?

Graham believed the figures he used in Vietnam were way too high.
Graham said there was no blocking of figures or infiltration reports,
claiming that if anyone was to block it, it would be he!

"Do you know Sam Adams?" asked Wallace.

"Oh, him. His figures were way too high. There was something
wrong with the man. He wanted to have Davidson court-martialed—
me court-martialed. He has a mental problem or something."

Everyone chuckled at this, even Sam Adams, sitting there at the
defendant's table.

God, it is so hard to know who's right, wrong, lying, telling the
truth. Everyone seems so sincere.

Graham claimed there were only 84,000 enemies fighting in the Tet
offensive.

All of this counting SD and SSD and guerrillas and the infiltrators is really centered around this event. The Tet offensive, which happened in late January 1968, was something of a surprise.

Tet was a big Vietnamese holiday, therefore the Tet offensive was so named. The enemy, according to the documentary and some testimony, had been planning this attack for a long time. Hence, we should have known about it and been prepared.

With all this hiding of figures and arguing over counting self-defense and assault youth, the numbers became out of sorts.

For instance, Graham claims that only 84,000 enemy had been involved in the Tet; 27,000 had been killed in the first two days; 45,000 had been killed by the end of February; 80,000 killed within seven weeks.

The thing is, no one ever counted in the SD and SSD and infiltrators, because they were not real soldiers.

Yet when they were killed, they were in the body counts. How could anyone keep track of numbers?

The TV interview ended, and after a short break General Graham, in the flesh, appeared on the witness stand.

This should be good. I perked up. The usual questions—name, address, children? He had seven; he was smaller in stature than I had envisioned. He had thick, thick white hair that wouldn't behave in front.

He was not a modest man, nor was he a braggart. He just matter-of-factly answered questions and seemed proud of his record and job history.

"What was your rank when you were discharged, sir?"

"Lieutenant general."

"And how many stars was that, sir?"

"Six," he answered without hesitation. "Three stars on each shoulder."

Laughter burst out in the courtroom.

Graham, indeed, seemed to have a bit of responsibility in Vietnam.

He was in charge of the daily INSUM (Intelligence Summary) and the WIEUs (Weekly Intelligence Estimate Update) that all the biggies attended for updating. He stayed on top of intelligence documents, and a couple of times, if I'm not mistaken, I believe he looked over at the mystery man before he gave an answer.

He didn't seem to have much use for CICV. He called them bean counters.

Graham felt that figures that weren't rounded off into tens of thousands were a waste of time and inaccurate.

If he looked at 123,321, he knew it was fake—whereas 120,000 to him would appear legitimate.

Everyone has a definite opinion, don't they?

The command position, according to Graham, was not the position of Westmoreland but an opinion reached by the entire staff of MACV.

Time ran out, and we were dismissed. I can't wait for tomorrow. We should see some fireworks!

October 31, 1984

We stayed at my father-in-law's last night. What a pleasure to stay in the city and walk out of your apartment, say good morning to the doorman, and walk to the subway.

It was a beautiful day, with a magnificent blue sky and a slight nip in the air.

As I walked down the steps to the subway, sounds of Mendelssohn's violin concerto greeted me, played by a young man whose violin was amplified by the subway tunnels. I tossed a quarter into his case and made my way to the end of the platform. Beautiful music followed me.

I got a seat. This had the promise of a good day. I could tell. I even got through another chapter of *On Wings of Eagles,* which I'm enjoying very much.

I arrived at Foley Square in plenty of time to have a leisurely breakfast. Bumped into J5 and we walked together to the courthouse. I was surprised he was still talking to me. I called him this morning and said: "This is your conscience; are you going to be on time today?"

Westmoreland and his attorney walked past us. It's strange, we stare at each other all day long but pass each other outside the courtroom with no verbal acknowledgment.

Graham was still on the stand this morning. I got the feeling that he thought that he was doing us a favor: moving around in his seat, checking his watch, making himself comfortable, one arm dropped over the back of the witness chair. Mr. Murry was still politely questioning him.

"Yes, we had evidence of movement in North Vietnam in September, but I wouldn't call it infiltration," he proceeded. "Infiltration is when they sneak over the border. We were having trouble deciding how to name it—when whole divisions are walking across, is it invasion or what?"

"And where was this taking place, sir?"

"Oh, around Khe Sanh."

Graham played with his tie, brushed at his shirt, moved around more in his seat, getting a comfortable position, draped his other arm over the back of his chair.

I looked for the others' reaction to him, but no one else seemed to notice his nonchalance. I found his wife in the audience. She looked like a nice lady, nondescript other than her red suit. She reminded me of Edith Bunker. Not in looks, but in demeanor.

Graham seemed open with his information. He didn't appear to be hiding anything. He offered more information than he was asked for, as many of our witnesses have. On more than one occasion, the judge reminded him to answer only the question and not to debate it.

He was asked for a definition of the Tet offensive.

Apparently, it took place January 31 and February 1, 1968. There were two main assaults—one in the north and one in the south the following day. They in the military surmised that there must have been some problem in communication among the enemy because the military analysts were sure the enemy had meant to have simultaneous attacks.

The enemy lost 27,000 in the first two days. The whole affair dragged on and by the time it was over, seven weeks later, 84,000 had been killed.

Those first few days we captured two or three thousand—some defected.

"How many casualties were there?" asked Mr. Murry.

"Oh, there's one casualty for every three dead, so there were about 40,000 total casualties. We knew they were using a maximum effort."

"And how did you know that, sir?"

"Oh, they were throwing everything into battle. People were still bandaged from their wounds—children were carrying rifles they didn't even know how to use. In fact, many of them were still in the cosmolene that they were stored in."

Graham went on. We got a firsthand account from him of what these battles were like.

"Did you ever falsify records, General Graham?"

"No!"

"Did you ever attempt to erase the data base on the computer?"

"No!"

"I'm finished with my examination." And Mr. Murry took his seat.

Mr. Boies stood up. "Good morning, General Graham."

I don't remember, but I don't think Graham answered. Mr. Boies turned around, casually looked at some notes, and began.

I was anxious to hear Boies cross-examine this guy. In spite of his self-assurance, I suspected Graham had holes in his testimony.

According to Graham, Sam Adams was the only one who wanted higher figures so far. No one else that Graham knew agreed with Adams. Graham made it quite clear that he, Graham, didn't even believe the figures MACV had. He felt they should all be lower, and he felt it was preposterous to include irregulars. To him, irregulars were guerrillas; he didn't believe the SD and SSD were worth mentioning.

"Adams even wanted to include another group called the assault youth," he added with a superior annoyance.

Boies began to read from a document and was shot down at each turn by the plaintiff's attorneys. Bad form, irrelevant questions. This witness has no way of knowing that. He hasn't laid any foundation.

Poor Boies—couldn't get past first base today. It was frustrating.

We broke for lunch. Cheryl (A6) and I decided to skip eating today, and we took a leisurely walk down Nassau Street. The weather was so glorious, we both wanted to take advantage of the balmy day.

We listened to a jazz band in the square down by City Hall and examined the magnificent facades. Gargoyles, statues, richly sculptured windows grace these buildings. All too often one does not have time to stop and admire them.

We bought some frozen yogurt and window-shopped.

We, of course, discussed the jury—Philip is quiet; Marion doesn't seem to be interested. Cheryl had made a comment in the jury room to the effect that a woman in the audience didn't look like Graham's wife. That woman would never have seven kids, she had said. Now she was concerned that Kate, on the jury, who has seven of her own, may have heard her and misinterpreted the statement. Kate couldn't be nicer. She is a warm, pretty, likable lady. It's hard to believe that she *does* have seven children, and grown at that. In fact, she has seven grandchildren as well. She's always telling us stories of this grandchild or that one. She's already started her Christmas shopping. I can well understand why—Christmas at her house must be like a huge party.

Time flies when you're having fun. Suddenly we had ten minutes to get back to the courthouse. We ran most of the way and got there exactly at two. Pat, the court clerk, was at the door with a make-believe stopwatch.

The clerk is the only one we have contact with. If we want to say something to the judge, we must pass a note to the clerk, who in turn gives it to the judge, who in turn reads the answer to us in the courtroom, in front of the entire congregation.

The clerk gets us cups, passes out our checks, and makes sure we stay together in the jury room and speak to no one.

Yesterday, David (J5) brought in some posters to hang on the walls of the jury room. We have a Chagall now on one wall, a Dali on the other, and Paul Klee's *Portrait of a Man* looks over the head of the table.

Pat seemed to be amused by this and told us we should all bring in paint to brighten the walls.

Then there's Wild Bill. He's a likable older man, quite bald, with a corpulent figure. He got his nickname from an incident when the key he had wouldn't open our jury room door.

He had told us his name was Bill—just plain Bill, he said. As he was trying desperately to unlock the door one day, he turned around and said.

"Just plain Bill is going to turn into Wild Bill any minute."

He's been Wild Bill ever since. Wild Bill is the one who swears in the witnesses.

He stands there with his left arm straight down by his side and his right hand raised and in an authoritative no-nonsense deep crackling voice says, "Take the stand please, and remain standing. Do you solemnly swear to state the truth—the whole truth, and nothing but the truth, so help you God?

"You may sit down. State your name and spell it *slowly, please.* Talk into the microphone."

Wild Bill then takes his seat at the table just below the judge. He answers the phone there—gives us dirty looks if we talk too much. He reminds the entire courtroom when there is deliberation going on at the side bar: "Court is still in session—you must remain quiet, please."

When the judge says court is dismissed, Wild Bill stands up and, in a booming voice, repeats, "Court is dismissed—the jury shall return to the jury room."

When one of the jurors brings in cakes or cookies, which is usually daily, we automatically send some in to Pat and Wild Bill.

We were called back into the courtroom, and Boies took up a new approach. This one seemed to work. At least he wasn't stopped at every turn.

It was evident the attorneys for the plaintiff did not want Graham cross-examined. They were passing notes back and forth, and Mr. Dorsen was always nudging Mr. Murry to object. A couple of times it seemed that Mr. Murry wasn't even sure why he was objecting.

Graham became a wise guy. He grasped every opportunity to make a wisecrack.

He did manage to get a few laughs from all of us.

Graham would say things such as: "I have a problem with these exact numbers—I have a problem counting the SD and SSD in the Order of Battle . . ."

"What was the political cadre?" asked Boies.

"Oh, I had a problem with them, too—they didn't belong in the OB," Graham replied.

"What exactly did they do, General Graham? Who were they?"

"They collected taxes," answered Graham. Everyone laughed.

"What else did they do?" asked Boies.

"They made policies, made speeches—just like politicians here," Graham answered flippantly.

"What else?"

"Oh, they'd round up people in the village and give them speeches on Lenin and Marx, and they gave horrible speeches." Graham sounded like he was looking for a laugh.

"And how did they round up these people?" Boies asked.

"Oh, they had guns—they'd shoot the people who wouldn't listen," Graham said.

Boies continued: "And kidnap them and threaten them, right? They were armed, were they not, General Graham?"

"Oh sure—of course—yes, they carried arms!" Graham shrugged.

Suddenly, I couldn't believe this man.

These political cadre were armed as well as violent, and he didn't believe they should be in the Order of Battle?

Who has a mental problem, Graham or Adams?

It was time to break for the day . . .

November 1, 1984

Court began at eleven this morning. Actually, we had been told to be present at ten-thirty, which we all were. But obviously there were a lot of ground rules and deliberations.

The defendants were eager to cross-examine, and the plaintiff was eager for them not to.

Boies began: Do you know what the Phoenix Program is? Simultaneously, the witness Graham answered yes and counsel for the plaintiff objected to the question.

Apparently, the Phoenix Program had to do with the political cadre.

Finally, after many objections, Graham was able to answer. He did so in the same manner he did yesterday—draped over the witness chair.

"Oh, the white mice—I mean the South Vietnam police—eliminated him, the man with the bull horn—oh, excuse me, the political cadre . . ."

This man was offensive.

The cross-examination went on: Komer—yes, of course, I had reason to believe he passed on the information to Washington. Oh, of course, I don't know for sure—I had no direct knowledge of it, but, yes, he passed it on, I would assume. He answered and examined his fingernails.

"Sir, did General Westmoreland contact you to be a co-plaintiff in this case?"

"Yes, he did, but I was advised by the plaintiff's counsel not to join."

We were told by the judge to disregard this testimony.

The cross-examination went on.

Mr. Boies brought up the question of infiltration figures in the MACV documents. Then the question of Graham's own methodology came up.

Apparently, Graham had his own way of doing things. Yes, he had inherited figures of infiltration and guerrillas, etc., when he arrived in Vietnam. But they were unreliable.

"I developed a way of, a superior way of analyzing these figures. Assuming that at the present time we have 550,000 enemy and assuming that monthly we called it the input/output study, losses varied from month to month, but they averaged 5,000 a month." He continued with an elaborate system of numbers and subtractions and additions. I listened very carefully.

Here was a man spouting off figures—numbers, reasons, and additions and decreases. He had the floor—no one interrupted him. He very authoritatively spouted off this elaborate system he devised about how to figure out the enemy's strength.

I watched and I listened—I didn't miss a word.

I looked at this man—I listened to his words—and I realized:

He's full of it. He doesn't know what the hell he's talking about. The minute someone gives him a soapbox, he wants to hear his own voice.

I started to squirm in my seat. I was embarrassed. He was a garbler. He didn't make sense.

I wrote on a separate note in my pad: "I am resisting a violent urge to stand up and shout: 'Graham, you're full of *shit*!'"

I let the foreman see the note. He sits to my right. He turned red and said, "Shh, shh, quiet—he knows what he's doing."

I gulped. Oh my God, I thought. I shouldn't have done that. I cannot give my opinion—we are not to discuss this with anyone, not even each other. I never thought for a minute that I was wrong about this guy. But I realized that some people could be influenced by him.

The idea that one of the other jurors could possibly believe that this man had all his marbles troubled me. I realized then and there that deliberations with this jury might be hell.

You are to talk to no one . . . you are not to let anyone influence you . . . you are to keep an open mind . . . when you have heard all the testimony, you are then to evaluate the information you have received.

Well, this guy's testimony, as far as I was concerned at this time, was bull—a waste of time!

Most people, when they are handed their deposition to refer to, are handed a bound document about one half to three-quarters of an inch thick. Graham's deposition consisted of two copies, one about one and a half inches thick and the other about three-quarters of an inch thick.

He did like to talk!

I watched the characters: the plaintiff and the defendant.

Westmoreland couldn't keep a straight face. The plaintiff's attorneys looked like the chairs couldn't swallow them up fast enough.

However, they were going to die with a grin on their face.

The defense attorneys were wallowing in this testimony.

Boies pulled out a large easel and attempted to follow Graham's arithmetic.

When it didn't work according to Graham, Graham said: "Oh, we don't use arithmetic in estimates." He continued undaunted—tried to bullshit his way out.

We broke for a longer lunch than usual—a chance to go back to Ha Ha's—Hamburger Harry's.

David (J5) loved this place. We—A6, J11, J4, and I— accommodated him today.

Ha Ha's was a brisk ten-minute walk. To my delight, the others were as exasperated as I was with this last testimony.

I guess I'm not as out of line as J1 made me feel.

However, no one dwelled on the issue; everyone was trying hard to keep objective. Sometimes it's just too hard to keep it to yourself. It's been four weeks now.

I have not spoken to a soul about the goings-on in the courtroom—not even to my husband, who is trying hard lately to get a feeling from me.

The other night as I was almost asleep, he started whispering in my ear. "Who's going to win? Who has the stronger case? The paper has been saying . . ."

I turned around and got hysterical. It was funny, but I realized how difficult this was going to be.

We've only seen ten witnesses, and we've been in court for a month. We have seventy witnesses to go.

I can't even talk to my own husband about it—of all people. Even though he's interested in history and this type of thing.

I knew instinctively that I couldn't even mention things to him, because he had very definite opinions. I just couldn't allow him to influence me. It was tough—I wanted to share things with him, but I couldn't.

"If you want to know what's going on, come to the court, but just don't talk to me about it."

I felt bad. I usually talk to him about everything, but this was something I couldn't share.

"Come on—it's about time," he said. "No one believes that you haven't discussed this with me, so you might as well . . ."

Conveniently, I fell asleep.

After lunch, the cross-examination went on. Graham was handed a series of depositions from numerous sources.

He was instructed to read them to himself and answer yes or no, and that was it.

At one point, he looked up and said: "This guy didn't like me too much, did he? I couldn't blame the guy—I guess we carry our baggage with us, don't we?"

The rest of Graham's testimony consisted of his opinion about whether we really won the war in Vietnam—maybe not politically, but militarily.

Boies questioned him on his present occupation. He is the director of a society called the High Frontier.

What is the High Frontier?

"It's a nonprofit organization to convince the country on the exploration of outer space for security and economic advantage. We advocate the use of superior space technique, looking for a nonnuclear defense against nuclear ballistic materials."

It sounds good on paper. But judging from the witness—the direc-tor—I began to have personal doubts about the organization.

Boies asked, "Did CBS adversely affect the reputation and name of the professional officer corps.

Graham answered, "Yes."

My feeling was: CBS didn't have anything to do with it. Open your mouth, Graham, and you'd do more damage.

We had a short recess—actually, most of the recesses were long today. But when we returned to the courtroom, another witness was on the stand.

Robert Michael Leverone: a Harvard graduate, entered the military on the NROTC route, was a commander on a couple of ships, was with command intelligence, worked in current intelligence at MACV. He was nice-looking, rugged, and had a nice manner. He spoke when spoken to, didn't go into elaborate, detailed answers. He appeared comfortable and direct. He worked in Estimates. His commander, two above him, was Graham—good old Graham.

Apparently, Leverone took Heon's place when Heon left Vietnam.

Leverone worked in something called the Tank. It was quite secret and dealt with confidential material. He more or less confirmed the CICV number of infiltration. He did say he felt quite comfortable knowing that good men were working on these figures and doing a good job. He felt they were accurate and competent. It sounded like he was in a different war from Graham's.

Sam Adams apparently called Leverone in late 1979. The telephone conversation lasted about one and a half hours.

Sam Adams seemed to be interested mainly in confirming the vari-ous positions that different individuals held. Then he used a code word on an individual, so Leverone stopped the conversation.

He said: "I told Adams, 'you're out of your mind—you don't have enough evidence.' When Adams mentioned Meechem's letters to his wife, I told him Meechem was a private individual, probably just vent-ing frustrations to his wife in letters."

I liked this guy. I felt he was credible. He looked like he kept his nose clean. He also didn't see anything that he didn't want to see.

If there were any irregularities going on, I'm sure he didn't know about them, for one—or would feel that his superiors would know what they were doing and probably not question it.

We were dismissed late today, at five-thirty.

Have a nice weekend—talk to no one about this case.

THE OBSERVER

November 2, 1984

We've all had the same experience, like a song we can't get out of our heads. The initials are plaguing us—MACV, SD, SSD, CINCPAC. Driving to the station, I still see the faces of the characters in the courtroom.

What culture shock it will be going back into the classroom when the trial is finished.

On the days that court is recessed, I must report to my regular job.

For years I've been questioning my regular job—teaching elementary school. It's not that there is anything wrong with teaching children—in fact, it's fun.

Going back twenty years ago, I had a major decision: What did I want to be when I grow up? I heard a lot of choices—I liked a lot of things—I finally decided, after a lot of soul searching, that I could incorporate all of my likes and talents in teaching art.

I had left the classroom for a while to work in a bank in California—with computers—then I owned and operated my own art studio, but I came back to a steady paycheck and a reliable, predictable en-

vironment when I returned east and found a good school district that I
was proud to be a part of.

I was captivated by my students, their individualities and dif-
ferences, their need to be guided. When working with them daily, they
became people. It's strange; when you see them outside of the classroom, they are children. Yet inside, among their peers, they are like
miniature adults—yet with childish wants and needs.

It's hard to explain, but when one goes out into the so-called world,
one sees the same thing among adults.

All those traits that we witness in children carry into adulthood:
shyness, verboseness, the need to be recognized, strong egos, weak
egos. For many, these things change along the way, but for many they
remain the same. Put a bunch of individuals together, and one be-
comes a leader, someone else tries to upset him. There are the fol-
lowers—the joiners—and individuals and the sheep. I'm witnessing
this phenomenon among the jury, a group of individuals randomly
chosen.

By chance, we have become a group—people whom I would have
had no other way of coming in contact with are suddenly my daily
comrades.

I'm already getting insights into these individuals and realize that
some are entities to deal with—others are non-opinionated in open
conversation—yet all of us will have a mind of our own when the time
is right.

Already I can feel a certain leaning. We were told to keep an open
mind until all the evidence is presented. Yet I can feel certain leanings
in both directions—for the plaintiff and for the defense.

Some have expressed a sympathy for the underdog, others for the
stronger one. In spite of this, I do feel they are an impartial group.

I'm curious as to what characteristics of ours brought us to the attention of counsel. What made them choose us out of all the other jurors
they had a choice of?

The same phenomena of group dynamics that I'm discussing among
the jurors and the children I teach I see in evidence in the witnesses
called from the military.

Some of these men are so strong-willed that I find it hard to believe
they were able to take orders. Yet others filled the role of follower.

I've tried to look at the defendants in this light, yet it's hard to
evaluate them. To date, all we've really had a glimpse of are Mike
Wallace and George Crile.

Sam Adams played a different role. He is skirting both sides.

I'm not trying to make decisions at this point as to the role all these people have played. I'm trying to evaluate their place in the game. That's not to say one is right or wrong—simply to establish their roles.

Even in the makeup of the military, because one happened to be a general and another a lieutenant does not necessarily make one smarter or more competent than the other—it's simply the role he was given to play.

One of the aspects of this whole experience—being chosen as a juror—that has overwhelmed me is the fact that here I am, an ordinary individual, chosen at random out of all the other ordinary individuals of voting age, and I am supposed to make a judgment on a group of individuals who have achieved a status I'll most likely never achieve.

A four-star general in the U.S. military versus a group of media people who are household idols.

Wallace and CBS reach millions of Americans weekly. Millions of Americans have never heard of Pat Roth the art teacher, or Myron Gold the IRS agent, or Linda Pasquale the dental assistant, Cheryl Raymond the librarian; David Lederman the researcher; Norma Parker the nurse's aid.

Yet we are chosen to make judgment in this case.

It's quite an overwhelming experience.

I cannot forget that I have two jobs. I must still try to maintain my place in them. Fortunately, as a teacher, I have a substitute who is quite capable. But I'm torn, because I still have a responsibility and the children expect me to be there. I've written them letters and tried to explain what I'm doing within the limits of what I'm allowed to say. Then there is my real estate job. Fortunately, it is not my sole source of income. If it were, I'd be destitute. There is no way I could maintain that job and be on the jury. Lastly, there is my work as an artist, whose main goal has been to achieve a standing in the arts. This whole experience is disturbing.

After only one month of jury duty, I'm experiencing an identity crisis.

Who am I? What is my occupation?

As a juror, you have none. You are an observer. You watch all day. I have found this one of the most tiring experiences of my life.

After being a doer—a main character, the center of a day (as a teacher)—to learn to just sit and observe is grueling. The first two to three weeks was fun—a change, learning a whole new vocabulary, new character, a new way of life.

But this last week has become more and more difficult, and today was extremely difficult. The same questions are asked of each witness—it has become harder and harder to take notes—the same answer in different forms. We are dealing with a five-month period before Tet—September, October, November, and December of 1967, plus January of 1968. The numbers of the Order of Battle.

Who was counted? Who wasn't? Why weren't they? What happened?

The event was important, the event and the goings-on made an enormous difference. The event and the documentary that CBS made of it is the entire context of the case.

Westmoreland chose to debate it, bring them to trial.

I feel like God is punishing me for having been an ostrich during the Vietnam War. Few other civilians have had their nose rubbed into the hard facts of a six-month period in Vietnam more than this jury . . .

In one month's time I have been made an authority on the subject of MACV, SD, SSD, guerrillas, infiltrators.

Today was simply more of the same—

November 5, 1984

Started off with more testimony from Leverone—he held his own without trying to. He seemed like just an honest guy doing his honest job. He was finally dismissed, this time with a thank you from the judge.

Was this thank you as I interpreted it—the first witness who seemed to warrant it? A Freudian slip from the judge? I felt so. This man seemed so far to be the only witness who was really open, in spite of the fact that he really was not able to put any new light on the entire issue.

The majority of the day was filled with the reading of a deposition taken of Mr. Hankins—a civilian employed by the U.S. Army, presently residing in Washington, assigned to CICV, Order of Battle during the period in question. Nothing basically new was learned; it was more of the same.

He talked with Sam Adams in reference to the book he was writing, called *To Circle a Square or to Square a Circle*, the first I'd heard of the title.

The title sounds as esoteric as this whole debate on counting the enemy, like more of the same argument.

Should we count SD, or should we not? Actually, the title makes a lot of sense in view of the subject:

What is the subject, anyhow?

What is the whole question?

Westmoreland is suing CBS for libel.

Was Westmoreland defamed?

Did CBS do this documentary with malice?

Did they present this with knowledge that the statements were false?

Was the broadcast defamatory?

What was the defendant's state of mind?

Was Westmoreland damaged by the documentary?

The two parties concerned sit in front of us each day.

Westmoreland sits alone with his counsel at one table.

Mike Wallace, George Crile, and Sam Adams sit at another with their counsel. We have yet to hear the main characters.

The counsel is all we can judge.

Mrs. Westmoreland sits in the audience—with friends! We watch the family, feel for the family.

We heard things such as: egomaniac; military; he's felt strongly; we are victims.

This testimony was painful because it was a deposition taken a while ago, and it had to be read to the courtroom just as though he were there. The attorneys from the bench took turns reading it. One attorney would ask questions, the other would answer as though he were Hankins. The day dragged on.

The mystery man was there again.

Parkins was Hankins's boss; he worked in the OB of CICV. He then worked in the Tank, the top-secret clearance center of CIIED.

His job was to work mostly on infiltration estimates, where he broke down the infiltrations into probable, possible, and confirmed.

Hankins felt that in early October infiltrators had reached 20,000 men. He kept referring to methodology and the Parkins-Pickey chart.

There were historic trends, wet- and dry-season statistic projections, back channel messages. It went on and on.

The long and the short of it was that Hankins believed infiltration was higher than you could document in official reports. He said, "I felt counterproductive—to have estimates, but couldn't report proper figures." He thought twenty to thirty thousand a month was accurate infiltration, but he needed hard infiltration sources in order to officially report.

No one worried about the numbers, according to this testimony. Colonel Parkins agreed that Hankins's numbers were probably accurate.

CICV believed the numbers. But Morris and Graham felt that they were too high. In particular, because it didn't agree with their numbers.

At three o'clock finally we had a new witness—live, in the flesh.

Colonel John Frank Stewart—I began to wonder how live he was. He was stiff and formal; his crew-cut head held as though he were permanently at attention. Only his hands moved, but in a very controlled manner. He was still in the military, and now in charge of sixteen hundred men.

Stewart was very knowledgeable and seemed eager to be accurate, painfully so. He would stop and think carefully before answering each question. He never said, "Ah," never said, "Let me think," or made any unnecessary nervous sounds—just plain silent, stared ahead, answer.

His vocabulary was straight intelligence. Soldiers—he called them "human resources."

Stewart was asked to characterize various individuals.

McChristian—the first MACV J2 he was subordinate to: He was a formal person, wanted written briefing.

Davidson—less formal than McChristian—would have the analysts give verbal briefings—he had freer contact with his men.

He described General Westmoreland as being businesslike and terse of manner, who questioned his analysts in depth. There was no way of giving Westmoreland a briefing without knowing your subject very well. He described one incident when the general was uncharacteristically nice. During the briefing, for which Stewart did not have absolute numbers to verify a point, he told the general that he had used the SWAG method of calculation. Westmoreland asked what the SWAG method was.

Stewart told him it was scientific wildass guess, and he laughed.

Always looking for comic relief, we all broke out in laughter. So did Westmoreland.

Burt, his counsel, overreacted. He jumped out of his seat and slammed the table and fell back into his chair.

Stewart was a talker. He could not answer yes or no—he had to qualify each answer and give an example. He was very informative, but he also described each incident like a robot—expressionless, except for his hands. Even they were controlled.

When asked what J2 stood for, he had to explain the entire code:
J1 stands for the person in charge of personnel
J2—intelligence
J3—operations
J4—logistics
J5—civil affairs
J6—communications and electronics

Boies stopped him here and continued questioning in a different vein.

What did you consider hard-core documentation? What did you consider a valid source of information on the subject of infiltration?

Answer—when we captured enemy documents, such as Vietcong diaries. These men kept involved diaries describing the ambience of these areas, their entire military experience, and they talked about their families a great deal. Their losses, according to these diaries, were great. They talked in great detail about their military experiences.

Boies interrupted and asked another question. It was a long afternoon.

Sometime in late November, NSA (National Security Agency) gave a warning that something big was going to take place. Strange things were happening—the enemy was changing tactics, they had reports of movement over the borders and throughout the DMZ.

4:45. It was time to be dismissed. Tomorrow is Election Day and we are due to appear in court on Tuesday at 1:00 P.M., after lunch.

November 6, 1984

I drove up to Carmel alone Monday night. Bob had work to do in the city and I was anxious to get organized at home.

My life had become one long blur since my jury duty began.

We had plans to go away for the weekend, and this was the only chance I had to pack and get personal things done—paperwork, banking, etc.

I bought food for the cat that my neighbor was feeding. I drowned all my plants, tidied the house, worked a little on my sculpture commission, which was due at the end of the month. I returned phone messages from my machine, and finally, by 2:00 A.M., got into bed.

I woke at six—was the twelfth person at my assigned poll to vote, and continued my chores.

I forgot till I waited on the steps of the bank that it was a legal holiday. In fact, most everything I set out to do was thwarted.

At ten-thirty, I set out for the city. I felt like I had only turned around—it was again a magnificent day; a little more fall-like in temperature, but clear as a bell. It was enjoyable to drive into the city at this hour. Traffic was light, and I was making good time. I decided not to switch over to the Harlem River Drive, but to take the Major Deegan down to the Third Avenue bridge.

As soon as I made the decision, I saw an enormous cloud of thick black smoke billow into the air hundreds of feet high. It couldn't have been a quarter of a mile in front of me. Traffic was still light and moving, so I didn't become alarmed—until suddenly I realized it was coming from my lane, and all cars came to a screeching halt. It was too late to turn off—there were no exits between me and the smoke. Within seconds, the southbound lanes became a parking lot; chaos was breaking loose.

A truck apparently had careened against the median divider. One of the other people who had walked up to see the accident firsthand said someone was killed.

I sat locked in this roadway for more than an hour.

All that kept running through my head were the words of Judge Leval: "It is your duty to be on time. Court cannot start without the presence of all the jurors. There are witnesses, attorneys, the plaintiff, and the defense all inconvenienced by your being late."

We had a number to call in case of emergencies. I locked my car and ran up and down the roadway, knocking on the windows of taxis, buses, limousines—does anyone have a telephone?

Finally, I spotted an emergency phone in the middle of the roadway. I climbed up over the wall and waited till the operator picked up. It was strictly for emergencies, a 911 number. I finally convinced the operator that it was extremely important for him to call the court for me. He did, as I found out when I finally arrived twenty minutes late.

It was only when I was sitting back in the jury box that I became upset at my actions. Here was a major loss of life that ordinarily would have overwhelmed me with emotion. All I could think of was to get to court. What was happening to me?

Colonel Stewart was still on the witness stand. His voice was one long dull drool in the background. I tried extremely hard to concentrate.

Real time—near real time—what was real time? When the act took place—that was historical in nature—I informed the decision-makers—the enemy went back to sanctuary.

I found Stewart's wife in the audience. She hung on every word. She watched him with total admiration. I wondered if she understood what he was saying.

I watched the others in the courtroom—the spectators, the counsel, the other jurors. Everyone sat expressionless, intent on his testimony. I tried again.

At this point, Stewart was finishing one of his examples and completed it with: "Do you understand, Your Honor?"

Judge Leval sat there expressionless, looked thoughtful for a minute, and simply shrugged his shoulders.

Oh, for comic relief. Thank God everyone in this courtroom had a sense of humor.

It was a long afternoon. We went from 1:00 to 5:45, with only two ten-minute breaks.

Stewart's testimony was more of the same that we've heard from others. But he told us of two reports that he had worked on after the Tet offensive—one on enemy capabilities, and one on the postmortem effect of the Tet offensive.

The accident that had held me up this morning was all over the news. It was horrible—eleven cars, a truck, a woman killed and a policeman lost his legs.

November 7, 1984

The questioning went on. Boies tried to find loopholes in Stewart's testimony—anything that sounded like a contradiction.

Boies was a whip—I pictured him never leaving the courtroom. I'm sure he didn't. I think he owns one suit and one sport jacket—both navy, so you're really not sure if he's changed clothes. He has three different shirts—a pin-striped button-down collar, blue and white; a blue and white checked shirt, and a solid blue oxford shirt. I think he has two ties. He was wearing his navy woven one today.

Without missing stride, he glides over to the table and picks up Stewart's deposition and, without opening it, walks over, hands it to the witness, and states: "Turn to page 246 of your deposition and read line 10. Take your time—read whatever you wish for context, and tell me when you have finished."

"I'm finished, sir."

"Was that statement true when you made it? You realize you were under oath when you gave that testimony, do you not, sir?"

"It is still true."

Boies proceeded to show that it disagreed with the testimony that was just given.

He did this for almost an hour. The plaintiff's attorney, of course, objected half the time—restate the question—this is irrelevant—Mr. Boies didn't allow Colonel Stewart to finish a sentence.

One point Dorsen got up to object but changed his mind and waved his hand, as if to say why bother—and he just sat down, resigned, like the rest of us.

Stewart didn't like to use *yes* too much. He usually substituted words like *exactly—precisely*. At one point, quite tersely, Stewart told Boies—Look, I'm telling the truth—I have nothing to hide—I am saying the same thing now that I did in my deposition—only reworded and elaborated on this in an attempt to have Boies back off.

Boies did not.

Actually, I believe Stewart was telling his truth—the only one he knew: his figures, his analyses, his observations, which were from a purely analytical point of view.

He was only interested in his job—to count the real established Vietnam regulars.

He believed, as Graham did, that the SD and SSD did not matter.

He said that the damage they did was insignificant—they were not trained and had archaic weapons. I wondered how he'd have felt if one of those archaic weapons had shot him. Would that have constituted an insignificant act?

Boies gave him an exhibit to review—a document with figures. According to Stewart, the figures were accurate. After cross-examining, they weren't, because it was impossible to get accurate figures. He recounted some figures to Boies: there were 125,000 enemy and 80,000 losses, and then losses of 90,000 later on, etc. Through a display of additions and subtractions, Boies showed that it left 20,000 enemy uncounted. The two men went back and forth in this verbal confrontation, and finally, the witness was dismissed.

We had an hour and a half for lunch, the longest we've had so far. I was interested to hear the other jurors. Most anyone who expressed an opinion reflected mine. They were a savvy group. For the most part, they were well aware of what Boies was attempting—when he had a case, when he didn't.

Our conversation on the way to lunch consisted of characterizations of Boies.

"Do you know where you are going to lunch? To the best of your knowledge can you answer that? Are you sure? Is that your best recollection? Did you know at the time that you were deciding where to go to lunch, that you would, in fact, do just that? Will you answer that?—if you can.

One of the jurors disliked him intensely; another felt sorry for Mr. Burt; one thought Dorsen too nervous. Another liked Mr. Murry. Everyone wondered where Miss Fingerlick was today—no one could get her name straight.

Everyone commented on the mystery man. Apparently, they all had noticed him.

Everyone loved Pierre—Judge Pierre Leval. Did you see his shirt yesterday? J6 loved his blue and pink polka dot tie.

We decided to write a letter to Mr. Boies or take up a collection for a new suit. Everyone wondered how Mr. Burt brought up his wardrobe from Washington—he had a different suit on every day. Each in a garish color. Actually, some were quite smart; others were something else.

Hardly anyone watched the election results at length from what I could gather. No one dwelled on the subject too much.

We had movies most of the afternoon. Act V of the infamous documentary was shown.

Mr. Burt gave his statements. Mr. Boies gave his.

Judge Leval took out his X chart again on how to receive the testimony and documents and gave us another long lecture on how in this case, because of its expected length, he is allowing the attorneys to give us summaries as we go along to keep us up-to-date on what angles they are attempting to convey.

We had an hour and a half of outtakes of interviews with George Allen, who apparently was the number two authority on Vietnam intelligence.

It was hot. I thought that I would pass out in the courtroom. I couldn't get comfortable. I could hardly pay attention. I wanted desperately to listen. I did, but I was having great difficulty focusing. When we finally got a break, the other jurors were having the same trouble.

The only thoughts that I grasped from the outtakes were that Allen thought the Vietnam War was perceived by many to be a temporary phenomenon—a part-time, secondary war. There was great difficulty getting support for it.

He seemed to honestly want to help, but was reticent on saying too much. He appeared to have admiration for Sam Adams as a worker, calling him eager and enthusiastic, perhaps overenthusiastic, though some of that element was needed.

Finally, we had a new witness in the courtroom.

Before the judge allowed him to take the stand, he called the attorneys to the side bar. We had a few minutes to chat quietly among ourselves in the jury box. I glanced over at the plaintiff and defense tables and spotted a deposition, marked *Carver*, on the table. I couldn't believe my eyes. It was three and a half inches thick. I gasped to myself and pointed it out to a couple of the other jurors.

"Oh my God—he talks more than Graham did!" Our suspicions were confirmed the minute he took the stand.

What is it about these guys? Do they feel they must tell us everything they know? Everything has to be clarified. There is no such thing as a simple answer.

Carver was short in stature, with a small pouch of a stomach and a full double chin. He parted his hair very low on one side to bring long strands of hair up over his crown to cover the balding. He had trouble with his eyes, changing glasses from reading to full-time, and they didn't seem to focus on what he was looking at.

He had a slightly high-pitched, hoarse voice and an extremely pedantic manner. He loved to hear himself talk and colored every statement with words one would find in a doctoral thesis.

We only had a half hour to go until court would be recessed for the day, and it took him half an hour to give us his educational and occupational background.

He was the youngest man ever to hold the high position he enjoyed. He impressed his professors with his doctoral thesis. He worked with—and he dropped names of the highest political and military people of the last twenty years. He was truly incredible. He mentioned at one point that working with the people he did, one had to be careful because egos became bruised so easily. I had to laugh. They were all from the same ilk.

Do you know a Robert Komer?

"Yes, of course. I worked with him. Of course if you asked him, he wouldn't put it quite that way," Carver added.

Komer was the ego that spoke to us several weeks ago. "Did you have clearance for highly confidential matters?" the attorney asked.

"Yes, on a scale of one to ten, I was cleared for ten—the highest confidential matters," said Carver.

Court was adjourned. We had the same orders: Speak to no one—report at ten.

November 8, 1984

I'm fast becoming a New Yorker. It was another gorgeous day—blue sky, crisp chill in the air. I finally was able to bundle into some real fall clothing.

The subway was packed today. I barely got on at my stop. I couldn't reach a strap or pole, nor could I move my arms to read, so I just stood there held up by the passengers surrounding me. The next stop was like a tidal wave—bodies pushed and shoved, and suddenly the term *packed like sardines* was an understatement. There was a stranger pushed flush against me. His face was so close to mine that I couldn't focus on his.

He apologized and said, "I guess they're more aggressive at Sixty-eighth Street than at Seventy-seventh." We both laughed, but we were uncomfortable because of our closeness for the next two stops, until the crowd finally lightened at 51st Street. He disappeared. I would never be able to identify him.

People complain about New Yorkers, but I was beginning to get a lot of respect for them. They're truly a hardy bunch of survivors. In spite of the circumstances and difficulty of getting places, they seem to arrive unscathed and in good spirits.

The security staff at the courthouse already knows me. Good mornings and how are you todays are liberally stated.

Where's your coffee today? You're the one with the bracelet that will set off the detector: These are the greetings.

The elevators' temperaments are routine. The court clerk has his quips.

The jurors arrive one by one, each with his or her account of the ride home last night and the morning's events.

Thursday we all have to recheck what happened on *Dynasty* last night.

The soap opera is timely: Alexis is on trial, and we laugh at the sham of her courtroom scenes.

At exactly ten, we are called into court. Carver is still on the stand. The questioning begins the moment we were seated.

What was the ONE?

It took him fifteen minutes to give us a full account of exactly what ONE was, how it worked, who was involved, and the importance of it. The ONE, a part of the CIA, was the Office of National Estimates, which published the NIE or SNIE.

The day was more of the first fifteen minutes. There were innumerable trips to the side bar, and some of these sessions went on for twenty minutes or so.

Objections and irrelevancies were the norm. Carver managed to sneak in many snide remarks about Sam Adams. Overenthusiastic—did things his own way—he sent a cable without approval, with his own ideas stated as if they were the department's—he jumped to conclusions and went off half-cocked.

We were told by the judge to disregard all of these statements—they're to be stricken from the record.

At one point, when the attorney stopped his questioning for a minute, Carver said, "Are you done, sir?" The judge laughed and said,

"Mr. Carver, *you're* on the witness stand. Mr. Burt is asking the questions!"

He gave us a rough idea of what the difficulties were between MACV's thinking and the CIA's:

MACV used a data-base approach—they were traditional, classical, and viewed data in a military way. They had stringent criteria for accepting information; you needed at least two documents or two accounts to affirm information, or to have sufficient confirmation.

CIA used a general concept of enemy casualties. It was a different perspective. They used the estimative approach.

If you knew there were three divisions and you knew one of the divisions had heavy weapons, we'd assume that each regiment had the same even though only one was confirmed. We'd make that tentative assumption.

Carver supported a broad range of numbers, rather than exact figures, for estimating the SD and SSD. Therefore, he preferred prose in reporting them as opposed to columns of figures.

The data base was inherited from the South Vietnamese, who had inherited it from the French. About the time MACV was asking Washington for more U.S. soldiers, the CIA discovered that the figures they'd been using were highly inaccurate. The actual figures were much higher than those they'd been using. This caused an enormous problem. They were afraid to let these new figures come to light for fear that they would be misleading—they, too, were concerned about the possible press coverage that would ensue.

The mystery man was not there today. I began to think that I was wrong about him. After all, here was a person with the highest of confidential clearance on the stand.

At one point a document was to be presented as evidence, but it had not been previously presented. The attorneys for the plaintiff and the defense took it to two men sitting among the spectators for their okay. There they were—two elderly, nondescript gentlemen, lost in the crowd.

Their cover was blown!

ABSOLUTELY NOT!

November 9, 1984

This was the day I'd been waiting for for weeks. Since our summer vacation had to be cancelled because Bob's mother was mortally ill— she died in September—we'd planned to get away later for a three-day weekend in Florida.

I was looking forward to collapsing on a beach. As usual, it wasn't going to be that easy. A flight leaving at 5:45 P.M. gave us ample time to get to the airport under ordinary circumstances. However, when I learned that court *would* be held on Friday, November 9, I panicked. We usually get out at 5:00. There is no way that a trip to La Guardia would be feasible in forty-five minutes in Friday rush-hour traffic. I sent a note to the judge, pleading that we get out at 4:00. I had tried to arrange other flights, but they were all booked. The first flight with an available seat left at 10:30 P.M.

He announced in the courtroom that a juror had requested that we be dismissed early on Friday. He said that we would be, but it had nothing to do with the request—he had other court commitments at four o'clock on Friday.

A couple of the jurors were miffed that he couldn't just say, Sure, you can get out early because of the tickets.

I didn't give a damn why or what he said the reason was, just as long as he let us out early. Then a few people got me concerned about traffic. There was a lot of construction going on in Queens, and Friday evening traffic was always horrendous.

We all decided I should take a helicopter to La Guardia. Even Bob surprised me and suggested a helicopter, so a helicopter it was. I'd never been in one.

Even though we started court today later than usual—eleven o'clock—it seemed the longest. Every time I looked at the clock, it was barely five minutes later than the last time I'd checked.

Carver was still on the stand. He was being questioned about the meeting at Langley in September 1967. Who was there?

He was being questioned about the Saigon conference. Who was there? Who represented the Washington delegation? Who represented MACV?

Cables were produced—copies of Carver cables back to Helms giving outlines of the meetings. The lawyer for the plaintiff read several excerpts from these cables.

"Frustrating and unproductive meeting—it seems like MACV is under orders by Westmoreland to not go over a ceiling of 300,000."

"What did you mean by that statement?" asked Burt.

"They were being unreasonable in my estimation, because they weren't doing things my way. So I unfortunately lapsed into purple prose. I had no idea, obviously, that these cables would be held in evidence in a court case seventeen years later."

"Why did you believe MACV was under orders?" continued Burt.

"They were so obtuse and difficult to deal with," Carver answered. "I drew the erroneous conclusion that they were under orders. I was annoyed that I had not been able to see Westmoreland, Bunker, or Sharp, whom I'd rerouted my flight to see."

"Did they know you were coming?"

"Yes, I'd sent cables informing them before my trip—of course they knew."

"Objection."

Many more cables were read, and I made notes to ask for them during deliberation. I couldn't believe the plaintiff was using them as evidence. It sounded more like evidence in the defense's behalf.

The only thing I could figure out was that the plaintiff was using this information to show that there was no coverup and that, indeed, everyone had been informed of the arguments between the CIA and MACV on the issue of counting enemy.

Finally, on September 13, Carver met with Westmoreland. They had two meetings—one private, and one with the committee that had been in a deadlock. Westmoreland denied he had ever given instructions to stay within a ceiling.

Westmoreland found NIE's prose acceptable and felt they could come to an agreement. (Actually, when we were given the total figures that each had been arguing for, there really was little difference. I felt that, indeed, the egos involved would argue just for the sake of arguing.)

The four sections that the enemy was broken up into were: administrators, guerrillas, political cadre, and the regulars.

Washington figures:	Agreed figures:	
35,000–45,000	35,000–40,000	administrative
75,000–95,000	70,000–90,000	guerrillas
80,000–90,000	75,000–85,000	political cadre
229,000–250,000	224,000–249,000	regulars

Carver came to believe, after giving the issue a lot of thought, that adding SD and SSD and guerrillas was like adding up apples, oranges, and kumquats—a single sum total was misleading as to what you were dealing with.

Carver stopped in Honolulu on the way back to the States and met with CINCPAC's J2, who was Peterson. He discussed what happened in Saigon. No, there were no written reports.

What did infiltration refer to? Personnel replacements from North Vietnam to the South for long periods, or to large units for short terms?

What was your source of information on infiltration?

Received reports from NSA or from POWs and confiscated diaries and documents, but the latter was unreliable—historical, out-of-date.

"Why was that, sir?"

"Because the NVN were not polite enough to become prisoners as soon as they entered the country," Carver answered.

The largest movement that Carver testified to was in the fall of '67—late fall, I believe, when they got reports of movement of three regiments and two divisions, moving from the North to South Vietnam.

We were finally dismissed. The other jurors pushed me out the door, yelling, "Enjoy—have a good time."

I found a cab down the block. He had no idea where the World Trade Center Heliport was. Just my luck!

As politely as I could, I informed him that as a cab driver, it was his duty to know places like that and to drive me in that direction and find it.

After stopping a couple of other cabs, we did find it, but traffic was slow—exasperatingly slow. We were shooting across side streets because the main streets were gridlocked. A bus stopped in the middle of the block and picked up a group of elderly passengers, who took forever to get on board.

It was hard to get on the West Side Drive—the light only allowed two or three cars to make it across the intersection. Finally, I was there.

Checked in—had to give my weight and the weight of my baggage, and at last, I was on the copter. My heart was in my mouth. The noise was deafening. You could hardly speak to the other passengers. There were five of us in all—two other women, and two young men in their early twenties. The copter took off—it tilts so that you look over the head of the pilot.

I felt like I was a bird flying and tilting, and the scenery was the most breathtaking I ever experienced in my entire life.

The sky was deep cerulean blue—the sun was low on the horizon—the moon was in full view. The lights of Manhattan were twinkling on. We were directly above the World Trade Center. The skyscrapers of lower Manhattan seemed an arm's length away from the Empire State Building, which was lit up white and blue. I made up my mind I wanted to learn how to fly a helicopter.

The young man next to me nudged me and pointed to the Long Island Expressway, which was bumper-to-bumper traffic. We gave each other the high sign—we'd made the right choice. This was truly the way to get to the airport.

Bob was waiting for me when we landed. We checked in and ten minutes later were on the plane.

Bob warned me that our hosts, Dick and Tobi, were very excited about the case and that Dick would want to talk about it—so just let him know you can't, and change the subject.

They were there at the airport. We hugged and kissed, carried our baggage, and jumped into Tobi's new pride and joy—a white Jaguar.

We weren't in the car three minutes when Dick turned around. "So how is the case?"

Without giving me a chance to answer, he continued. "I know everything that's going on—Carver's on the stand now, he's showing these guys there was no coverup."

"Dick, stop. I can't discuss the case. I know you're interested, but talk to Bob about it when I'm not around."

"Oh, okay. How much are they suing for—it's 142 million, isn't it?"

Tobi and Bob jumped in and corrected Dick that it was only $120 million.

"I don't blame him," said Dick. "These hot reporters have got to be put in their place. *60 Minutes* is a witch-hunt, but it's entertainment—anything to get a story."

"Dick," I yelled. "Stop it, don't say another word. I'm a juror—I'm going to tell the judge on you."

"He can't do anything to me down here. I'm from Florida—he's in New York."

"Dick, it's federal court. Besides, you're trying to influence me."

"I'm not trying to influence you. I'm not discussing the case, I'm just telling you I think that the press has got too much leeway—they've gone too far, they'll do anything to get a story, and I think that Mike Wallace has got to be shown a thing or two. I wish I was on the jury."

By now we were doubled over with laughter.

"You're too biased, Richard. You'd never get on a jury," his wife yelled.

"What do you mean, I'm too biased? I'm not biased—I'm just stating a fact."

It was no use—no convincing Dick he was biased. The next three days were wonderful. Dick had said his piece and didn't bring up the subject again.

We ate, we drank, we went deep-sea fishing. I relaxed—I read and got a lot of sun. Too soon it was time to go home. My plane landed on schedule.

November 13, 1984

Suddenly it was Tuesday morning. Back to court.

"How was your trip?"

"I thought about you."

"How was the helicopter ride?"

"Look at your tan."

"Oh, I'm jealous!"

Everyone talked at once. It was Myron Gold's birthday. We collected fifty cents from everyone, and Kate bought a birthday cake.

Carver was still on the stand; Burt was still questioning him.

How many people in your department did you have monitoring the information of NVN (North Vietnam) to SVN (South Vietnam)?

How many people in SAVA (Special Assistance for Vietnam Affairs) were monitoring infiltration?

Other than communication intelligence, how did you receive information on infiltration?

The questioning went on and on.

MACV's reports were all based on collateral information.

What is collateral information?

When the information is received from documents and diaries confiscated from the POWs.

What is real time?

It took Carver ten minutes to answer each question.

A witness previously had told us real time was when the act occurred.

Carver went through a long, involved answer, using examples—big words, metaphors—and finally gave us the four-word answer.

"Could MACV have suppressed reports of infiltration?"

"Absolutely not!"

Objection. This is the witness's opinion.

In your opinion, Mr. Carver, would it have been possible for MACV to suppress information of infiltration reports?

Ten minutes later, with long involved comments, he gave the same answer.

The plaintiff had new documents to offer as exhibits—four copies of George Crile's notes from interviews with Carver.

More trips to the side bar with the attorneys. We, the jury, talked quietly in our seats.

Finally, the interview notes were accepted. We had excerpts read to us by counsel.

In the notes, Crile asked Carver about Sam Adams. What were his abilities? How did he approach his work?

"Adams was enthusiastic, energetic—I got him his last promotion, which he deserved. However, his enthusiasm was not tempered with judgment. He considered anyone that disagreed with him to be a fool. If he was an intelligent person in disagreement, then he was a knave—he had ulterior motives."

"It says here, sir, in the notes that you had more respect for Gains Hawkins than anyone you'd worked with in twenty-five years."

"That's an exaggeration—I respected some of Hawkins's work, but I never elaborated any more. That's a figment of Crile's poetic pen."

Crile looked dismayed—eyes wide open in disbelief.

"It says in the notes that you said General Westmoreland was under a lot of pressure."

"I said Westmoreland may have felt that he was under pressure—I never said that he was."

George Crile's look was again of dismay.

His notes say you stated there was a good deal of fiddling.

I said nothing of the sort—what I said was—people—each side thought that the other was fiddling.

The look on the defendants' faces was not only of dismay, but of exasperated humor.

"You," the notes continue, "claim that the White House and the Pentagon manipulated the statistics."

"I said nothing of the sort!" Carver practically yelled. "I didn't say that! What I said was, the White House and the Pentagon were overfixated with numbers, so much so that they were capable of manipulating statistics—I never said *the* statistics."

The defendants' reactions were such that it was difficult to believe that Crile had fabricated the notes.

Carver offered a piece of information: President Johnson could never understand why there was so much disagreement over the number of enemy. After all, everyone was working from the same information.

The judge once again reminded the witness to answer only the questions: Don't elaborate, you will get a chance to say what you wish when the opportunity arises. This is not a debate.

Yes, sir.

It seems as though Carver was not asked to be interviewed before the documentary in question was completed.

The interview took place eleven days before it was to be aired. When he was informed of this, he stated that this conversation was pointless.

Did you see the documentary when it was aired?

"Yes, I did."

The plaintiff's attorney read from a transcript of the documentary: "The President, Congress, and the American people were told that the Vietcong had only 247,000 left."

Before Carver was asked to reply, he yelled into the microphone louder than he had spoken in three days of testimony, "That statement is a lie!"

"When in fact the enemy had over a half million," the plaintiff's attorney continued.

"That's a lie!"

We are quickly given a break. Boies is to cross-examine when we return.

Mr. Boies began: "Mr. Carver, do I understand you to say that the enemy never totaled more than half a million—500,000?"

"Order of Battle was not the purpose of NIE!"

Boies produced exhibit 226-A.

It was a cable from Carver's office to the Department Director of Intelligence. It stated something to the effect that MACV's Order of Battle of communist ground forces—of confirmed Vietcong and North Vietnamese, the political cadre, and Vietcong infrastructures—listed as 277,150 was far too low and should be raised, perhaps doubled.

Carver went through a long, elaborate analysis of the cable, the wording, the semantics of SD and SSD, and said that the definition later changed to Vietcong infrastructure, and he couldn't remember when the term changed. It was either early 1967 or late 1967. He went on and on.

I write in my notes: Carver is trying to bullshit his way out of this one. I tried to think of a more acceptable way of stating this.

Boies produced one of the exhibits—notes from George Crile's interview with Carver.

Boies read—Crile's words—"Carver sidesteps main issues with artful fillibusters."

I couldn't help but admire Crile—what a gentlemanly way of stating it.

However, the comment had the same effect—sparks flew over the courtroom. We were dismissed for lunch.

I went shopping. Cheryl came with me. Linda went with Eileen. David went to Chinatown. Everyone else went his or her own way. Our courtroom popularity as the Westmoreland jurors was being usurped by another trial.

Cameramen were all over the place, but not interested in us. A new case began today—*Sharon* vs. Time *magazine*. It, too, was a libel case—this one for a mere $50 million.

Time magazine seems to have accused Sharon of being responsible for the murder of civilians in the Lebanese-Israel skirmish last year. The case is being tried upstairs. They expect it to last a month.

We all returned around two-fifteen and surprised Myron with the birthday cake. We just finished cutting it when the clerk called us into court.

The judge began with, We've been here for a long time and will be for a lot longer, so there are times that business other than the courtroom procedures will be addressed. It has been brought to my attention that it's Juror 8's birthday, so we'd like to wish him a happy birthday.

Everyone in the courtroom applauded.

We will now continue cross-examination.

The air has changed. Sparks have been squelched and the atmosphere is nothing but politeness and agreement.

We are now back to the figures that had been argued at the Saigon conference. I found it hard to believe that it took four or five days for MACV and ONE or CIA to finally accept a meeting of the minds.

They both refused to give exact numbers, but instead used ranges—a low-of and a high-of estimated enemy.

MACV's range was 219,000–249,000—take it or leave it.

The CIA's range was 229,000–250,000.

The final agreed range was 223,000–248,000. Then Carver argued that they really looked at the mean. According to my calculations, they were arguing over a difference of 1,500.

All the testimony up to now has been to the effect that everything was an estimate. There was no such thing as an exact figure.

I couldn't imagine why they would argue so emphatically for four or five days over these ranges, which, to me, were so similar. Maybe they knew something I didn't.

The longer I've been here, the more confused I've become. Not about the issues—what is being given as testimony—but about the whole situation.

CBS produced a documentary. The overall documentary, from what I have seen, was an account of a portion of the Vietnam War—the Tet attack: the counting of the enemy.

I have always watched TV with a slightly jaundiced eye, taking statements, news accounts, and even eyewitness-news accounts with a grain of salt. I have felt up till now—and the testimony we have heard to date verifies this—that ten people can be in the same room, witness the same happening, and each will give a different account.

A couple of years ago I did a series of paintings of three plastic cubes from different angles—I also wrote a poem about the grouping—and meant it to encompass not only a visual reality, but a psychological and spiritual one.

Capture each moment. It's been touched by its own fingerprint—It
will never exist again.
Even if with great care you put together the same ingredients.
The sun will never repeat its angle—the wind its force or direc-
tion.
The spirit will not be the same.
Nor will your state of mind be able to see it
That way again!

I have had no doubt that for the most part, the witnesses we have heard testify have been giving us their accurate account—some, of course, with reservations.

The hard part is to decide what the real truth is.

I have watched Westmoreland for almost six weeks now. He is a proud man: his deep-set eyes give away years of concern and worries. The lines on his face tell of decisions. His chin is one of determination. He braces his youthful-looking shoulders like a soldier. When he walks through the courtroom or on the street, you can't help but take notice. He walks with importance. He has an unfaltering gait. He sits alone with utmost discipline.

Mrs. Westmoreland comes to the courtroom faithfully each day. A charming lady—she emits class. She seems warm to the spectators around her and almost seems to take under her wing the wives of witnesses who appear each day. There is an air of socialness, yet interest and concern with the goings-on in the courtroom.

It appears that the Westmorelands have a good personal relationship. A warmth emits from them when you see them together. She appears to be the perfect general's wife—gracious, social, concerned, yet she puts out her stamp of individuality. She often does needlework.

The courtroom is like a who's who in the higher echelons of the military and top government officials of the late 1960s. Sitting among them are the individuals interested in the defense.

George Crile's wife appears now and then—there are a group of people who gravitate to her. George Crile and Sam Adams sit side by side each day, joined by Mike Wallace on occasion.

There is an electric youthfulness surrounding the defendants. Even their counsel is youthful. Though Westmoreland's attorneys are not elderly, there is a conservativeness emitted from them that seems to express his stand.

It's occurred to me that this is not a trial of *Westmoreland* vs. *CBS* but a trial of Old-time Military Thinking and Youthful Idealism.

The old-line military used circumstances and enemy figures in a pragmatic way. The public will not understand—so we change numbers or don't tell them. Men are fighting—we've fought before—this is how to handle it—we do this.

A reporter comes along and says, This is what the truth was. The reporter has no concern for the outcome—the whys, or the reasons—just plain this is what happened.

The generals are playing chess; the reporters are simply reporting the game. Did the reporters report the game accurately?

Did they make the main player, Westmoreland, look bad? Rightfully—wrongly? If you can answer that.

We can't yet—we still haven't seen all the evidence. "Let me be sure of what you said—you stated that . . ." Boies's voice broke into my thoughts.

Carver answered in his usual long-winded way. "I remember saying something like that, but I'm not sure if that's exactly the way I stated it."

"Turn to page 495 in your deposition for the record—line 10," said Boies without referring to notes or a deposition.

"You sent this cable, sir, did you not? Exhibit 296-A, in front of you, sir?"

"Well, there's nothing to indicate that I did draft this, but most likely it came from my department, so I most likely okayed this—I probably, in that realm, I guess you can say I sent this, yes. I sent it."

The document was enlarged before us on a large screen. It read: "We strongly suspect that much of recent urban excitement was caused by personnel drawn from secret self-defense components, perhaps assault youth, and other elements currently written out of the records by J2 MACV on the ground that they have no military significance."

"What were you referring to, sir, when you stated other elements currently written out of the records of J2 MACV?"

"Well, er, this is a slightly purple sentence. I'm not sure what I was referring to—but I know it was not what I meant."

"Sir." Boies pulled out 297-A—paragraph 3, February 1968. "'We believe that 30 January '68 Order of Battle was too low.'" He went on.

"'Paragraph 5—OB too low.

"'Large numbers of small specialists who (Sapper, Special Action) which undoubtedly participated in attacks were almost certainly absent from OB.

"'City units (which almost certainly were involved in urban offensive) are by and large missing from OB.

"'Some larger units identified in attack apparently not in OB.

"'A review of recent evidence indicates enemy made large-scale re-cruitment drives prior to offensive and finally certain classes of enemy manpower (who were probably in attack)—not in OB at all—for ex-ample, guerrilla, secret self-defense and assault youth.'"

Boies read on: "'Our assessment of the situation is that the enemy, who was stronger than we acknowledged prior to the offensive, may have some short-term problems because a relatively high proportion of his better soldiers were among the casualties, but that in the long run, barring major setbacks for him in the countryside, he has capabilities for main force warfare.'"

Carver again used his artful fillibuster method to answer these state-ments.

We were dismissed.

You will discuss this with no one . . .

November 14, 1984

Someone finished the jigsaw puzzle I brought in to amuse us on our breaks. Now we have another. Everyone at some point has contributed a piece or two—some more avidly than others. The one completed was a Big Mac hamburger. The new one is a crossword puzzle—it is truly nervous-breakdown material.

Carver is still on the stand. We are told to disregard the testimony from yesterday afternoon. I can't even remember what we are sup-posed to disregard.

The morning was spent going over a document, a cable that was sent. *Declassified* was stamped all over it, like the majority of exhibits we've gotten; lots of areas were blacked out. We spent at least an hour discussing what was blacked out—whose names, what does CONF stand for, where did the cable originate, who drafted it, who arranged its being sent.

Allegedly, it was a cable Sam Adams sent after hours, without any-one's approval, and Carver had been rather miffed because of it.

He has called Adams impulsive more than once—actions not tem-pered with judgment, and so forth. Of course, Carver talked himself into a hole.

He had been aware of Adams's views even back then, and he even had recommended him for a promotion. Sam Adams's letter of resig-nation to Carver stated something to the effect that he, Sam Adams, was unable to work in an area that accepted MACV's Order of Battle estimates, which he called a monument of deceit.

This questioning went on all morning. Apparently, Mr. Carver had testified at the Pike committee hearings—well, actually, he couldn't remember if he testified or not, but he had assisted Colby with his written statement.

Finally, there were no more questions.

Mr. Burt gave a summary of the past few days.

"As you can see, you've heard fourteen witnesses all testify. There *was* a lot of noise—everyone knew there wasn't agreement over the figures. As you can see, there was no coverup. And you are going to hear General McChristian in a taped interview with CBS, and just watch how they put words into his mouth."

Mr. Boies spoke. "You have heard fourteen of the plaintiff's witnesses testify. You have heard them testify that there was a ceiling—you have heard these witnesses testify that they themselves believed there were at least 400,000 to 500,000—even 600,000 enemy—that MACV refused to recognize. Yes, you will see General McChristian on taped interviews with CBS. You be the judge. You decide if CBS is putting words in General McChristian's mouth."

General McChristian's face came on the monitor; so did George Crile's voice.

"Were you put under any pressure to keep below a ceiling?"

"Yes, George, I was—it was never stated that way, but it was said to me: Take another look at those figures—are you sure they are correct? What is your criteria?"

"What did you think of Gains Hawkins?" asked Crile.

"I felt he was a man of great integrity—he was a conscientious worker."

Crile read to McChristian that Hawkins thought the same of him, calling him a white knight—a rarity in the times, a saint in so many words.

"What do you think of the allegations that numbers were falsified? Is it against any laws or statements in the military to not report all the figures?"

"No, Mr. Crile, it's not, but I wear a ring from West Point that has engraved on it: DUTY, HONOR, COUNTRY. It may not be against the law to falsify records, but it's dishonest. I can't live like that."

This was the only part of the interview that was used in the documentary.

McChristian stated he had a cable that he had given to Westmoreland with very high figures on it—Westmoreland wasn't too pleased. He asked McChristian to let him keep it for a few days to look it over.

McChristian was shaken by Westmoreland's reaction. He said, "I argued with Westmoreland that we shouldn't have any troubles passing this information on because they know we were trying to compile it."

McChristian was in the middle of leaving Vietnam at that time, having been transferred back to the States, so he never knew if the cable had been sent.

George Crile asked McChristian if he knew about a report in a Jack Anderson column on November 30, 1967, that claimed he was transferred because he had reported higher estimates. McChristian told Crile he had heard about the news story and that friends had said things to him along those lines, but as McChristian said: "Perhaps I was naïve at the time, but I had never been aware, or felt that I was being transferred to get me out of the way."

He went on with an account of General Westmoreland's wanting him to stay on in Vietnam and command a troop, which is what McChristian also wanted to do. But apparently there is some kind of ruling that two years is the limit of a tour in Vietnam, so his request was denied. Instead, he was given a command back in the States.

"I just reported it like I saw it—the enemy was capable of carrying on for an indefinite period."

"Would you have kept the figures down so as not to jar the American people?" asked George Crile.

"George, *no*!" was his straightforward answer.

McChristian continued: "I decided to be an officer when I was six years old. One must expect criticism and welcome it. There is no such thing as lying a little. A lie is a lie—you'll be found out in the end.

"I had seven hundred sons of American mothers to protect. They came here for a chance to live and prevail against the enemy, not sent here to die. The commander out there needs the best information on the enemy he can get."

"Help me understand Westmoreland's predicament," said Crile. "What was his dilemma?"

"Not just General Westmoreland, but anyone up to the President. How would they look at a figure change of that magnitude?"

McChristian refused to conjecture on the feelings of General Westmoreland.

More questions—answers. The main thing of consequence that he said in addition was that he had had notification of his transfer before the cable incident. He thought his move had something to do with Bob Komer's arrival in Vietnam.

"I think I may have been looked upon as in Komer's way. I had begun organizing the Phoenix Program and Komer was taking it over; he was using it for a different purpose.''

McChristian seemed like a sincere, feeling person.

November 15, 1984

I couldn't find a parking space on the street, so I put the car in a lot downtown. It took me only fifteen minutes to get there—traffic was almost nonexistent. Rumors were flying that Westmoreland was to testify. I don't know where these rumors came from because there had been no hint of it in court—at least not in front of the jurors.

Sure enough, there he was on the stand when we filed in.

It was strange to see him on the witness stand after watching him for weeks at the plaintiff's table.

He's a striking man. He carries his age well: he said he was seventy and one-half years old. I guess those half years count as much at seventy as they do at seven. He was asked all the usual questions: Where were you born? Where did you go to high school? College? What is your work experience?

He graduated from West Point in 1936 via South Carolina, the Citadel and a few other assorted places. He graduated as a second lieutenant.

He went to Harvard's business school, did some studies in military engineering. He was a helicopter pilot. (I wondered if he could teach me how to fly a helicopter.) He was a major or a captain in World War II. He mentioned places like Casablanca and Morocco; he fought against Rommel in Tunisia. He fought in France and Germany. He mentioned various battles that I was sure any student of military history would have been impressed with. When he was a major general, he said, he had two stars—on one shoulder.

It took almost an hour for him to give us his history, which ended with him as a four-star general in Vietnam.

Along the way he had been superintendent at West Point for three years, appointed by Eisenhower. (It must be exciting to have the top position in a school you had proudly attended.) When he was in Vietnam as COMUSMACV (Commander of U.S. Military Assistance Command Vietnam), the only people he had to report to were the ambassador and CINCPAC commander in chief Pacific, who was Admiral Ulysses S. Grant Sharp.

While Westmoreland was in Vietnam, the ambassadors had been

Henry Cabot Lodge, Maxwell Taylor, Lodge again, and then Ellsworth Bunker.

Bunker is the only one we seem to be dealing with in the time span that this trial is interested in. Apparently, Westmoreland did not have a duty to report to the President.

He was asked to give an account of a typical day in country (they all refer to being in Vietnam as in country).

He breakfasted at home, was in the office by 7:00 A.M. Briefed by operations staff.

If anything of major consequence happened, he would be telephoned at home, regardless of the hour.

Four days a week he went out into the field. It was a requirement he set for himself. He made sure he hit the crisis points. He visited every-where—I Corps, II Corps, III Corps, IV Corps. Talked to soldiers and generals, visited hospitals, talked to POWs, American advisors—ev-erywhere at least once every three months.

"Vietnam was a sizable piece of real estate," as General West-moreland put it. "It was six hundred miles north to south and one hundred twenty miles wide—thirty-five miles wide at the DMZ."

His job was also to entertain visitors from Stateside. They got a lot of visitors, and that became quite burdensome. He had asked Washing-ton to please try to control visitors—they were taking too much time from his commander's schedule.

He did his paperwork at home, on planes, in helicopters. He worked seven days a week. His family was not with him in 1967.

Operations was his number-one job, and trying to anticipate where the enemy would attack. Fifty percent of his energy was devoted to troop deployment.

He gave us a rundown on the major components of MACV—CICV—between 430,000 and 440,000 American servicemen were there.

These military people love ranges—figures are never exact. He, too, had to think hard for some of the information, reminding us it had been sixteen years ago.

I tried to remember what I had done sixteen years ago. I lived in San Francisco at the time. I had an art gallery—I also had worked at the Bank of America. I can picture many incidents, but ninety percent of the names escape me.

I promised myself not to sue anyone whom I had anything to do with out there at that time—I'd make an utter fool of myself on the witness stand.

General Westmoreland said he had learned more about what many of these people and departments did during the trial than he had ever known when he was their commander.

He really did not refer to the Order of Battle summary like many of these men did; he said he had no occasion to. He said it was historic data that was of no use to him. Current intelligence was what he was concerned with—he needed to make judgments of the capabilities of the units that would be particularly dangerous to us.

He had requested more troops in April 1967. He had two requests:

List 1 was the minimum essential force of 100,000 men.

List 2 was the optimum force of 200,000. With the latter request, he claimed he could bring this war to some conclusion, but it would take five years.

The President did not make any decision on his request until July, after McNamara visited Saigon.

At that time, General Westmoreland had a new plan. If he could get 80,000 U.S. troops, he could hire Vietnamese for support strength. This request was granted.

On July 10, General Westmoreland's mother died. When he went home for the funeral, he was asked to speak to Congress. He asked if he could elaborate on this and his lawyer said he'd rather that he didn't. I felt sorry for him. A general isn't even allowed time to mourn a family member, his mother.

Mr. Burt asked about the cable incident with General McChristian. Westmoreland gave pretty much the same account as General McChristian did. "Why do you think General McChristian showed you the cable?"

"My feeling was he wanted to get my endorsement, which was highly irregular without having been briefed. There was a tremendous increase in these irregular enemy troops and guerrillas and political cadre."

He continued, "I wasn't about to dispatch or endorse this cable—it could be terribly misleading. I told him I wanted to hold the cable [or the draft message as the court, after clarification of terms, named it] until I could be properly briefed."

About ten days later, he was briefed. He said he was rather impressed with the work and detail that had gone into the briefing.

Not only was the enemy broken down into the various categories of SD, SSD, political cadre, guerrillas, etc., but also the listing and numbers for each province, of which there were forty-four. He was led to believe that the numbers were arrived at by going into each district.

It was a numbers exercise.

Two documents were presented as exhibits and subsequently as evi-

dence: General Westmoreland's appointment book and his diary—
which was called "Historic Notes," General, Volume 7, May
1–August 18, 1967—and is presently in the L. B. Johnson Library.
He said he began keeping the diary about a year after he was in Vietnam, on the advice of Eisenhower, who said he began keeping one
much later than he should have.

"You have an entry here, sir, dated May 19—8:00 P.M. IHO. What
does that mean, do you remember that, sir?"

"Yes, I do—it was a dinner in honor of Admiral Sharp."

"What does IHO stand for?" asked Mr. Burt.

"In honor of!" answered Westy.

There were a lot of trips to the side bar—the lawyers love to talk to
the judge at the side bar.

Miriam, next to me, said that she liked Mr. Burt's hair today—you
can tell he set it.

I said I didn't think men did that.

She said that of course they do. Look at the court recorder—he has
his nails done.

I looked at my nails. The polish was all chipped. I kept my fingers
curled the rest of the afternoon.

We were dismissed rather late for lunch, about one-thirty. Cheryl
and I went around the corner, where we had our plates overloaded for
$4.50 with good Italian food.

Cheryl said that she hoped we wouldn't have to find Westmoreland
guilty and that maybe all of them were right—he and CBS—and that
everyone was just overenthusiastic over their jobs. He looked like he's
basically an honest man and that he had strong convictions that he was
doing the right thing. I told her I felt the same way, but that the judge
told us we can't be swayed by anything but the evidence.

I'm sorry she is an alternate. I would like to have her deliberate with
us. She listens to the evidence, and she's a very feeling person as well.
I believe she would be quite fair.

Actually, I really feel that the group of people I've spent all the time
with in the jury room the last few weeks is basically a fair group of
people.

One of the girls really lets her feelings show: I don't like Sam
Adams's eyes, I don't like Mr. Burt's suits, and so forth. I just hope
she's all talk, like this, and when it comes down to deliberations, that
she'll be fair.

We got back into the courtroom at three, and Mr. Burt told us he
was going to show us a taped interview of General Westmoreland
by CBS.

Notice how friendly we were in the courtroom, how General West-moreland was not under any stress. Notice how they try to trap General Westmoreland with a fourteen-year-old memory without the benefit of briefing him—in front of a TV camera with George Crile lurking in the background and Mike Wallace firing questions at him.

Burt didn't quite state it like that, but that's what he implied. General Westmoreland was not in the courtroom during this, or for the rest of the afternoon.

Mrs. Westmoreland was, though. She was very busy with her embroidery during the entire procedure.

Mr. Boies put his two cents' worth in: "What is a more logical explanation of what happened—what you heard on the witness stand now, or what you are about to see on the TV monitor—what he told Mike Wallace? You be the judge."

General Westmoreland says, "Let me hasten to say" a lot. Actually, there wasn't much else new said on the tapes. Mike Wallace does like to fire questions. He has an authoritative voice, and he has guts. Some of the things that he asks about take, I guess, a newsman. George Crile has a sensitive way of asking questions. Mike Wallace jumps right in, but he does get answers. He also gets it back.

General Westmoreland at one point said, "Stop it, Mike, stop it! I don't know where you were in 1967–68, but I was in Vietnam!"

General Westmoreland said he felt that the American press distorted the Tet offensive—the Vietcong were incapable of winning a military victory, but they won a political one. Thanks to the press and the state of mind of the American people.

Johnson apparently was very sensitive to public opinion. He watched all three networks at the same time on three different TVs. He even had a TV in the bathroom.

God, I hope my husband doesn't get any ideas!

General Westmoreland said that the enemy was really scraping the bottom of its manpower pool. Kids too young and frightened to fight were trying to escape and go back to North Vietnam. But pistols were put to their backs to make them keep on fighting.

He said that MACV was right on the scene: They were the best judge of what was happening—the CIA was too remote.

Washington was not sophisticated enough to evaluate the information accurately—neither was the press. This was all, of course, in reference to the numbers—the almighty uncounted numbers.

The TV monitors were shut off at 4:45; we were given orders to return to court at 1:00 P.M. tomorrow after lunch.

Have a good night—speak to no one.

Traffic was brutal. It took me one hour and fifteen minutes to get from court back to my father-in-law's apartment on the Upper East Side—the same trip that took me fifteen minutes this morning.

I went to sleep early.

November 16, 1984

I spent the morning doing things like taking an extra long shower, leisurely reading the morning paper. General Westmoreland was on the front page—it was a very unflattering picture of him. He was walking up the steps of the courthouse with his chin sticking out.

I walked all the way down Madison Avenue to Grand Central Station.

I stopped at the bank and deposited my jury check. Tried again to stop in at that antique store that Bob told me had a desk we were looking for. It wasn't open again. I had a nice visit with an art-glass shop two doors down. I stopped in a lot of other shops on my way. It was like being on vacation. I went to Sam Flax to pick up the missing knob for my drawing table. I even talked to the owners of a crazily painted Porsche that I've seen on the street. I had a nice morning.

The trains were all crazy. I waited for twenty-five minutes for an express.

I picked up a Nedick's hot dog and carried it into the jury room. My soda had spilled all over it by the time I got there, so I had a soggy roll.

Westmoreland was on the stand when we took our seats in the jury stand.

Mr. Burt was still questioning him. Burt had on a hairy gray suit and a delicate pink knit sweater vest. Burt paced back and forth a lot. He's been getting frisky lately. I'm certain that he has watched Boies in action and he is attempting to use the courtroom tactics that Boies does—thumb through pages while a witness is answering, turn his back to talk to a colleague—but it doesn't have the same effect.

I think that the light in the left-hand corner of the courtroom ceiling talks to Burt. Every time he formulates a question, he stares up at that light. Once today it failed him because he looked up at all of the lights at one point, grasping for the right word. He even tried the fixture in the back of the room.

Westmoreland answered:

"Of course, McChristian could have sent that cable without my approval, but because of the scope of the cable, he wanted my approval.''

''No, I didn't say bombshell—that's not in my vocabulary.''

''I told him, Joe, if that cable goes, it will be a public relations problem.''

''No, I never told anyone to reduce the figures.''

''The SD and SSD had little attack capabilities . . . Admiral Sharp—you mean Olie—that was his nickname . . .''

''Of course, those statements were accurate when I sent the cable—why would I have sent it otherwise? . . .''

''No, Ambassador Bunker was my boss—he was in total charge.''

The judge showed us his X chart again on how to receive the evidence we were given.

The evidence was on the truth, not state of mind. He took ten minutes to make sure we had it clear.

Burt read a long line of numbers and letters that sounded like a New York State driver's license.

Westmoreland told us that the numbers and letters were secret codes.

We heard the contents of the cable, and Westmoreland explained to us his dilemma of that gray area—how to count orderlies and pool typists into the Order of Battle.

Westmoreland said Davidson made sure all his ducks were in a row. He was very thorough and made sure he could defend his estimates and documents.

He said that Davidson and General Godding had briefed him on the estimates. (I thought that yesterday he had said he hadn't met General Godding. I'd better look up my notes.)

Today he said he never heard of Hamscher.

Davidson recommended that Westmoreland endorse a document. Westmoreland trusted him and took his advice: ''I didn't have time to dig into those matters, he was my authority in that department.''

Westmoreland said he had an open door policy and instructed his officers to do the same: ''Problems need venting—if there has been poor judgment or an injustice done, I want to know about it.''

Vietnam was his eighth command; you learn a lot about soldiers and people in that time. He said he welcomed anyone to come to him with a real problem. The only thing he wasn't interested in hearing about was a complaint about the food.

He pulled a card out of his pocket that he said he carried with him all the time and had printed up for all of his officers.

It was titled "Guidance for Commanders in Vietnam." There were fifteen points:

- make the welfare of your men your main concern;
- mess, mail, and medical aid are foremost;
- recognize outstanding work;
- be smarter than the enemy;
- be sensitive to the detection and correction of injustices;
- keep an open door policy for complaints; etc.

The card was passed around for all of us in the jury stand to read.

He told us about a former soldier he had met recently who had used the open door policy—to tell him about an officer who was verbally abusing him, and he was sick and tired of it.

Subsequently, the officer was relieved of his duties.

A cable that Westmoreland had sent from the Philippines was put in evidence. Why were you in the Philippines?

Westmoreland thought very hard. He looked up at the same light that Burt talks to and exclaimed, "Oh—to see my wife. That was very important, you know."

I turned to look at Mrs. Westmoreland embroidering in the courtroom. She was nodding in agreement.

Everyone in the courtroom seemed to get a kick out of the incident. Everyone got serious again when the contents of the cable were presented:

SD and SSD were only old men and women—they were no threat . . .

Press reaction of much greater concern . . . if you release figures of 420,000–431,000 newsmen will seize upon the figures as an increase . . . they will jump to erroneous and gloomy conclusions . . .

"Why were you so concerned with press reaction?" asked Mr. Burt.

Westmoreland thought for a minute and asked if he could answer in more than one sentence because it was a complicated issue.

He was granted permission.

He began slowly: "Vietnam was an unorthodox war—it was fought halfway around the world." He was quiet for a few seconds; the courtroom was too.

"It was the first war without censorship, and I want to hasten to say I was all for it. I did not approve of press censorship. It was covered by TV. It was a unique experience and unique to the media. The troops did a great job. I was proud of them. They were proud of themselves. It was a difficult job. They did it magnificently.

"But they never felt that they got a fair shake from the media. They were sensitive to that. They would get newspaper clippings from home—poor reporting was detrimental to their morale.

"There were five hundred reporters at my headquarters. There was great competition for lead stories. Most were good, but many were distorted. Of course I was sensitive to press reaction." (His voice rose with emotion as the speech went on.) "I felt an obligation to my troops.

"Suddenly I'm told to put a new figure of a hundred thousand people into an Order of Battle that were not fighters. They were old men and women, home guard, they were civilians. We didn't want to kill civilians. It would have been detrimental to my troops to add this figure.

"Yes, I was sensitive to press reaction. They would have drawn erroneous and gloomy conclusions.

"I agreed with General Abrams. I did it then, I'd do it now, and I'd do it again if I had to."

I felt tears welling up in my eyes.

We were quickly given a break.

A couple of jurors said they felt like crying. Eileen said she heard the "Battle Hymn of the Republic" playing in the background. Phil, the reader, said he wasn't moved at all.

But no one could stop talking. Nobody, as it turned out, looked over at the defendants. Westy had mesmerized the jury—just as I'm sure he had mesmerized his troops.

His little talk was like that of a general leading his men into battle.

The TV interview of Westmoreland was anticlimactic when we returned from our break.

Mike Wallace was pounding Westmoreland.

Westmoreland told him he talked to the wrong people. You only talked to those people in intelligence—they were hyped on numbers.

You should have talked to Graham and Davidson.

No—he never heard any of the Parkins-Morris incident. Why didn't Parkins come to my office?

Could Morris or Graham have kept information from you, General Westmoreland?

Westmoreland never really answered that.

Mike Wallace asked Westmoreland about Danny Graham.

"He had a rapid rise to fame," said Wallace. "Could he have been a keystone to blocking reports?"

"If he did, it was for a good reason—I considered him a very competent man," answered Westy.

We were dismissed for the day.

We are to meet Monday at ten.

November 19, 1984

When we went into the jury box, the judge ordered the first alternate to take Marion's seat. The judge said that Marion had had a personal tragedy—her mother in Atlanta had had a stroke. She would not be rejoining us.

Loretta Brown was now J3.

Everyone teased her at the first break.

"Did you see all the artists sketching you? They had to erase Marion's picture and superimpose you on top of her!"

"See, you're not getting away that easily. Pack your bags—you'll be sequestered with us. Now you'll get your chance to take a trip to nowhere." She'd cancelled a cruise to nowhere last weekend.

Westmoreland was on the stand during the morning session.

He said that the CIA had a different view of the war—they were obsessed with increasing the number of enemy we were fighting.

We knew best—we were there on the ground.

Another cable was introduced. Burt talked. Westmoreland asked the judge if he could correct Mr. Burt. USIB stood for U.S. Intelligence Board, not Estimates Board.

The new cable named the people who were at the Saigon conference: Generals Abrams, Komer, Sible, Kern, Davidson, Godding, and Carver.

More cables were introduced—secret, top secret, secret eyes only—more numbers of troops—more estimates. January 1968 was the first month for reports of infiltration reaching 25,000.

No, those other reports in the earlier fall were not infiltration—infiltration is secret. We knew that those divisions were there.

How many in a division? Seven to ten thousand.

I wrote a note to myself: could it be that we are having difficulty with semantics? The numbers were there, but MACV refused to call them infiltrators? We finally got to the interview with Mike Wallace and George Crile.

In April or May of '81, Mike Wallace called Westmoreland on the telephone and said CBS was doing a special educational program on Vietnam. No, it was not *60 Minutes.*

George Crile called a few days later. They had some give and take on the telephone. The program was to be built around the Tet offensive.

Westmoreland did some research on Tet and came up to New York.

Some stocky five foot seven or five foot eight guy picked him up and took him to CBS. You could see Adams and Crile trying to figure out who was the stocky five foot seven or eight guy—Westmoreland had met Mike Wallace in Vietnam, where he spent one full day on a field trip with him.

He said he immediately felt somewhat uneasy because Wallace had been warm and friendly in Vietnam but was all cool and business this time.

George Crile had promised to send Westmoreland a checklist of what was to be discussed—however, he got it at his hotel room when he arrived at the Plaza. It was quite different from what he'd been led to believe.

At the interviews there were two cameramen, Mike Wallace, George Crile, and a girl.

George Crile and the girl sat behind Westy, to his right. Westmoreland felt that Crile had been holding up cards to prompt Mike Wallace on questions he should ask.

No, Westmoreland was not prepared for the questions that they fired at him.

"Did you lick your lips from time to time?" Mr. Burt asked.

Westmoreland said, "Yes. I had these bright lights on me—and I was parched, and I have dry lips, and when Mr. Wallace was talking, I didn't realize the cameras were still on me—I was trying to keep my lips from cracking. They were interviewing me for over two hours.

"Since then my wife gave me some waxy stuff to keep on my lips."

"Could you tell me in your own words, General Westmoreland, what you felt about the interview?" asked Burt.

"It wasn't an interview—it was an inquisition. I didn't know what I was participating in. They were going for the jugular—I was ambushed."

Mr. Boies objected, and all the lawyers went to the side bar.

When they returned, the judge told us to disregard the last statements; they were stricken from the record.

"Sir," Burt continued. "Were you asked questions you were not prepared for? Did you lose your temper?"

"My first impulse was to walk out—but I didn't, because so many times I'd seen on *60 Minutes*—"

Everyone objected—Mr. Boies, Mr. Burt, the judge.

"Did you consider walking out, General?"

"Yes, I did!"

"Why didn't you walk out?"

"So many times I've seen on *60 Minutes* . . ."

The judge interrupted, "Are you objecting, Mr. Boies?"

Boies jumped to his feet. "Yes, sir!"

"Do I have to guess?" asked the judge.

"Limit your answers, please, General Westmoreland," reminded the judge. "Did you think it would be an admission of guilt if you stopped the interviews?"

"Yes I did!" answered Westmoreland.

"What did you say?" asked Mr. Burt. "If anything. Can you answer that if you will, please, sir?"

Burt has been prancing around the courtroom, sipping water, looking at papers—he's trying very hard to look cool.

"I told Mr. Crile, looking him straight in the eye—I have been deceived, I have been rattlesnaked!"

There were more objections. You will disregard that.

On June 9, 1981, General Westmoreland wrote CBS a letter. We heard it in the courtroom. It was civil and tactical—well written. He called the interview interesting and included several documents that he thought they might find helpful. He suggested that they interview Bunker, Komer, Graham, Carver, Colby, and Morris. No one from CBS ever acknowledged the receipt of the letter.

It got cold in the courtroom—downright frigid. We were given a break while someone shut the windows.

When we came back into the courtroom, the judge gave us a lecture about tone of questioning. Westmoreland had mentioned tone, but we are not judging whether CBS can be held libel for the tone of an interview. The question we must ask is did they make false, defamatory statements?

We had a new witness, William Bundy.

Mr. Reiss, another lawyer for the plaintiff, was now examining him.

Mr. Reiss has been in court every day. He's young, quiet, stoic-looking—trim beard, trim figure—and now that he is questioning a witness, I see that he is also a monotone, and boring.

William Bundy had impressive credentials, like the rest. He went to Yale and Harvard Law, taught history at Princeton. Had worked for the CIA in the Office of National Estimates. He had been a deputy of international security affairs under Kennedy and assistant secretary of defense under Johnson. He recently gave up being editor for *Foreign Affairs* magazine.

He knew them all—Johnson, Rostow, Carver. William Bundy was tall and stiff—quite intellectual looking—very controlled. He blinked a lot and pursed his lips a lot. I became fascinated watching his facial expressions. He spoke in a monotone, but accurately. None of these men we have seen as witnesses believes in blanket statements or generalities. Every word—every period—is precise.

It was a long afternoon. We were dismissed at 5:15.

November 10, 1984

We were all there at ten, but we were not called in until ten-thirty. By eleven-thirty I was trying desperately not to fall asleep.

There were a lot of trips to the side bar—long ones. There was, I'm sure, a lot of discussion on the validity of Mr. Bundy's testimony.

It is evident he is an intelligent man. However, the information he had was received through a variety of sources—mainly George Carver and Fred Green, his intelligence briefers.

He received a long questioning from the judge, who was trying to establish if Bundy simply took the information he received and passed it on to the Subcommittee on Asian Affairs or if he had formed any of his own opinions.

Mr. Bundy tried hard to convince us that he had fourteen to sixteen years of experience dealing directly with Vietnam and that he did indeed combine his views with the intelligence that he received.

In retrospect, Bundy said he believed that we should go back and revise the infiltration figures before Tet upward, as far back as November.

We broke for a short lunch.

General Westmoreland was on the stand when we returned. He read a letter into the record that he had sent to CBS.

We then saw an interview of Mike Wallace and George Crile on a show emceed by Diane Sawyer. It was aired on the Thursday before the Saturday airing of the infamous documentary.

The Uncounted Enemy: A Vietnam Deception. Cuts of Westmoreland being interviewed were shown, then cuts of Hamscher.

The most unflattering cuts from the documentary of Westmoreland were shown, of course, and then an intellectual discussion followed with Miss Sawyer playing straight man and Mike Wallace and George Crile the exposers.

Westmoreland was taken aback by the program, claiming it was humiliating.

He saw the program and received about fifty calls from family and friends, who expressed astonishment, concern, disillusionment, bewilderment, and questioned if they should believe it or not.

We were shown newspaper articles that were sent to Westmoreland and we were shown a letter from a woman in Houston, Texas.

Part of that letter stated:

You ordered our sons and husbands, brothers, fathers, and friends, to fight a hopeless battle against insurmountable odds.

How could you have such little regard for our young Americans? . . .

You played God. American parents are still grieving. If anyone deserves to be stripped of their so-called honors, it's you. . . .

We were also shown a cartoon. A picture of Westmoreland holding a machine gun and three bodies lying on the ground, dead.

One had *Duty* written on him

The other *Honor*

The other *Country*

It was titled "Body Count."

He was visibly shaken when he saw the cartoon again. He said it was a humiliating experience. We were given a break.

The courtroom was so cold that our teeth were chattering. The artists were bundled up in coats and hats and gloves when we returned. Boies was cross-examining:

"Didn't you say you didn't have a reporting obligation to the President?"

Westmoreland said that he didn't recall that. (I thought that he had said that also.)

He said the President was well briefed by Rostow, but now that his mind was refreshed, he saw that he had discussed things with the President. They talked about a trip he took to the LBJ Ranch. He and Mrs. Westmoreland had a press conference there.

The rest of the day was more of the same. We were dismissed at four-thirty.

Tomorrow we would meet from ten until two—no lunch—and the judge told us that we would be off from jury duty from December 21 to January 1.

November 21, 1984

Today court was like what you see in the movies.

The witness being cross-examined by the opposing attorney.

All the testimony you've seen up until now sounds so sincere—so credible.

Suddenly the defense attorney questions an inconsistency—a hole in the testimony.

For a few minutes sparks fly—tension hangs in the air, the judge pounds his gavel, the witness's attorney yelling for an objection, and no one listening to anyone else.

It lasted for thirty seconds. But it was just like in the movies. Movies leave out the boring hours in between—in this case, days, months.

But only a person who has sat through every bit of testimony, every witness, every question asked over and over and over again, can feel the true impact of the thirty seconds of flaring emotions.

It started out as a normal day. All of us were looking forward to the four-day weekend.

We exchanged our schedules for Thanksgiving; some were cooking, others weren't—there was conjecture on traffic and weather.

We had been told that we would go straight through without lunch, ten to two. Many of the jurors brought snacks and shared them. Cheese and crackers, cookies and fruit were all over the place.

When we were called into the courtroom, all the characters were in position. Boies was still questioning General Westmoreland. Mrs. Westmoreland was still embroidering. Mike Wallace was there. (Bob told me he had been in Ethiopia.)

I'm sure that a person in his position must feel that he lives in a twilight zone—one minute in the midst of Ethiopia's starvation and drought, and the next sitting in a courtroom filled with well-dressed women, seasoned reporters, and four-star generals accusing him of warping the truth.

After the testimony yesterday and the general's story of not receiving an accurate account of what questions CBS would ask him in an interview, and not having the courtesy of returning letters and so forth, it doesn't look great for CBS.

I am beginning to know the real meaning of there being two sides to every story. Now I suspect that there are really three sides to this story.

As it happens—if I got the dates accurately (so many float around, it's hard to recall exact dates without my notes)—it seems as though CBS contacted General Westmoreland one weekend and the interview took place the following weekend. If not the following one, it was no more than ten to fourteen days later that the fateful meeting took place.

Boies was driving at something because he kept questioning the general about being out of town the week before his interview. The point was never resolved, but it led one to believe that CBS had been trying to reach him by phone the week before the interview, and the general was unavailable.

A whole hour went by of questioning and requestioning on the cable that McChristian wanted sent.

Westmoreland kept saying that his meeting with McChristian was insignificant—the cable (notifying Washington that there were twice as many enemy) was nothing.

Boies went through Westmoreland's diary and found entries about lunch with a nephew and what they discussed. He even had an entry about recommending a doctor to a soldier with a head cold.

When Westmoreland was questioned on this insignificant entry, as opposed to a meeting with his J2, Westy said it was a human interest note.

He, Westmoreland, started referring to the so-called Order of Battle.

Boies got mad and started: "When did you start calling it the so-called Order of Battle? When? Did you ever call it the so-called Order of Battle back in 1966 or 1967? No! General, you just started calling it the so-called Order of Battle in this courtroom, didn't you?" The judge kept yelling, "Mr. Boies—Mr. Boies!" Mr. Burt jumped to his feet, yelling, *"Objection, objection!"*

Westmoreland was answering with controlled emotion and Boies just kept firing his questions, listening to no one.

It did wake you up—the episode was over as quickly as it began, and we were dismissed for a break.

Boies had regained his composure when we returned. In fact, if you hadn't seen the incident, you would never guess that emotions had flared. Everyone was nicey-nice.

Westmoreland was now defending his statement that he had never used the word *bombshell* when he spoke to General McChristian. As he said: "Bombshell just isn't in my lexicon, I would have said it could result in a political relations problem to report new high estimates of enemy irregulars."

Well!

Boies had him refer to page 642 of a deposition he gave over ayear ago.

As General Westmoreland read it, he looked up over his reading glasses and laughed.

"Yes, Mr. Boies, I see what you're driving at!" Everyone in the courtroom laughed. Boies looked at him like the cat that ate the canary.

"Well, General, was it not part of your lexicon—your vocabulary?"

General Westmoreland took off his glasses and laughed nervously, and said: "Mr. Boies, after fourteen days of depositions with you, you thrust the word *bombshell* right into my lexicon."

Loud laughter in the courtroom.

"Look back in your deposition, General Westmoreland, and you find for me where I thrust it into your lexicon."

The judge looked up, unbelieving, and said, "Through all sixteen hundred pages?"

The audience fell apart.

General Westmoreland answered, "If I knew the word *bombshell* would become such a big issue, I sure as hell would never have used it."

He continued: "I was pounded and pounded in that interview, there were bright lights on me. I felt like a criminal on the witness stand. I told Mike Wallace it was a nonissue—that whole meeting with General McChristian."

Well, naturally Mr. Boies found several accounts of the general using the term *bombshell*, and he beat it to death.

It was obvious *bombshell* was indeed in General Westmoreland's lexicon. There was another tense incident when General Westmoreland ended a statement with: "You know *that*, Mr. Boies."

"No, I don't *know that*, General Westmoreland," he answered.

The judge reprimanded Mr. Boies, and Mr. Boies told the judge to tell the general not to say that or lead him and the judge told the general what Mr. Boies said, and everything was nicey-nice again.

I don't think that David Boies ever goes to sleep. I am certain he only owns blue suits, blue ties, and blue and white shirts, so that he can get dressed in the dark. Maybe he's color blind and his wife only lets him out of the house in monochrome. Anyhow, he certainly does his homework.

Out of the clear blue, he starts referring to General Westmoreland's book. The copy in his hand had slips of yellow paper sticking out all over the place.

"General Westmoreland, do you recall on page 432 in your book, you discussed your request for more troops?"

"Yes, Mr. Boies—I'm quite familiar with that book," answered the general.

Naturally, before Boies presented this exhibit he had laid the groundwork with thirty minutes of questioning on exactly how many troops the general had requested and the fact that he didn't get his optimum request.

Westy made a point of emphasizing that he was quite satisfied with the number of troops he had finally received.

Mr. Boies is like the spider—he weaves his webs quite masterfully.

"Well, General, according to your book, you were quite dissatisfied."

"Oh, well! Er, Mr. Boies, that was in my book," he answered.

That brought down the house.

The rest of the afternoon was filled with questions, explanations, repetitions. At two we were wished a happy Thanksgiving by the judge and given his usual cautions—don't read articles pertaining to the case, etc.

Is there life after court? If there is, it is frantic. Traffic was somewhat hectic, but not horribly so. I arrived in Carmel by five, just in time to stand in long lines at the supermarket. I never shopped so quickly for Thanksgiving dinner. I literally charged up and down aisles, throwing things into the cart. I had no time for comparison shopping or label reading.

The turkey was thawed—by midnight I had stuffing made, vegetables peeled, and table set and all systems go. By 2:00 A.M., I had the house clean enough to greet my twelve Thanksgiving guests.

Thanksgiving went well. Everything came out of the oven on time and okay. Everyone left stuffed to the gills and carrying doggy bags. The sign of a successful holiday. By 11:00 P M., all signs of our company were gone.

Leslie and Tracy, my step-daughters, stayed. Leslie was playing backgammon with Daddy, and Tracy was sweating over some physics problems for her pre-med tests. At last I could work on my sculptures, which were due Saturday morning at the art gallery for the Christmas show.

This trial has really put a damper on my life. If I'd had any idea I'd be a juror on this case I never would have accepted this commission.

Cheryl was the biggest help. Being in charge of the picture collection at the New York City Public Library, she got me the photographs I'd needed to get inspired. I spent all day Friday on them.

The sculptures were okay—I had to finish painting and varnishing them. I wasn't totally pleased, but then again, I never am, so they were par for the course—the important thing was that they would be completed as I'd promised.

On Saturday I helped set them up in the gallery, did some Christmas shopping, and spent the rest of the day taking advantage of the beautiful warm weather. I cleaned outside. A house in the country is wonderful unless you have no time to keep it up.

Commuting daily is no help. Thank the Lord for a four-day weekend!

However, it was over in a blink. The next thing I knew, there I was on my way back to New York, with clothes for the week. We decided to spend a few days with my father-in-law.

November 26, 1984

The moment we got back into the courtroom on Monday morning, I got depressed.

I felt like I was serving a prison sentence. I looked over the characters, all in place. I looked at the same familiar faces in the audience and the same familiar reporters, artists, court reporters, court deputies.

Are they enjoying their work? Is this fun? Do they get bored? Can they hear? Some were there by choice, others were not.

One man looks like a derelict. He shuffles in every day—sits in the back row in the same red plaid shirt.

I've been trying to decide who he is, what his life is like—does he come here to get out of the cold? One day he threw me a curve. He came in, dressed in a suit. Nothing spiffy, but a suit nonetheless. I've made up a lot of stories about him. He seems to pay close attention and watch with interest.

The artists, of course, are always busy—at least one a day manages to drop all their brushes at a crucial moment. They, I can identify with—time flies when you're busy sketching.

Judge Pierre Leval wins my admiration. He renews my faith in the jury system. He is bright, fair, patient, humorous. He never seems to miss a beat. He interrupts to clarify statements, picks up points—I could go on and on with how well he maintains a positive tone in the courtroom.

I can well imagine how much more difficult this whole ordeal could be with someone in charge who wasn't as warm a person.

The day proved to be boring. Boies was still on the same line of questioning. He had made his point, I thought, but he was trying hard to break down the general.

I wondered if he used any of these tactics at home—or did he save it all for his cross-examinations?

He smiles—he's polite, and he has a preppy look about him—but what an iron will. At one point the judge asked him to start on another line of questioning, and he unblinkingly told the judge he wasn't finished yet.

Leval is wise. He knows when not to press a point—he had made his. Boies made his—he asked one or two questions more on the same subject, but then shifted quickly to a new line.

A couple of cables had gone back and forth—Wheeler to Westy and Westy to Wheeler in response. Westy didn't recall the cables at all.

Apparently, a Mr. Apple had written an article in *The New York Times* to the effect that it's strange that General Westmoreland comes to the United States saying how well the war is going and we're winning, etc., but then returns to Vietnam and requests more troops.

Wheeler immediately sent a cable to Westmoreland.

The pen, I guess, is mightier than the sword. Everyone seemed to be worried about the press.

Westmoreland went through a long, involved explanation about how cables are answered, who writes them—he only puts an okay on them. His J3 probably wrote the cable.

Boies went on with another line of questioning—the fact that in several documents and testimony, Westmoreland's reaction to increased enemy estimates was that of surprise.

A discussion of semantics evolved. I wasn't surprised—question: Who gave the estimate? Whose estimates were they?

Those intelligence people always inflated numbers and so on and so on.

"You don't understand how I held a meeting," said General Westmoreland.

He went on to tell us what a good general he was and how he gave everyone a chance to air his views, and then the fact that he was the general and he made the final decision.

He went on to tell us what a good soldier he was because Ambassador Bunker was his boss and they were always on the plane together—there were no secrets between them.

"Intelligence was not an exact science," Westy said. "It's like trying to estimate how many roaches you have in your kitchen; we knew there were administrative services in Cambodia, but had no idea how many—there was no way of estimating."

Exhibit 284 was brought in—a bar graph that showed the Vietcong, North Vietnamese strength for the third quarter of 1965, 1966, and 1967.

It was a graph that had been taken to the conference at Langley to brief the President.

Mr. Boies naturally couldn't believe that it didn't include SD and SSD or political infrastructure, and he found some other charts from the same period showing in essence the same figures that did.

Fur started to fly when Westmoreland said to Boies: "You don't know how to read bar graphs."

He went on to say that Rostow didn't know how to read them either and that he had given faulty testimony back in October.

The judge interrupted to give a lecture to General Westmoreland about debating the attorneys.

"Direct your answers to the jury. When I ask you a question, answer to the jury. When Mr. Boies asks you a question, direct it to the jury."

Westmoreland proceeded to explain how the bar graph should be read. It was a long, contrived process of eliminating this group in one column—hence you must eliminate it from the others to get a sound reading—and on and on.

I am a college graduate. In fact, I have had courses way beyond a master's degree—I have been well educated in the use of bar graphs, line graphs, charts, and so forth.

Visual aides are meant to clarify; they are meant to put complicated information in a form that can be well understood by the simplest of minds.

I sat there dumbfounded. Why would anyone go out of his way to complicate the information?

We were dismissed early. Scratching our heads—I'm glad there are twelve people on a jury—the decision we must make looks relatively simple on the surface. But both sides leave a lot of questions—

November 27, 1984

I was in a happy mood. We went to a Mozart concert last night at the Metropolitan Museum, a birthday gift to my husband from my father-in-law.

The concert was wonderful. The pianist was superb. Everyone was praising the performance. I mentioned that I'd seen *Amadeus* the other night and how the line "Mozart, you have too many notes" made me laugh. This pianist handled them with skill not to be believed.

The mood carried me through the subway trauma and back up the courtroom steps this morning. I bumped into two of the defendants, Crile and Adams. It's disconcerting to meet outside of the courtroom. We have been amply warned about such meetings. We exchanged quick smiles of acknowledgment and moved on quickly.

A few days ago the same thing happened with Westmoreland, so I felt it was even.

It's a strange position to be in. I'm a gregarious person. If I see someone I vaguely know in unfamiliar surroundings, I'm usually the one who acts like we're long lost friends.

All the jurors were in the jury room. Everything was as usual. One found an article in the *Daily News* captioned: JURORS FEEL THEY ARE ONES BEING PUNISHED.

We all read it with interest. Kate brought in a new puzzle—chocolate chip cookies was the theme. I wanted to kill her—here I am, trying to go on a diet. Being a jigsaw puzzle freak myself, I knew immediately that those cookies could be my undoing.

The court clerk came in and counted us. Closed the door. We all went back to our diversions. I was trying to go over my bank statement. Myron and Harold and Loretta were reading the papers. Kate and David were getting the puzzle started. Eileen and Randy and Richard and Linda were playing cards. Philip was reading a novel.

The court clerk came in again and said it would be a few more minutes.

Jean was clipping coupons from the newspaper. Lili was reading a book in Chinese. Michael and Cheryl and Norma were talking, and Carmine was writing notes.

We were settling in. We no longer felt the need to be formal or on guard—everyone was beginning to do his or her own thing.

The door opened again, and we lined up and filed into court. Everyone was smiles from ear to ear in the courtroom. Something funny must have transpired, I thought. The judge began.

"Ladies and gentlemen of the jury: You will have a day off!" If he had said "You have just won a million dollars" I don't think I would have reacted differently. You know, this is news that you hear that you really aren't sure you've heard. This was it. It was ten-fifty—a full day! A gorgeous day at that. It was clear and balmy outside—a perfect day to do New York City.

Within ten minutes we were all out of the building. Some were going to work, others home, others shopping. If only the judge knew what he did for the economy of New York City today!

I went holiday shopping—celebrating Chanukah and Christmas can be detrimental to one's purse. I didn't care. SoHo was the scene. No store's doorway was left unshadowed by Juror 2. Many stores received my sheckels—others were left my signature. It was a truly fruitful day. I called the phone number we were given in court, at three o'clock sharp. "You are not to meet in court tomorrow. You are to report to your usual place of work," was the message. I had to think—where is my usual place of work?

November 28, 1984

I went to school. Back to the country, the kids, the paint on the floor—the voices. Voices, voices everywhere—running feet, it was as though I had never left the building.

"Mrs. Roth, Scot just kicked me." I still had my hat and coat on, walking toward my classroom. "Hey, Mrs. Roth, you feeling better? Maryann just fell out of a tree and broke her arm. She's okay, though—she came back to school the next day, and she's learning how to draw with her left hand! The substitute stinks—she won't let us talk."

"Hi, Mrs. Roth—when you coming back? Is the case over? What's the general look like? Is he guilty?"

"Hi, Mrs. Roth. Oh, can we come in and work before school—I want to finish my work."

I made it to my classroom and locked the door behind me. Everything was so clean I didn't think I was in the same room. The projects the kids were doing looked wonderful. The paintings they did were even mounted.

How easily we all can be replaced!

The day flew by. Before I knew it, it was over. I went home exhausted. I poured myself a drink, opened up a package that had been sent to my house.

There were a bunch of letters the reading group had sent me, not knowing I'd be in school today.

Dear Mrs. Roth,
How are you doing? What's new in the big city? It's the same old thing here. I've improved a lot since you've been gone. How was

your Thanksgiving? Mine was pretty good. I can't wait when you get back.

We all miss you a lot.

Your friend,
Brian

Dear Mrs. Roth:
I hope you come soon. How are you feeling? Mrs. Jensen is a nice substitute teacher. Hope you come back soon.

From,
Jerry

Dear Mrs. Roth:
How are you? What have you been doing? Do you enjoy that book? In art we are drawing snowflakes. I hope you come to see us. WE ALL MISS YOU.

Your student and friend,
Liz

To Mrs. Roth:
How are you doing? I hope your not bored? Do you like the other jurys? So far art is pretty good. Were finished the boxes. Were doing the snowflakes. The other day we helped Mrs. Jensen hang up some stuff and put the boxes in the showcase.

From,
Susan

Dear Mrs. Roth
How are you? What are you doing? Are you still reading that book? As reading is going by it is pretty fun, but now that Mrs. Jensen had a conference with Mr. Kirk and Mr. Farrington reading has gotten much harder, and I am doing much harder. So far in my folder, I have gotten all 100's (mostly). Mrs. Jensen is sooooo nice to us, she has a nice temper and gives us snacks to eat while we do our work, It's really fun. In art we are making snowflakes, by the way I'm trying not to sit with the boys, and since I haven't art is a lot of fun. Well I have to go. Chorus in a little while but I'll write you again.

Miss you!
Your student,
Alma

Dear Mrs. Roth
How's life, mines fine my grades have been getting very high, how

was you Thanksgiving? I'll tell you what I ate for Thanksgiving. Prime ribs, pumpkin pie, golden potatoes.

> Your
> pupil,
> Greg

I thought about how wonderful my students were, and fell asleep.

November 29, 1984

It was another one of those days. Boies was still questioning General Westmoreland. It was a painful day. The questions—the same old questions. What did this figure mean—how did you arrive at that? I didn't arrive at that, my intelligence estimated that—this—then— probably—probable—possible. I couldn't stand it.

I listened—I watched—and I realized: There is something very wrong.

Either the general was still ill (we had been told he was ill, which is why we had gotten time off), or he was trying to cover up something.

They had been on the same question all morning. Boies was trying hard to get the general to admit that the combat support was really, or had become, the administrative services. After all, the figures carried over were the same exact figures.

Westmoreland kept denying it, kept going through long involved explanations and asking that questions be repeated.

I was getting tired. It was difficult to concentrate, my patience was wearing thin. I wondered how Boies was keeping his cool. I knew what he was driving at.

It was obvious, looking at all these documents in front of us, that the figures were skillfully veiled. If anyone could contrive a compli- cated way of arriving at figures, it was the military.

This group really belonged here, and we took this segment and placed them in this category and then added the militia from here (and it was incredible).

The man was so sincere. If I dared say I am questioning your in- tentions, I'm certain he would honestly be crushed.

I think he really believed he was doing it the best way. His boys told him so. I thought back on his boys. Davidson, Komer, Graham—he kept mentioning those names. When they appeared as witnesses, I was less than impressed. I didn't trust them at all.

What happens? When does it start? We've had a lot of witnesses. Some I liked, believed, with others I was uncertain. But with the ones that Westmoreland seemed to feel most credible, I definitely didn't like them and didn't believe them.

I felt Graham was a smart aleck, Davidson sly, and Komer pompous. These were the men that Westmoreland had put his faith in. "If these numbers do not represent the same categories, how come they are so similar?" Mr. Boies continued. "I asked the same question when I was briefed," answered the general, "but it was strictly a coincidence!"

Boies presented the documents to compare:

Exhibit 1412-A	January 31, 1967	PERINTREP
Combat	— 113,492	+ 3,480
Combat support	18,953	+ 300
Militia	112,760	N/C
Political cadre	39,175	N/C
	284,380	+ 3,780

Exhibit 199-A	February 1967	PERINTREP
Combat	113,087	(−405)
Admin. ser.	18,953	N/C
Irregulars	112,760	N/C
Political cadre	39,175	N/C
	283,975	(−405)
Maneuvers	102,002	−375
Combat support	11,085	− 30
	113,087	(−405)

Westy tried to explain that there was a transition period where troops or enemy were being recategorized. Then he insisted on reading definitions of what the combat support category consisted of and what was the makeup of the administrative services—doctors, logisticians, administrators.

I wondered if the general was on painkillers. He was acting confused, or he was aging or nervous. I couldn't believe that he was as unintelligent as he was sounding—or was he trying to cover up? It sounded like some not so skillful fillibustering.

Boies changed his line of questioning: When did you last discuss these numbers with your attorneys?

Did you read Rostow's deposition?

Did you read McChristian's deposition?

Rostow said that you *didn't* do a retrospective estimate—that you said it was impossible.

The general asked if he could give an anecdote in answer to his own words. He was given permission.

He said that he hadn't remembered that Rostow had briefed congressmen on the charts. He hadn't remembered until he went over his own history notes.

When he had come back Stateside for the briefing of the President, he was a guest at the White House with Mrs. Westmoreland. They were given their own apartment. Mrs. Johnson approached Mrs. Westmoreland and said that if she had friends in Washington she would like to entertain, feel free to invite them to the White House as her guests. Consequently, they were given menus and a staff, and the Westmorelands gave a dinner party in their suite.

In the meantime, President Johnson was entertaining some Democratic congressmen and he asked Westmoreland to brief them at their dinner party—so Westmoreland had to leave his own party.

Rostow was the briefer and he did a good job, Westy said. Then he went back to his own party.

Dorsen, the nervous lawyer for the plaintiff, returned. Dorsen hasn't been around for a while. He looks the same.

The two CIA guys were back—I was sure we were going to be getting some information close to classified. The subject changed to infiltration figures. We were given the report that General Westmoreland had sent to Crile and Wallace, showing figures of infiltration from September 1967 to January 1968. It amounted to about 43,000 for the five months.

Boies kept referring back to the documentary—the interview that Westmoreland gave Wallace and Crile.

But you said in your interview that the 20,000 figure for infiltration a month was accurate.

Yes, then you contradicted yourself on the program *Meet the Press*.

Westmoreland kept saying he was ambushed. He had no time to go over his documents.

Out of the clear blue, Boies mentions a new name—Vince Demma, the archivist in the history department at the Army History Center.

How many times did you visit Mr. Demma? Before the interview? After the interview?

As it turned out, Westmoreland received the same documents before and after, according to Mr. Boies.

We broke for lunch. Everyone was concerned about Westmoreland. Is he still sick? Is he on medication? Why are they keeping him up on the stand? Why don't his attorneys stop the testimony? He doesn't know what he is saying. It was obvious—everyone felt as I did. Something was wrong.

There are certainly a lot of places to choose from for lunch, but I didn't feel that ambitious. Cheryl and I went across the street for Italian food. David joined us. We didn't even mention the trial.

It reminded me of selling real estate. The times my clients are quietest are the times when the most thoughts are going on in their heads. It was usually a sign they were thinking about the house.

When we resumed after lunch, we were back on infiltration. "Weren't you aware, General Westmoreland, that infiltration was widely regarded as the most important indication of what was happening in Vietnam?"

General Westmoreland answered, "Well, troop movement was important information and we were sensitive to that."

Was it all semantics? Are we all talking about the same thing and using different words?

"And wasn't it true, General, that you were up against the best soldiers in the world? The North Vietnam troops?" pressed Boies.

The general answered, "Well, they were well armed, well trained, and well led."

Boies questioned him for a long time about the troops he had requested.

There was something about the 101st Airborne Division and the 11th Brigade in Hawaii. They were scheduled to come to Vietnam, and Westy pressed a great deal to get them into the country as soon as he could.

They arrived sometime in December. Boies is trying to find some correlation between the intelligence reports of infiltration in the fall of 1967 and the arrival of these troops.

When did Westmoreland get the news of infiltrators? When did he request more troops?

The general went on for quite a while about two of the northern provinces where infiltration was a problem. He described the terrain and the weather—the monsoon season, the trails that could be used, the treacherous mountain paths.

It was the most interesting testimony so far. A picture of the fateful area was painted. It's so tiring listening to the same numbers over and over.

He went on about the fact that he had a lot of experience as a soldier. He'd been in Vietnam for three and a half years at that point. He knew the enemy. He anticipated their moves. He didn't have to rely on intelligence—he relied on his intuition a lot.

"My memory was as important as the information I received from intelligence."

The enemy had capability—I wanted troops—bureaucracy moves slowly.

There was greater activity at the DMZ than we'd ever seen.

We had a break.

A new jigsaw puzzle was going on in the jury room. Some of the ladies were exchanging shopping coupons. Wild Bill came in and passed out our paychecks. This was the end of the eighth week.

When we returned to the courtroom, the judge said, "There are seventeen people walking into the courtroom with wide smiles on their faces. They just got their paychecks. Do not spend them, please, until you leave the courtroom."

Anything for comic relief—the audience laughed.

A new exhibit was presented. "But, General, you told Washington the enemy was running out of troops," said Boies as he presented a document stating that.

I've already learned the game. If the attorney asks a question, he knows something we don't know. He doesn't ask questions of a witness to learn something. He asks questions to get the witness to say something out loud in front of the jury.

The trouble seems to be that General Westmoreland hasn't learned that yet.

David Boies would say: Didn't you say the enemy is running out of troops? Didn't you say that to the President?

Westmoreland would vehemently deny that and go through long, elaborate denials.

David Boies would come up with several documents proving General Westmoreland had indeed said that.

"General, didn't you characterize this whole fact—enemy running out of troops—with, 'Some light at the end of the tunnel'?" asked Boies.

"I never used that expression. I never had that degree of optimism. It has been attributed to me, but unfairly. I believe Henry Cabot Lodge used that expression," answered Westmoreland. "I did express optimism when I went to Washington. I never intended to connote that the war was over. 'Light at the end of the tunnel' was very optimistic—I never had that optimism."

Westy didn't learn.

Next thing you know Boies produces a declassified cable from Westmoreland, and passes it out to the jurors.

There, in black and white, were the words Westmoreland had just so sincerely denied. "We want to give the American people a light at the end of the tunnel."

This phrase was actually not all that important in the major context of things. Why did the general keep denying these small points?

Boies tried to present some information from the Pike committee. Again, the plaintiff's attorneys kept on objecting.

We got as far as: Were you aware it was published in the newspapers? Westy said he thought it was classified information.

No, a portion of it leaked to *The Village Voice*. There were a lot of trips to the side bar. Boies brought out some newspaper articles that had been printed back in the seventies.

He was trying to show that General Westmoreland's reputation had already been in question and that CBS had nothing to do with defaming him.

Why didn't you sue Sam Adams back in 1981, when he wrote that article about your not reporting all of the enemy?

In fact, isn't it true that in view of some of the atrocities that the Japanese and German generals were accused of, you would be a war criminal for some of the things that went on in Vietnam?

I froze in my seat—I couldn't believe what I had heard. I couldn't look at the general, Boies, Burt, or the judge. I stared straight ahead. Had I heard correctly?

I saw the headlines for tonight's paper flashing in my head: "Westy Accused of Being a War Criminal." I expected to see the reporters in the spectator's box climbing over each other to get to a telephone, like in the movies.

But no one moved—except Burt, who was yelling objections.

They all went to the side bar.

I didn't catch angry words, only guidance coming from that direction. I think Boies's face was red when he got back into position, but he continued:

He passed out a copy of the *Time* magazine article of January 18, 1981:

"Of Guilt and Precedent." Westmoreland's picture was next to Yamashita—it was the article linking My Lai to the Philippines tragedy.

The article did say Westmoreland was cleared of any guilt.

However, the implication was there.

Nuremberg and Vietnam—an American tragedy.

A WARNING FLAG

December 3, 1984

Monday morning comes quickly. Between all the usual chores of keeping house and trying to get ready for the holidays, I didn't sit down for a minute. Suddenly, I was back on the subway.

Boies was still questioning Westmoreland. We were back on the Pike committee report.

Boies asked Westmoreland if he had seen the portion of the report on which *The Washington Post* wrote an article.

He said he doesn't read *The Washington Post*. Boies gave him an article from the *Daily News*.

Did you see that article from the *Daily News* back in 1975—September 22?

"No, I don't read the *Daily News*."

A snicker of laughter could be heard from the row of spectators where the *Daily News* reporter was sitting.

Boies kept bringing out newspaper articles that were highly critical of General Westmoreland. Of course there were objections, but the judge allowed them to be presented on the damages question.

He made it very clear to us that the articles were not to be interpreted as telling the truth, but they were simply to prove that General Westmoreland's reputation had already been in question and that CBS had had the articles at the time of the broadcast.

We were given the exhibits, which were put into the evidence.

Exhibit 348: Jack Anderson's column—"Numbers Game on Tet Offensive."

Exhibit 341: September 19, 1975, *The New York Times*, "False Troop Data in Vietnam Sighted."

Exhibit 343: *Daily News*, "Faked Viet Data and It Costs Lives."

Then Mr. Boies brought out a book written by the former prime minister of South Vietnam, Mr. Ky. He was the prime minister during the Tet offensive.

Boies introduced a variety of articles written by Sam Adams. You didn't sue Sam Adams when he wrote these articles—why do you now?

I felt sorry for the general just on human principles—to have all these articles thrust in your face is pretty difficult to deal with, no matter what level of life you live on.

Even Boies was presenting this evidence with an air of apology.

We were back on the briefing at the White House that Rostow had given.

Boies kept asking the general if he was certain that Rostow had given the briefing.

A warning flag, of course, goes up in my mind when I hear one of these points questioned.

Westmoreland started denying a quotation that he had attributed to him.

"Sure of victory"—never said that.

When would the general learn? Boies never presses these issues unless he has proof of something.

Westy kept going off on tangents—actually, I enjoyed these little stories because they were a diversion. I was tired of hearing about numbers on SD and SSD and infiltration.

The general talked about the monsoons, that the enemy went on attacks every year in winter and early spring because the trails were dried up. He said that his goal was to have the Americans withdraw so that South Vietnam could fight its own war.

He talked about a difficult mountainous area that was a military problem. In general, it was interesting—but both the judge and Mr. Boies kept stopping him to get him back on to the issue in the courtroom.

Boies presented a document and it kept getting objected to. Yet he kept persisting in asking questions. It was exhibit 949-A. I looked back on my notes. As I suspected, it was the Pike committee report.

Mike Wallace was there today. I started to study him. Aside from the evidence, much of which is beyond my realm of experience, you rely on intuition and body language. I began to draw on my background as an artist. The stance one takes tells a lot—how you sit, act, your body movements tells a lot about a personality.

I tried to put myself in their shoes—General Westmoreland, Sam Adams, Mike Wallace, George Crile. How would I feel if I were they in the position they were in in the courtroom?

The general always sits erect. He sits alone. He sits like the commander he was. His appearance is impressive—white hair, square jaw, intense, deep eyes. He doesn't make small talk; he seems patient and able to sit day after day—alone.

Mike Wallace has not been here every day, I assumed he still has to work on his programs. When he is here, he often sits low in his chair, head tucked into his shirt collar. He cranes his chin a lot and looks up at the ceiling to think. He likes to move his mouth and often wipes expressions on and off with his hand. When he's not sitting thinking, he is buried in documents or books, or his briefcase.

Sam Adams sits like a bull, his head down and his eyes staring straight out ahead. He looks like he's going to charge any minute—the whites of his eyes shining under smoldering pupils. He looks pretty serious. But when something amuses him, his whole face softens into a jolly countenance.

George Crile usually sits between Adams and Wallace. Crile looks proper—every hair in place, a thin, alert face, thin lips, small eyes that dart everywhere. His eyes are the only part of him that give away his feelings.

None of them—Adams, Wallace, Crile, or Westmoreland—appears to wear criticism exceedingly well. They all appear to be people with strong convictions—people who believe they are right.

Boies was now on another document. They were going over it sentence by sentence. We had no idea what they were discussing because they were referring to pages and lines: I agree with paragraph 2, line 7. The eighth line is an overstatement. I'm not sure of line 3 in paragraph 3. I totally disagree with line 4.

The wind was picking up outside. The windows were shaking. There were long minutes of silence in the courtroom while the general read over the document.

The background sounds of the wind made it sound like a horror movie.

The court bailiff, Wild Bill, had his eyes closed, his hand over them. I was certain he would start to snore any minute.

There were questions—lunch—a break in the afternoon. It was just more of the same.

What did the President say? What did the President know? When did you write this cable? Could McChristian send this cable without your approval? You did have a ceiling, didn't you? In Carver's testimony, page . . . of his deposition, he said . . .

General Westmoreland, did you not have the responsibility for the men in your command?

The general went off on more tangents. He talked about some of his tactics, hoping to get the Vietcong to the negotiating table. As altruistic as his intentions sounded, it still did not resolve the question of counting SD, SSD, and guerrillas.

After all, that's all that we are interested in, is it not?

A few cables were introduced—one from Wheeler to Westy, and one from Westy to Wheeler, and one very short, strange cable from Westy to Wheeler stating something to the effect that all documents pertaining to something or other had been destroyed, and instructing Wheeler to do the same.

You usually see something like that in a spy movie, don't you?

December 4, 1984

Today is my seventh anniversary—no big milestone, but certainly not a day to sit and listen to long hours of objections. It is David's birthday too, so we spent most of the morning sneaking fifty cents to each other to buy him a cake.

Westmoreland was still on the stand. They were still discussing the cables from yesterday. Again, the general went off on his speeches. The judge brought him back to the courtroom on several occasions.

We read and reread the cables—I thought one statement quite interesting in a cable from Wheeler to Westmoreland in reference to Westy's opinion on quantifying the SD and SSD: "I appreciate the comments in reference B concerning . . . [intelligence duplication and disputation] but, realistically we cannot ignore the broad statutory responsibilities of the Department of Central Intelligence.

"I will undertake to insure that such quantification (of SD and assault youth) are realistically described and full consideration is given as to the manner in which the numbers are handled."

I understood this cable to mean: If I wrote it to a subordinate—

okay, I respect your opinion, but give me the information and let me worry about it.

Suddenly Westmoreland was dismissed. A new witness took the stand—Ambassador Paul H. Nitze.

One of the counsels for the plaintiff, Mr. Dorsen, was examining him. Mr. Dorsen is the epitome of nerves—I have watched him sit at the plaintiff's table and the guy cannot sit still—he frowns, preens, he folds his arms, searches his pockets, shifts, scratches, smoothes the little hair he has—all in short spurts of movement. No wonder Dorsen has little hair left on his head—it just falls out with all the movement underneath.

Mr. Nitze, in contrast, though small in stature, sits fixedly in the witness chair, hands folded. He has very white hair that is quite a contrast to a good complexion. The only fault I find is that the dark navy pin-striped suit he wears overpowers him.

Before he could even speak, there were objections from the defense and many long trips to the side bar.

Finally, we heard his credentials, which began with him graduating from Harvard in 1929 and ended with him currently being on the committee negotiating with the Russians for arms control.

He was deputy secretary of defense during the years that this trial is concerned with and had spent some time involved directly with Vietnam—sometime in the early to middle sixties, maybe 1965 or 1966. I thought perhaps that the fact that he was not directly related to Vietnam in 1967 and 1968 was the reason for the side-bar trips.

But apparently, he had access to every source of classified intelligence during the period we are concerned with.

He claimed he relied on individuals who gave the information as much as he did on the information. Carver was one of the people he relied on. When did you meet—? Do you know or have you met George Crile?

To make a long story short, Crile had been a guest at Nitze's home in northeast Maine. The Nitzes, as it turned out, were very good friends of Ann Patten's parents (Ann Patten was George Crile's wife), and they were quite fond of Ann. As it turns out, Ann is no longer married to George Crile.

Nitze's daughter herself was in the midst of a bitter divorce. We do get down to the nitty-gritty, don't we? I could see the soap opera unfolding already.

George Crile mentioned the proposed documentary he was working on—about the uncounted enemy—and Paul Nitze recounted the advice—or cautions—that he had expressed to George Crile. There was great uncertainty and error in the figures of enemy in Vietnam. Nitze knew Westmoreland, believed he had a deep knowledge of his character, and Nitze felt he would not have set out to deceive the President.

Nitze went on further to explain his view of the war as one of complexity: it was a political war, a psychological war, a guerrilla war. You had the main organized forces of the North Vietnamese and the Vietcong. It was a defense against a terror campaign.

He did say—either in the deposition that was read or in the courtroom—that he did believe the SD and SSD were terrorists, but he wasn't sure how the Vietnamese considered them. The judge reminded us that the only purpose of this witness was to testify on the state of mind of the defense—George Crile, and the fact that Nitze and Crile had a conversation.

Nitze did say that in 1965 they couldn't make an estimate of numbers of SD and SSD. He said that areas, some areas—mainly I Corps (I believe)—we, the U.S. forces, controlled them by day, but the SD and SSD controlled them at night.

Nitze went on to say that since 1981, when he met with George Crile, he had read a lot of information on the SD and SSD and the unresolved questions of Vietnam, so that he could not precisely recall exactly what information he may have related to Crile, or what his own, Nitze's, state of mind was at the meeting. But at the time he felt that it was not a fair assessment to aggregate SD and SSD and political cadre with regular forces—it's like adding elephants to flies, and then you get nonsense.

The witness was dismissed.

Judge Leval gave us a peek into our schedule for the next few days. No court Friday, December 7–December 10. December 11 we will meet at 1:00 P.M., after lunch. No court Friday, December 14, and he wished David Lederman a happy birthday.

We had a break, and then General Westmoreland was back on the stand.

They were back to all those cables, particularly one that seemed to leave a lot of questions. There were supposedly eight copies—only one could be found. The date that was stamped on it for historical archives was six months after it was written—the handwriting on it was in question. Westmoreland claimed it was his. I wondered if a handwriting expert would be called.

Westmoreland claimed he racked his brain to remember what exhibit 306 referred to—the cable telling Wheeler to destroy documents. He couldn't recall.

Westmoreland talked about Colonel Dac, a defector from North

Vietnam to South Vietnam. He claimed that he was the highest ranking officer to defect, equivalent to a U.S. brigadier general.

Colonel Dac had never heard of the category assault youth.

They talked more about the McChristian cable incident.

Boies asked to question General Westmoreland on voir dire. He read testimony from the courtroom that the general had given that stated he had never read certain documents, and the general had just finished saying he always read those documents. There was long questioning on a certain document that kept getting objected to. Typical courtroom procedure.

Who wrote this document?

Objection.

Who proposed this document?

Objection.

Who signed this document in front of you?

Objection.

The judge stepped in: Why don't you ask whose signature lies on the signature line?

No objection.

They went on to discuss a May 1967 meeting that was in question. Apparently, Admiral Sharp was present. There was a briefing—charts, etc.

Did anything obstruct the admiral's view?

"That would have been intolerable," the general answered quite curtly. "The briefing was also in English."

This evening, we celebrated our anniversary with my father-in-law. We went to the Van Gogh exhibit. It was overwhelming—not the exhibit as much as the fact that the work on display involved only two years of his life.

All I could liken it to was the SD and SSD count of 1967 and 1968. Two years in Saigon—two years in Arles. What a horrible analogy. I resent the fact that I have been forced to face an area of life that I have gone out of my way to avoid—war: who fought it, what it meant, who believed what.

I'd rather look at paintings than look at figures involved in war. I wondered about the difference between the torment of Van Gogh and the plight of General Westmoreland. I have no doubt that Westmoreland had strong feelings and convictions about what he was doing. I have no doubt that he agonized over certain decisions. I do have doubt about his judgment. I think he was fighting this war from a European viewpoint. He trusted the enemy. He was used to dealing with a gentleman's war. I do not know the Orientals, but my gut feeling is they fight differently. I dispelled my train of thought and continued to enjoy Van Gogh.

Dinner after the show was a delight, so was the walk home—in spite of the piercing wind that picked up. My spirits had been uplifted, nothing was going to interfere with my high.

December 5, 1984

The weather has become brisk. The general is still on the stand. This time the judge poses the questions—he had asked for an entire rundown on the chain of command. Who reports to whom? He posed several theoretical questions: if it pertained to just the army? if it was a question of changing uniforms? if it was a question involving logistics?

The general was quite helpful—sounded in full capacity and eager to clarify points for the jury, ranging over the responsibilities of everyone in the chain of command from the President to Secretary of Defense to Joint Chief of Staff to CINCPAC. We did get an armchair briefing.

I was quite delighted to have this information clarified. Again, my esteem of the judge was reinforced. He was articulate and thorough. He was not afraid to ask questions, and he asked questions that were disturbing me also. Again, the military had ways of making the most ordinary information seem like it was Greek.

No fault of Westmoreland's—just a fact.

How does one become COMUSMACV? Appointed by the President? Yes? No! Secretary of Defense? Oh! When given the order, can you refuse? Civilian? Yes. Military? No! Resign? Escape clause? Senior officer—retire—oh! Could ask for reconciliation!

Wallace appeared at eleven, in the middle of this. George Crile was not here for the first time—in fact he disappeared after a break yesterday, at three. Dorsen makes me nervous just sitting here—God, he doesn't stop moving!

We were to be shown a portion of an interview of Westmoreland and the tapes wouldn't work, so we were given a long lunch—an hour and forty minutes. Cheryl and I went shopping. Everyone made elaborate plans, several stayed in for lunch.

After lunch, we saw the interview. Nothing new—Westy still licking his lips, Wallace still firing questions. I felt sorry for Westy, but Wallace was still making points—after all, it was his interview.

Why was the plaintiff showing us this? I know why—but they really weren't making points.

After it was all over, the plaintiff offered it as evidence. The judge said, "About time!" in so many words. Suddenly, George Crile was on the stand. I was taken aback. Why was the plaintiff calling him?

He gave his credentials—not as in depth as the usual (education, background, etc.)—however, credentials.

How old are you? Thirty-nine.

What is your present position? Producer for CBS.

Since when? What did you produce? How many programs before 1981? When were you hired? Who was your supervisor? Did they like your work? Were you ever criticized? When did you meet Sam Adams?

George Crile was nice-looking, very neat and trim—brown hair with tinges of gray. He dressed neatly, in browns and grays. He had small but penetrating eyes, very controlled mouth. Looked like he dotted his *i*'s and crossed his *t*'s. His voice was smooth and pleasant, and he had a million-dollar vocabulary.

George Crile has been a producer with CBS since 1976, where he produced five or six documentary-type programs as a producer/reporter.

Previously, he was an editor with *Harper's* magazine. There, he met Sam Adams. He became reacquainted with Sam Adams on a visit to Washington in 1980, when he contacted Adams because he wanted to take his three-year-old daughter for a visit to Sam Adams's farm in Virginia to see cows, because, as he said, the child's only contact with nature was Central Park.

Burt was not interested in anything but what he called a blue sheet.

The blue sheet amounted to the work sheet that one would produce to sell an idea to the network—a proposed plan.

Having worked with ideas to be presented, I knew it was just that— a theatrical presentation of an idea for a film. In my mind, it had nothing to do with the documentary that was ultimately produced.

Burt, however, tried his best to discredit Crile with the blue sheet. During recess and side-bar meetings, I realized that it was indeed influencing some of the jurors. The juror on my left side felt that Crile was boring—she couldn't understand what he said. (He did have an Oxford vocabulary, and he used it.)

Burt asked Crile if he did any research before he had made the documentary.

Crile said yes and outlined every avenue he had taken—not just Sam Adams, whom he relied on a great deal. He outlined the information he obtained from him, but he went on and on with all the documents—the Pike committee findings, Tom Powers, Greg Rushford, congressional reports—all going in the same direction as Sam Adams: there was a conspiracy!

Burt asked for the monologues to be stricken from the record.

Burt said, "I asked if he had done research—not what research had been done."

The judge said, "Too late!"

It surely was. Indeed, Crile had done research!

As George Crile said, as soon as General Westmoreland expressed political connections, he felt they were off the track.

The documentary never really focused on General Westmoreland, but collectively on intelligence officials who had the responsibility to report information.

Burt kept asking questions on whom he had questioned for the blue sheet. Crile kept saying no one—it was just a proposal.

I know the blue sheets were bullshit, but a lot of the jurors did not.

Finally, the judge said the blue sheets are not in question—they were a preliminary proposal, they have nothing to do with the trial.

Then the other jurors discounted them. We were dismissed at four forty-five.

December 6, 1984

The morning started out terribly.

I had dinner with a friend last night in an Indian restaurant. It was fun. I took care of writing matters, bills and such, when I got home. But I went to bed rather late.

The morning came too fast. I was still all right, but by the time the fourth subway came by, I became a New Yorker. I just shoved till I fit on the train. The only thing that sustained my sanity while I politely but tensely waited for a train was the violinist hoping to pay his rent by playing Beethoven. At nine o'clock the only thing I find tolerable about the subways is an opportunity to read. This train was so packed I couldn't get the book out of my purse. Even if I did, I wouldn't have been able to hold it up far enough away from my face to read it.

I had just enough time for breakfast when I arrived downtown. Cheryl joined me unexpectedly. The conversation relaxed me. The day took a new turn.

When we were beckoned into the jury box, a new witness was on the stand. When he was sworn in, we discovered it was Robert S. McNamara.

The day became rather interesting.

I liked him even before I knew who he was. He sat comfortably in the witness seat and didn't appear to be the least bit ill-at-ease.

He was asked to give his credentials, which were numerous and impressive. He, too, graduated from Harvard and taught there at one time. He was secretary of defense under Kennedy and under Johnson (of course—that's why he was here as a witness) and president of the Ford Motor Company and president of the World Bank until he retired in 1981.

He spoke in a gravelly voice. His hair was thinning, but he had a wonderful face. When it broke into a smile, which was often, he had a playful look about him.

I was impressed with him throughout the day. He never was satisfied with just being handed a document. He would ask if he could read it in its entirety. He would take as long as he needed, making notations with a pad he brought with him. He was handed numerous documents, many that were literally volumes of paper. He read them all, using the Evelyn Wood method. We sat for ten to fifteen minutes at a time while McNamara poured over documents.

There were numerous moments of humor. It was obvious McNamara was used to being in control. On more than one occasion he answered a question intended for the judge—but good-humoredly, he would apologize when this error was evident.

He wore gold wire glasses. They looked like a part of him. Though his hair was thin and slicked back, he had fluffy gray sideburns.

He knew Westmoreland well, he had a close working relationship with him. McNamara made a number of visits to Vietnam and saw Westmoreland there and also saw him on Westmoreland's trips to Washington.

He felt Westmoreland was well qualified professionally and characterwise to assume the post of COMUSMACV.

McNamara had felt Westmoreland had tremendous integrity and was above being involved in any kind of coverup. That didn't mean they did not have major policy disagreements, but Westmoreland served his country well.

There was constant controversy among the various departments and agencies involved in the Vietnam War, so he paid little attention to the allegation that Westmoreland was not reporting accurately.

McNamara was contacted by Mike Wallace in June 1981 by telephone. George Crile also got on the phone to ask McNamara if he wouldn't appear on camera.

McNamara declined the invitation, but agreed to talk off the record on the phone.

As it turned out, we learned George Crile taped the conversation. Burt made a big deal out of it. I found out later he was fired for doing it.

McNamara declined the invitation for an interview because first it was not his policy to make interviews, plus he didn't have a staff to help him do research work. This all had transpired seventeen years ago and he didn't trust his memory.

Actually, McNamara was quite a thorough individual. He brought a briefcase filled with notes.

Boies was not too delighted with that fact. At one point he asked McNamara if he could read his notes. McNamara said sure. As Boies reached over to get them, McNamara pulled them back and said, First can I see the questions you'll ask—then I'll decide if you can see my notes.

The courtroom fell apart—even Judge Leval. But then the judge instructed Mr. McNamara to rely solely on his memory.

McNamara said that he had come to the conclusion some time in 1967 that the war could not be won militarily.

Boies questioned him on this issue and asked if his opinion was recorded anywhere. McNamara claimed that in his notes, volume 7, marked January 1, 1967, to March 1, 1968, he had recorded a great deal of information as to his experiences as secretary of defense.

There was also a cable or memo that stated his views.

He didn't believe the figures that Westmoreland called the crossover point. But apparently he was alone in thinking so. According to McNamara, some called him a communist appeaser.

McNamara didn't believe that the bombing of North Vietnam was effective. He didn't believe that the current course of action would lead to peace—if anything, we'd get China and Russia involved.

McNamara claimed that Henry Kissinger and two Frenchmen were attempting to negotiate peace talks. He had more faith in them.

There were a couple of documents that McNamara appeared to have never seen. A session did go on over one bar graph and how to interpret it.

McNamara, as we would suspect, fell into debates with Mr. Boies on several occasions, but he, too, was reminded by the judge about his role as a witness.

The day ended on a pleasant note.

We were off for the weekend as of Thursday night. I didn't feel so hot. Friday, I was still feeling the beginnings of a cold or flu type of condition, so I called in sick. I slept most of Friday and felt like a million dollars when I woke up.

I hoped no one saw me running around over the weekend getting caught up on my errands. We even went out for a wonderful dinner Saturday night.

December 10, 1984

George Crile was back on the stand. Burt was still at it. They were back on the blue sheet and back on the telephone interview.

It sounded like the plaintiff was grasping at straws. Burt kept asking the same questions over and over again. He didn't even bother to change the sentences around.

It was getting tedious. Crile held up well and never lost his cool in the least. He'd just calmly restate the answer and add, "as I just previously testified."

Burt brought out a chronology sheet that Sam Adams had compiled. We were all given copies. It was interesting. I read through as much as I could while I sat waiting for the counsel at the side bar.

It was interesting—the entries of the characters involved in the intrigue, along with characterizations of them.

I loved the one that said McChristian loathed Davidson and Komer and couldn't tolerate Danny Graham. I could understand this.

McChristian's opinions made him seem most credible to me. I was disappointed in Sam Adams's handwriting. It was tiny and difficult to read. It didn't look like it belonged to the person sitting at the end of the table for the defense. His observations and comments on the individuals, though, were to the point.

At about four-fifteen, Dan Rather made an appearance. He quietly came in the door in the back of the courtroom and sat down with, I assumed, his wife. Not a person in the jury box missed it. I had a hard time not stealing glances in his direction. He makes a striking appearance.

Cheryl and I brought in ornaments to decorate the jury room.

I brought in crayons and construction paper, and every one of the jurors made a stocking. I was truly surprised at how everyone got into it. They even started to fight over the different colors. It was fun.

Otherwise the day was tedious.

December 11, 1984

George Crile is still on the stand. Today is most painful. Burt is really disorganized. He can't get the right numbers on the right documents.

The TV never seems to work when he wants it. He tries to act dramatic and it is just out of character.

At one point, the judge stopped his line of questioning and gave him advice as to how to handle a particular situation.

The same has happened to Boies, but at least his mistakes are not so obvious. They usually involve wording or procedure.

Burt goes on for hours on one issue and then the judge throws out the issue as not being relevant. The blue sheet was one of those. It had nothing to do with the trial.

At one point, Burt took a phrase out of the documentary and said "And, Mr. Crile, you know that is simply not true!"

Crile came back with a ten-minute dialogue on why it was true—or why he believed it to be true.

He had every ounce of evidence memorized. He sure was convincing.

Burt would let him go on and on and then ask him the same, exact question.

I guess he intended to do that until Crile said what Burt wanted to hear. It didn't happen, and the judge would ask him to go on to another line of questioning.

Though we began today at one o'clock, after lunch, and were out by four-thirty, the day seemed long.

We were given a document. On the cover page was a quotation from *The Price of Glory:* "The War Office kept three sets of figures—'one to mislead the public, another to mislead the cabinet; and a third to mislead itself'" (Asquith).

Burt couldn't get off the document. He started comparing pages in this exhibit to another document. Finally, after twenty minutes of this, the judge asked Burt if he was trying to test Crile's ability to compare charts.

Then he started to compare the transcripts of the documentary to the text of an interview by Colonel Hawkins.

One part of a sentence was deleted in the documentary. Actually, about a hundred pages were deleted. Only a few sentences were used. Burt was attempting to show that the deletion changed the meaning. I didn't think it did, but then I thought perhaps I might be becoming prejudiced. Burt was so offensive and Crile was so professional— maintaining his composure thoroughly under this examination. On more than one occasion I personally would have gotten up and screamed at Burt if I had been in Crile's position.

I reminded myself not to be swayed by the personalities, especially an attorney's.

Westmoreland was on trial here, not Burt.

As a matter of fact, Westmoreland really is not on trial—one portion of his life is: how he handled one aspect of the Vietnam War, which was how, or if, he counted all of the enemy.

I was not to judge Westmoreland on what kind of a father or husband he might be. It was a play of sorts, watching Mrs. Westmoreland day after day faithfully sitting behind her man.

It was obvious watching her frown, grimace, continuously bury her head in her needlework. I liked the woman from what I saw. She felt her husband's pain deeply. Watching Westmoreland day after day—it was hard not to get a feeling for him.

He appears to be very proud. I'm sure the documentary cut him deeply. I'm sure criticism isn't worn well by Westmoreland—in spite of his eagerness to tell us what an open policy he had with his men.

He said "After all, I was the general" once too often in his testimony. He wore that title proudly. He acted according to his convictions. I did not discount that point at all. What I did question was the judgment he used.

I had the feeling he was too embedded in that old affliction of those in power, who begin to feel they are above the law—the old Nixon and J. Edgar Hoover syndrome. I'm certain if we looked back through the ages—if we really knew what went on among the decision-makers—we would be shocked.

I tried to imagine what it would be like to be in a command position, having to send a battalion of soldiers into a battle.

Math and statistics become your war. The enemy has one thousand men—I have one thousand men—they engage in battle. Five hundred men will be injured—two hundred will never recover—one hundred will die. You didn't—you couldn't—think in terms of flesh and blood. You would simply think in terms of numbers, supplies, guns, bombs.

The thought makes me shudder. Yet someone has to do it, I guess. Using this line of reasoning, I wondered why the general would not count everybody who could be a potential soldier?

The Vietnam War is not on trial here!

The words of Judge Pierre Leval flashed like a neon light in my head to abruptly stop my train of thought.

The numbers—the evidence. Did CBS defame the general? Did

CBS have a reckless disregard for the truth? What is the truth? What was the truth?

Westmoreland belonged to a club—the hale, hearty, well-met boys—they all went to Harvard or West Point together.

One lied and the others swore to it. Were they lying? They all seemed so sincere in their quest for the numbers.

Was I too ignorant of this type of statistics and Order of Battle issue? Or was it they who couldn't see the forest for the trees?

According to my math and my own common sense, I personally came up with a lot more enemy than 294,000.

But I was beginning to doubt my own reasoning.

You know: You hear something so much, you begin to believe it. Maybe that was Burt's tactic. He was still on the part of the sentence that had been deleted in the documentary, portraying Colonel Hawkins's remarks. "Was it an accident, Mr. Crile? Was it an accident that that particular part of the sentence got cut? No! Mr. Crile! You did it on purpose, didn't you?"

Give me a break!

We were dismissed at four-thirty. I wrote a letter to my class.

Dear Boys and Girls,
Just thought I'd write a note to say hello and to see how you are doing.

How did you like the snow last week? We had it down here, too. It only lasted one night and it didn't stick on the street. But it was so beautiful. A lot of the holiday lights were up, so that the snow looked like a winter wonderland. Big giant flakes were falling and they stuck to your eyelids. When we got up to Carmel the following night, we couldn't believe how much snow was still on the ground, because it already had disappeared in the city.

The trial is still going on. Sometimes it is very interesting and sometimes it's very boring. You cannot imagine how much time they spend arguing about grammar and punctuation. Everything has to go down into the court records absolutely perfectly, so that no one can possibly misinterpret the meaning. Sometimes, where the comma is placed can change the whole meaning of a sentence.

I'm beginning to understand why legal papers sound the way they do. It's interesting in that respect. I feel like I could get 3 college credits toward a law degree listening to what goes on in the courtroom.

There is a man who sits in front of the judge, down a step. He sits and faces the spectators and makes sure they are quiet. Yesterday he went over to someone drinking a cup of coffee and made him leave.

You kids had better pray that this trial gets over soon. Because the longer I'm here, the more I like how quiet and polite everyone is.

Maybe I'll hire the court bailiff to keep order in the artroom. He's the man who helps out the judge. Only kidding.

Well, take care of yourselves. I'm not sure when I'll get another day off. The judge did say that we'll have off Dec. 20 and 21, so I'll see you then.

Keep up those good reading reports. I enjoyed getting your letters very much.

Hope to see you soon,

> Your art teacher and reading teacher,
> Mrs. Roth

December 12, 1984

We were called into the courtroom. The judge greeted us with his usual hellos and gave us a short lecture with his X chart.

The information we are obtaining from Mr. Crile is to be received on the defendant's state of mind. It is not to be received on the truth. Mr. Crile was not there in Vietnam, he has no firsthand knowledge of . . . and on and on.

Burt resumed his position and began to question Crile. The first question was objected to and all the counsel and the judge went to the side bar. I began to notice that my notes were becoming elaborate doodles.

I was fascinated at the turn they were taking. Today they appeared quite linear. Other days they had been rather flowing—in fact, they were getting tight.

I wondered what kind of a field day a psychologist would have interpreting them.

But Boies, the judge, and assistants came back and we continued. Burt was now picking apart an interview given by George Allen.

Crile was defending his documentary and editing. God, it was hard to sit with a blank face, trying not to give away any feelings.

Everyone could watch us—the plaintiff, the defense, their lawyers, the press, the judge, the witnesses.

The witness talked to us. The counsel would pose a question, and the witness would answer us. As he talked, he made eye contact—he gave us his side, he elaborated on points.

What a demeaning position it must feel like to be a witness—on trial. Looking into these seventeen faces in front of you, not knowing how these people feel about you—do they believe you?

I thought Crile was quite believable. He was articulate, calm. Made his points, knew what he was talking about.

That didn't mean he hadn't used poor judgment on some issues. That taping of McNamara's conversation probably wasn't a good idea, yet I could easily understand how a reporter—in his zeal to capture each word accurately—could be tempted. I wondered what I would do. I think if I did it I wouldn't have told anyone—and once I got it transcribed, I would have destroyed it. Obviously, it didn't work that smoothly for George. He got fired, or suspended for a year, from CBS for doing so.

That restored my faith in CBS—the fact that it stood strongly on a conviction like that. Personally, if I had been at the other end of the conversation, I wouldn't have liked it too much. It's the old: "do unto others" issue.

I had a gut feeling, though, that this guy was honest—straightforward and sincere. I liked the way he sounded when he interviewed people. It sounded like it came from kindness. He seemed to be able to put himself in the guy's position when he was questioning. Yet he seemed to be able to hold his own.

We were given a break, and filed into the jury room. The first words out of Kate's mouth were, "This guy *is* lying through his teeth—I don't trust him!"

Cheryl spoke up, "Oh, Kate, I thought he was sincere. I believe him."

"Oh no," Kate answered emphatically. "I don't believe a word he says—he's lying."

"Kate," I said. "We aren't to influence each other, but I can't believe that you would feel as strongly as you do. Why?"

"I have this gut feeling that he's no good."

My God, I thought to myself, this is going to be tough. We are a jury of extremely diverse people—backgrounds—thinking. How are we ever going to arrive at a decision? What a nightmare I envisage for deliberations.

It's not just evidence, it's not just witnesses—it's how credible you believe they are. Kate liked Graham—because he had seven children, like her. I guess we all gravitate toward our own experiences.

"We talked to the head of the MACV's delegation, and he said . . .

We were watching a portion of the documentary. Then we were instructed to read the transcript.

General Godding had been the head of MACV's delegation representing the numbers at Langley. But he never appeared on the program. What CBS had done was to use Hamscher, who as it turned out, was in fact Godding's assistant, or deputy.

CBS hadn't lied. It never did identify Hamscher as the head of the delegation. However, it was implied by the broadcast. Naturally, Burt beat it to death. I had to remind myself that was his job. However, I personally felt it was a moot point.

Technically, CBS had not lied. So it could not be accused of an untruth. But judging from my little experience in the jury room, I realized all Burt's efforts *would* probably pay off. All it would take is for one of the jurors to believe him.

Burt started on Westmoreland's interview: "And you eliminated a portion of General Westmoreland's answer here."

Burt passed out transcripts of Westmoreland's interview and we had the transcripts of the documentary. We sat there like kids in a comparative literature class.

"First look at the transcript for the documentary—do you all have that page? I'll read it into the record."

"Westmoreland . . . 'Politicians or leaders in countries are inclined to shoot the messenger that brings the bad news . . . certainly he wanted bad news like a hole in the head.'"

Burt continued without taking a breath.

"Now, do you have the transcript for Westmoreland's full interview? Turn to page so-and-so. Now do you see that answer? Notice—in the full interview, Westmoreland had continued with 'he was given the good news and the bad news. Johnson accentuated the positive'—do you see that, Mr. Crile? Do you see that, jury? Why did you choose to cut that part out of the documentary?"

Burt pulled out McChristian's full interview; we again compared the transcripts.

The documentary transcript read, in answer to Crile's question: Why were you sent to Fort Hood, Texas? Because you wouldn't keep down the numbers?

McChristian: "Evidently people didn't like my reporting—because I was constantly showing that the enemy strength was increasing," the full interview read.

McChristian: No, because nobody ever asked me that, because I reported it as I saw it—and evidently people didn't like my reporting, because I was constantly showing that the enemy strength was increasing.

This issue stayed on the floor for some time—in the midst of this it came out that Westmoreland had contacted McChristian after the documentary was aired.

Apparently, Westmoreland asked McChristian if he wouldn't care to join him in a lawsuit against CBS for taking their words out of context.

McChristian declined the invitation.

Lunchtime came. I spent it browsing in bookstores. I never realized how much material was published on the Vietnam War. I began to wonder if it wasn't a world conspiracy—*war*!

It gave generals something to do, soldiers on the front a chance to be macho, workers at home a chance to make bullets, and writers something to write about. The shelves were filled with books on Vietnam, Korea, World War II. I didn't notice any for World War I—I guess that is out of vogue today.

Mike Wallace had his picture on a book—I was tempted to thumb through it, but I didn't.

Instead, I bought a few children's books for stocking stuffers for some of my little friends. I kind of missed my classes, in spite of all their problems—the kids were so innocent and naïve. I hoped they wouldn't ever have to count enemy.

Was war really a fact of life? I was beginning to wonder if I was really a fair juror.

We all were back at one forty-five, as instructed, but were not called in to the courtroom until two-ten. In the meantime, we planned a Christmas party for next week. We'd order out and have it sent in. Some wanted Italian, some wanted Chinese, others were for deli.

How was this group going to make a decision at the end of the trial?

The judge apologized to us for the delay but informed the courtroom that he had at the last minute been engaged to suppress counterfeit Cabbage Patch Kids!

Burt started reading from another document and in the middle interrupted to ask his assistant to pass out copies to the jury as he continued reading.

Poor planning—he was finished reading the passage before the first one of us got a copy. It was exasperating. He was already onto another issue.

Crile had posed a hypothetical question to McChristian on the film. Burt was badgering him about the question being hypothetical.

Crile gave the explanation that it was quite unusual for a major intelligence chief to come forward and speak out on public TV.

The hypothetical question was, in fact, the only honest way to answer that particular issue.

Burt badgered him on another issue of how the documentary was filmed.

Apparently because of low budget, which these documentaries have, they take only one camera on an interview. They focus the camera on one speaker, with all the questions and answers, and then focus it on the other speaker and go over the same questions and answers, and then edit the two takes together.

We've seen a lot of outtakes—thank God we are not bored with all of them on our home screens. More than once I've felt, after watching these takes, that my home movies aren't so bad.

We ended the day reviewing a *Meet the Press* interview with Lawrence Spivak and comparing it to the documentary. The Comparative Analysis of Transcripts class was dismissed at four forty-five.

December 13, 1984

I had a wonderful breakfast in the Thomas Street Inn—I love that place.

I try to take a train as early as I can to avoid the inevitable delays on the infamous New York subway system. Sometimes I get down to Foley Square just in time for court—sometimes I have an hour to spare, and then I try various breakfast places. The biggest bargain in New York City is breakfast—it's even less expensive than breakfast specials up in the country.

This morning I had my doubts about getting anywhere. Three trains pulled up and stopped, so crowded that the people on the platform just stood and watched the sardines on the train watch them. It's a humorous sight if you're in the right mood. Being late does not establish the right mood. I cursed under my breath and felt myself getting annoyed and angry. The other people at the stop just looked up and with total resignation went back to their newspapers or paperbacks. New Yorkers must be the most well read people in the world.

Everyone carries a book or a newspaper. So far I've completed two full books just riding the subways.

The fourth train pulled up relatively empty and the entire platform was taken care of. By the time we reached 34th Street, I was practically the only person left on board.

The day was beautiful. They had predicted rain, but I had my doubts. The temperature was balmy, and my ankle didn't hurt. (My ankle, which I broke two years ago, is a much better forecaster than any radio station meteorologist!)

The Thomas Street Inn is a little place with heritage blue tablecloths and white napkins, plants and mirrors, and terrific food. I have yet to be disappointed.

Everyone was planning our Christmas party when I arrived in the jury room. What shall we order? Finally, a unanimous vote was cast for deli.

They called us in to the courtroom and the day began with us watching the counsel at the side bar.

I'm taking fewer notes. Nothing of any consequence is being offered—George Crile is still on the stand.

He gives elaborate, long answers to each of Burt's questions, often going into depth about each issue.

He has the patience of Job. After a lengthy, explicit answer, Burt asks the same question again. It gives Crile more opportunity to elaborate.

Burt has a lot of bad habits—he points; he grins; he asks questions like your little sister would when she discovers that you got more candy in your stocking than she did; he paces back and forth in front of the jury box; he turns his back when Crile answers—in general, he lacks good manners.

It was another comparative literature lesson. We spent the day comparing this document to that document. I've never seen so much paper in my life. You could hardly see the witness—he had volumes of documents all around him.

We looked at takes of a Meechem interview and compared transcripts of a conversation he had with George Crile.

Burt was trying to characterize Meechem as overly emotional and an unwilling witness.

We saw him on camera—he did look uncomfortable and nervous, and quite uncommunicative. But there was something about this difficult soul that touched me. I felt he was very intelligent and very sensitive, with idealistic standards.

I learned a new word today—*hyperbolical*. One of the men who used to work for Meechem, a man named Cooley, said that Meechem had a penchant for Shakespearean drama, that he never liked anybody or anything. He came out with statements like, "The imperial war machine has done it again!"

Apparently, Meechem had spoken to Sam Adams for some twenty hours. He had urged Sam to go to his former wife and get letters he had written home. We had heard excerpts from some of the letters previously, and they were filled with things like "the lies going on here are not to be believed."

The whole issue of Meechem centered around his accusation that Graham had erased part of the data base on a MACV computer in respect to the enemy infiltration numbers. It's hard to piece together the story because we get it in dribs and drabs, but if I have it correctly, the sequence seems to be this:

Davidson was the J2. Danny Graham was his right-hand man, but apparently Graham called the shots. (Having seen both characters in court, I could believe that.)

Davidson and Graham came to Meechem and Cooley, who were in control of infiltration numbers and the computer, and asked them to erase the numbers they'd been using so that they could add in the enemy killed during Tet and have the numbers make sense.

Up until now MACV has been sticking pretty close to 294,000 as the number of enemy—a figure that many people questioned. At Tet, 80,000 enemy were killed in the first four or five days of fighting, and according to statistics the army used, for every one killed, three were injured. Out of those three, one more would die and one more would never recuperate from his injuries. So the question came up. Who were they fighting? There were no enemy left!

In order for the numbers to come out right, they felt they had to go and erase the data base and put in figures that would work.

Meechem and Cooley felt that would be improper. Another way it could be handled was to just add in the new figures and start at the present point.

Graham wouldn't hear of it. He apparently found a computer operator who would do it in spite of Meechem's protests.

The questions now turned to Meechem, who worked in London as a military affairs correspondent for *The Economist*. George Crile went all the way to London to interview Meechem, and Meechem would only give him a three-minute interview.

He had been quite open and talkative on the telephone but seemed to get cold feet when it came to discussing any of the information on camera.

(I know a lot of people like this—they can write fluently and talk on the phone, but in person they clam up. I wonder if Meechem was this type of person?)

Some of the jurors speculated that with the position he had in London as a military correspondent, he may have been concerned about his job.

It also could have been the fact that he felt his letters said it all and that here it is, fifteen years later, and he honestly couldn't remember some of the daily happenings that he had written about.

He said in one of his letters that he personally felt they were losing the war. He could see mistakes being made all around him, and he felt powerless to do anything about it.

Burt went on at length, accusing Crile of taping phone conversations he had with everyone.

Burt stood there with one hand on his hip and the other hand pointing at Crile. Then he accused Crile of making up that whole sequence about Graham changing the data base on MACV's computer. "Why would someone like Graham do that, Mr. Crile? He was very, very intelligent—was not Danny Graham a very intelligent man?"

Mr. Crile thought for a second and answered, "General Graham was *clever,* and in some respects capable."

Burt went back to the Westmoreland interview. "You never gave General Westmoreland a chance to do research—you never gave General Westmoreland a chance to retape an interview?"

Mr. Crile answered quite curtly, "He had all the opportunity in the world. I called him on the telephone and read him my letter, to give him ample time to do research. He never asked for another taping. He sent that letter with the documents and simply said that the documents might be helpful to us. In fact, we had already had all of those documents in our possession."

We were dismissed around four o'clock, wished a good weekend.

I even had time to do a little shopping on the way home to the country.

December 15, 1984

I spent Friday getting reacquainted with my class and the rest of the weekend getting caught up on paperwork, writing cards, and cleaning house.

December 16, 1984

Sunday night sure comes around quickly. We headed down to the city to have dinner with my father-in-law and be rested for Monday.

It gets dark so early these days. After dark the country takes on a "day is done" look—few cars are out, a few holiday lights can be seen here and there. But once Manhattan comes into view, it takes my breath away. It reminds me of a precious jewel: the George Washington Bridge, the high-rises, and blinking lights in the sky.

Manhattan is another world.

December 17, 1984

George Crile was still on the stand when we filed into court.

Burt went back to the letter that Westmoreland had sent to CBS. It got picked apart, line by line. "Didn't you know what he meant by this statement?" "Didn't you know what he meant by that?"

We got another comparative analysis lesson. We had to compare the letter Sam Adams and George Crile sent to McChristian and the letter that George Crile read to Westmoreland over the telephone and later delivered to him at the Plaza Hotel. The accusation of course was that the letter to McChristian was much more explicit and sent five weeks prior to his interview.

George Crile's answer was that the letters were to two different people of whom they were asking different questions. Furthermore, Westmoreland had claimed a busy schedule and that he was traveling, giving lectures, and conceded to give an interview to CBS if they could see him at his convenience, which was in two weeks. There were also indications in the letter that he had asked for something like three thousand dollars for his troubles, and there was some mention of the fact that giving money was not CBS's practice—but George Crile was trying to get him some compensation.

It's been my feeling right along for some reason—I have no literal foundation, just a feeling—that Westmoreland is quite conscious of the dollar. I could be quite wrong, but CBS seemed willing to go all over the country to interview people. How come they didn't go to South Carolina or wherever Westy was and instead he came up and stayed at the Plaza?

We also had read to us a memo or note that George had sent to Mike Wallace concerning his telephone conversation with Westmoreland.

It was quite candid: George Crile said something to the effect that Westmoreland puzzles him—he's not sure how bright he is. He doesn't seem to understand that we are talking about American intelligence, and Crile was afraid that Westy would start stonewalling when he got to an interview. George mentioned he planned on calling Westy again to go over the planned interview once more.

As the characters unfold, as candid notes like this get read to us, my own feelings are becoming confirmed.

Westmoreland doesn't seem to be that quick or bright. He has a tunnel-type vision—he sees what he sees on his own terms. This could explain his fascination with types like Komer and Graham. They possess a quickness that he doesn't have. However, I feel they are all trapped by their own egos. In different ways, perhaps, but to the same detriment.

At one twenty-five the judge interrupted Burt and said, "How about lunch?"

Thank God for Pierre the judge.

When we got back from lunch, Burt was back on the memo. There was a section in there in which Crile was giving his opinions to Mike Wallace on how to handle Westy, and at some point in there he said, "We covered our asses"—and something about breaking Westmoreland. Well, needless to say, Burt got a lot of play out of that.

How did Crile mean *break* Westmoreland? Was it a figure of speech?

Westy was all smiles in the corner. Burt acted like the cat that ate the canary.

No one on the defense side seemed even to blink.

Burt gave Crile a lot of opportunity to give his lengthy explanations.

Crile was a good talker. He was cool—good at eye contact—he explained situations in a context so that they were interesting stories as well. However, they tended to run a little overtime. Burt just let him ramble and then when Crile was finished, Burt would ask the same exact question. Crile just answered all over again, not even changing the form of the sentence. It became tedious.

Once the judge even asked Burt to ask another question. So Burt went back to the letter that Westy sent to CBS with all those documents attached.

Crile said the documents were the same documents they had shown Westmoreland at the interview.

We had a break, and afterward, Walt Whitman Rostow was on the monitor, Wallace being the interviewer. I like Rostow. He has a pleasant countenance and a wonderful way about him.

He said a lot of the same things that we had heard in court when he was here. It seems like a year ago.

We watched an hour and a half of unedited tapes. It was interesting. I learned a lot of interesting side points—unfortunately, none of it was admissible as evidence.

Burt simply showed us all the tapes so that he could accuse CBS of not using one second of any of them.

Rostow tried very hard not to implicate Westmoreland in any way. However, there were loads of things he just was not the least bit aware of. He knew about the disagreements that MACV and the CIA were having, but he was totally unaware of many of the accusations that we've been hearing.

Rostow said that former President Eisenhower had told President Johnson that Westmoreland's job was much more difficult than Eisenhower's ever was in Europe. It was a different kind of war—a guerrilla war—and none of the methodology used in Europe would be effective in Vietnam.

I wondered why the hell Westmoreland wasn't satisfied with just letting a statement like that from Eisenhower suffice.

Wasn't that enough? Why didn't he let this documentary just fade and die?

It certainly isn't repeat material. It's not a *Gone with the Wind*, which will be played twice a year for the rest of our lives on TV. It buzzed people three years ago and so much else has happened since. The news is dead and gone.

Actually, Westmoreland's act of suing has only continued the question about his integrity (the way I see it). He should have used a little of the Oriental psychology—let it die by itself.

So now we are not only seeing *The Uncounted Enemy* over and over again, but we are also seeing "The Making of the Uncounted Enemy." We have seen every inch of material that was left on the cutting room floor. I fear we'll see even more.

Wallace pounded a lot of questions at Rostow. Rostow has a pleasant, relaxed face that has the beginning of a pleasant smile engraved on it. He's contemplative yet quick.

"Now listen, Mike, you're going to do great damage to the country—listen, you're going to get it wrong."

Rostow was a protective father. He was quite certain his boys had done the right thing over there. He had all the answers they'd given us.

"Johnson heard good news and bad news . . . the tortured Order of Battle debate is not the main issue . . . the complexity of the war without a main front . . ."

Then we started to hear answers like: "You're telling me something that I don't know."

Wallace posed a hypothetical question. "What would you think of a general who has his men keep a ceiling on infiltration figures?"

"That would be bad business," answered Rostow.

The takes were finally over. The only ones still awake were Crile, Boies, and Burt and the latter had been reading the transcripts like he was reading a humorous novel.

When we got back from our break, Crile was back on the stand.

More accusations, questions, long answers—and then we were dismissed.

It was the same old subway. The ride home is a lot more pleasant than the morning. I get a seat at our stop and can usually get in a good read. I finished my book and felt that I'd just said good-bye to a friend. Ending is always a bittersweet thing for me. I'm glad it's over, but I wish it weren't.

I took a short nap when I got home. I made dinner for my father-in-law, and then Bob and I went to a holiday gathering at Cheryl's house. She had about five or six couples in for a wonderful buffet (she must have cooked all weekend).

Her friends were most interesting and we reluctantly called it a night at twelve-thirty. The food and drink and conversations were uplifting—I was in a romantic mood all the way home. The stars were out, the taxi radio played wonderful Mozart, and the weather was unseasonably warm—it must have been sixty degrees outside—and Bob was in a good mood, also.

WAS THERE LIGHT AT THE END OF THE TUNNEL?

December 18, 1984

Well, it happened today. I almost lost my mind. The same questions over and over again.

Crile was on the stand when we filed in—Burt was in firing position. I can't even remember what the first words were or if there was a lead-in, or what was said—but all I can remember was something like:

"And here on this page of the blue sheet, Mr. Crile"—(I didn't hear another word)—out of somewhere, way down deep, a sound escaped from me—much like a growl. When I heard the noise, it shocked me. The foreman next to me jabbed his elbow in my side. I looked up to see what had happened, and everyone was racing to the side bar.

Richard was whispering loudly in my ear: "What did you do? What's wrong with you? Crile heard you—he heard you."

I glanced up at the witness. He was buried behind some document, obviously dissolved in laughter. His face was crimson red! Oh my God! I could feel my own complexion become hot. I can't remember this feeling of embarrassment. If there were a hole somewhere—anywhere—I would have disappeared. But the fact remained, I was losing it!

They were at the side bar for a long time. I wondered if they'd heard me. Every thought known to man raced through my mind.

By the time they resumed position, I was composed—so was everyone else.

Burt read one whole page from the transcript of *The Uncounted Enemy*. When he finished, he said, "You wrote that, didn't you, Mr. Crile?"

I wanted to dissolve in laughter, but I didn't dare. I forced my mind to go somewhere—I chose a babbling brook somewhere in the mountains, with evergreens all around—and when I returned to the courtroom, Crile was giving a lecture on the tone of the war in 1967.

I couldn't believe how Burt let him go on. Crile told us that Rostow told him he was involved in a propaganda campaign to let the American people believe we were winning the war. They even made sure it hit the foreign papers. I had to chuckle when Crile said, "I could go on at length about it if you'd like."

Burt declined the invitation. Instead, he finally changed the subject and got into George Allen, who was Carver's deputy, and the fact that he had a couple of interviews. Crile explained that it was a joint decision. Burt wasn't happy with the answer and played that to death—then, out of nowhere he announced he was through questioning Mr. Crile.

Boies stood up, smiled, apologized for his cold, buttoned his jacket, greeted the judge, the witness and the jury, and began his cross-examination.

He brought up "the cable" and Crile proceeded to begin one of his dissertations on the Order of Battle. Boies let perhaps a minute go by—excellent timing—and interrupted with, "Excuse me one moment, Mr. Crile. I want to make sure I understand you correctly. Is it my understanding that you just said . . ."—and Boies proceeded to capsulize the answer.

"Is that correct, sir?"

"Yes, Mr. Boies," answered Crile.

Boies continued, "Now, what happened then, Mr. Crile, to the best of your understanding? What step took place after . . ." And then Boies repeated his capsulized answer.

Crile continued . . .

I really had to hand it to Boies—he had everything I learned in Debating 101 down pat. He not only regained his position of authority, but he put the lectures we were getting into understandable segments. He was allowing us time to digest each portion of Crile's statements.

It was a marvelous symphony.

We learned quite a bit today: CBS had lots of ammunition. We saw the tip of the iceberg. I think I have it straight—no, to the best of my understanding. The following is a brief synopsis of what I think I understood in today's proceedings.

George Crile was the editor of *Harper's* magazine in Washington back in 1975 or 1976 or sometime in there. Sam Adams approached him with a story on the coverup of infiltration in North Vietnam during 1967 and 1968, the time surrounding the Tet offensive.

George Crile printed the story. The story sparked so much interest that a House select committee on intelligence, headed by Otis Pike, investigated the allegations.

Apparently, the CIA was asked to find holes in Sam Adams's article, and it couldn't. There were many secret hearings—some public. A few more issues were presented, but it kept coming back to the Pike committee.

Adams's name came up: Why did you think he was credible? What did you know about him?

Crile went on at length about the fact that Adams had written to Carver in his resignation letter the fact that he, Adams, felt he was involved in a monument of deceit, and that he, Adams, had still been interested in working for the CIA. He was just not leaving—he was trying to remove himself from an area he felt totally uncomfortable in.

I have to admit—that struck me also! It seems that it's been Adams, the main one, sounding the bugle.

It's like another Bernstein and Woodward episode. A lot of other people knew, but if it hadn't been for Adams, no one would have bothered letting the cat out of the bag!

The fact that he wasn't just outright fired after having written a letter like that struck me. I felt that if indeed that had happened, the man was on to something.

There was a long trip to the side bar. All the jurors were buzzing: It was obvious that Boies had the ability to make a boring episode interesting. A couple of the jurors were misquoting facts. Eileen asked me what month was the Langley conference? Was it the one in the spring or the fall? Did the Saigon conference come before the Honolulu conference? I think we got it all straight.

Crile used an analogy today that really hit home. He said that Rostow had told him that the SD or the guerrillas were an insurmountable type of enemy to them.

Rostow used the analogy of ten terrorists in New York City. How many policemen would you need to control ten terrorists in New York City?

Well, that's what it was like to fight the guerrillas and SD. Their deeds—those secret booby traps and bombs, etc.—accounted for one third of the American and allied casualties.

This blew my mind. Of course, deep down inside, the idea of guerrillas and SD and SSD and political cadre bothered me a lot. But the MACV types (who were there on the front) belittled their effectiveness. A fact that always puzzled me. Rostow's analogy made sense.

So did Crile's interpretation of the tone of the world in 1967–68. A lot of people weren't buying the light at the end of the tunnel.

The Vietcong were instigating a psychological campaign on the U.S.—the same as they had done to the French in the '50s.

A lot of little side points of interest came out today—secret cables and such. Carver's code name was Funaro. I thought that was apt.

We were presented with another piece of evidence—on the defense's "state of mind."

Readings in current military history—a West Point text. It reminded me of one of my readings on the history of education texts. However, this one had a section on the Vietnam War. Right there, in black and white, they were quoting infiltration numbers of thirty thousand or so in the fall of 1967.

Westmoreland was a superintendent at West Point at one time, wasn't he?

The judge gave us a lecture on the admission of the West Point text and the Pike committee findings as evidence.

We could only attribute it to the defense's state of mind. It could not be admitted as the truth.

A lot of other things happened today. We kept hearing about the "Wise Men" and Cooley and a book written by Tom Powers.

We were dismissed.

Traffic was hectic getting out of the city. I picked up Bob, and we headed north. We made it to my real estate office party by seven-thirty. It was spectacular. A lot of people kept asking me where I had been.

Some I told, some I didn't—but when the husband of a colleague asked me a question, I was shocked.

"I know you're on the Westmoreland-CBS jury, and I know that you can't talk about it, and I'm not asking you to—but I must ask you one thing."

"Yes, John, what is it?"

"Do they mention the 'light at the end of the tunnel' a lot?"

I looked at him cross-eyed: "What do you mean, John? Obviously, you read the newspapers. Whatever are you asking?"

John said: "No, I don't read the newspapers—I could give a shit about the trial. I was there in 1967. And all I heard was, 'There's a light at the end of the tunnel.'"

I stared at him, and walked away. How could I possibly tell him that's all we have been hearing and not give away my deepest feelings?

December 20, 1984

I fought my way back to the city with the sunrise. It was spectacular— giant ball of fire, pink clouds, red tones throughout the sky.

It was all mirrored in the reservoirs that I raced past. It was a sight—the sky, the reflections, the white swans silhouetted against the steam rising off the waters.

I had wonderful background music on my tape deck (new again—I just had the third radio in my one-year-old car installed).

It was a tedious trip once I hit Yonkers. I hadn't passed an open bakery, and I was beginning to get nervous—I had promised cakes for the holiday party.

In Yonkers I filled the gas tank and the attendant directed me to Yonkers Avenue and a wonderful bakery. I came out of there laden with delicious things—and a cake for Richard's birthday—he is our foreman.

By the time I got downtown, there was blinding rain. Cars were backed up trying to get into the parking lot.

Finally my turn. I got into court at exactly ten.

I was greeted with: We have bad news. Loretta is sick—Juror 3. I knew she was—she sat next to me and had been popping pills for the last two weeks. Everyone groaned.

We were called into the courtroom in spite of Loretta. I wondered what would happen.

We were given the day off—SHOCK! The judge delivered the message with flamboyance, and he used the opportunity to go through very serious reminders of our situation.

I got the dubious honor of cancelling the food for our party. Everyone exchanged grab bags. We had pulled a name out of a hat last week and set a five-dollar limit.

Norma Parker gave me a beautiful shawl. It was a wonderful gift— soft and warm, and just a lovely thought. I'm not sure that David liked my gift—I thought it was so perfect!—*Zen and the Art of Motorcycle Maintenance*—he's into both. Maybe he's read it already. Anyway, we were dismissed.

Cheryl and I went for an early lunch, shopped a little, and by two-thirty I was heading out of Manhattan, not to return to court until January 3.

Happy Holidays!

January 2, 1985

I can't believe I'm writing the date, 1985. Orwell's 1984 has passed (I have to read the book again). How many of his predictions came true? I had to teach school today.

One thing about the classroom—children still possess an innocence and naïveté that keeps one in touch with oneself. Somewhere deep down inside, I am still one of them.

In small, short doses, as I've been experiencing these past few months, the children are a total delight. Even their noise level doesn't disturb me. I feel like I'm more effective than I've been for years. I miss them, and they seem to be delighted to see me.

For several years now I've been looking for ways to get out of the classroom—to mingle with the adults in this world. But by some strange twist of fate, I'm mingling with the adults in this world who carry awesome titles—the adults who hold stations of the leaders that we look up to.

When my name was called and I entered the jury box, the counsel for the defense asked me a couple of questions. One of them was, "Who do you most admire in this world?" My answer was, "I wish there were someone." Three months later my answer remains the same.

The men who have testified before me in the last three months have been intelligent, competent men. I have no doubt in my mind about that. But the glaring fact that they are just that—men—has been the thing that has most impressed me. They, too, are human. The emotions and values that plague me, plague my colleagues—my family—seem to be the same emotions and values that plague all these men. Some more than others, of course. I have yet to witness one who stands above all—unscathed by the petty emotions of self-respect, and from being worried about looking good in front of others, and so forth.

The things that seem to be my curse of late are things like art budgets for next year, getting ready for fire inspections, organizing projects that will incorporate all the skills that must be taught at each stage of development so that my children will progress and become adults.

At eight-thirty I arrived at school to begin these things. I looked at the clock, and it was three o'clock. It seemed like only ten minutes later, yet it was time for them to be dismissed.

Teaching days, as much as I've complained about them, fly into the next before you can blink. I didn't leave until five-thirty, and I still had to take work home with me. My revised budget is half done. If only the courtroom drama could pass as quickly.

January 3, 1985

When I left work, my classroom work, I rushed into New York. Bob had stayed in the city to keep a late appointment and an early one in the morning. I met him at his father's, had dinner, and got ready for another bout with Westmoreland.

It was somewhere in the middle of the night that the clock radio went off.

Heavenly music was playing—an oboe concerto that compelled my soul to dance in mid-air.

I lay enthralled. As my eyes focused on the face of the clock, my heart sank lower than I can remember ever. It was time to rise.

Something inside me—someone—got me out of bed. I stood in the bathroom splashing cold water onto my body. I resorted to slapping my face like a bad TV commercial, and stood in the shower for what seemed like an eternity.

The last thing in the world that my body wanted to do was to leave where it was and travel to Foley Square.

But it did those earthly things like getting the car off the street before the tow trucks came, and getting it to the inspection it needed, before going to court.

The car had to be inspected after our second robbery claim. Hence, at 8:15 I found myself in a foreign land—under the Williamsburg Bridge, having some stranger taking pictures of my car. It was relatively painless. Fifteen minutes later, I was having breakfast at the Thomas Street Inn.

By nine-thirty I was back in the jury room. One by one we all arrived—the jury.

Similar stories of getting up this morning were told by all.

At ten sharp we were filing into the courtroom.

The same players, same parts—but the witness stand was empty.

The courtroom was filled to capacity. Pierre Leval played host.

Happy New Year greetings. Hope all of you have had a good rest. Hope all of you had a chance to think about what has been happening here in the courtroom.

I had to laugh to myself. Think about it? I've been plagued by it. I even dreamed about it. As I prepared hors d'oeuvres for a festive New Year's Eve, thoughts of SD and guerrillas planting punji sticks ran through my head. I awakened each morning with visions of the plaintiff and the defense in verbal combat. I have envisioned the characters before me in every conceivable act of living.

Cheryl told me at lunch that she had been shopping up in Springfield, Massachusetts, and she looked up and thought George Crile was standing in front of her. I imagine that each of the·jurors had similar experiences.

Pierre Leval continued. He brought out his X chart and reviewed the meanings—the documents—the data that we've witnessed for the past three months.

He went over the five elements of this case again:

1. Was the broadcast, the documentary—*The Uncounted Enemy*—defamatory?
2. Were the defamatory statements and accusations directed at General Westmoreland?
3. Were the defamatory accusations false?
4. What were the defendants' state of mind? Did Sam Adams, George Crile, Mike Wallace, and CBS know that these accusations were false, and did they have a reckless disregard for the truth? (I found out in the jury room this morning that Mike Wallace had been admitted to the hospital a couple of days ago for exhaustion.)
5. Did the false accusations or defamatory statements damage General Westmoreland's reputation? (What was his reputation before the documentary? What was his reputation after the documentary?)

Judge Leval reminded us about the evidence that had been admitted and which documents pertained to what.

Some pertained to the defendants' state of mind. Some evidence pertained to the truth. Some pertained to General Westmoreland's reputation—such as newspaper articles and cartoons and such.

He thanked us for our patience and then proceeded to invite Mr. Boies to continue questioning his witness.

George Crile took the stand. He looked terrible. He had a slight tan, but he looked like he'd aged ten years in ten days. His hair was grayer, his face taut, his eyes red. He sat up in the witness stand with a box of Kleenex and a jug of water.

His coughs echoed throughout the courtroom. It was obvious that many of the reporters were also suffering from bad colds. If you shut your eyes for a minute, it sounded like an infirmary—even one of the alternates was so sick she really shouldn't have been here today.

Boies smiled, buttoned his jacket, greeted the judge, the witness, and then the jury. He too went through a coughing bout—but with a bit more style. He was wearing a new tie. It had white squiggles all over it. The background was his customary navy blue. He was wearing his pin-striped navy blue suit and a new white shirt, button-down collar.

Boies began: "Mr. Crile, there are some questions that neither I nor the counsel for the plaintiff has asked you. Could you tell us what you did before you joined CBS and under what circumstances you became affiliated with CBS?"

Crile started out in Cleveland, Ohio. He then went to Trinity College in Hartford for another degree. He then was a reporter with Drew Pearson and Jack Anderson in Washington, D.C. He worked for a newspaper in Gary, Indiana, in the early 1970s.

Then he was editor for *Harper's* magazine in Washington, where he became acquainted with Sam Adams. He recounted his professional reporting career as a producer and documentary producer.

There were many impressive credentials and many controversial topics that Mr. Crile worked on: battle for Panama; battle for South Africa (a black liberation attempt to overthrow the government); Three Mile Island; Francis Gary Powers; gay rights or gay politics in San Francisco; many shorter broadcasts; critical choices of men of power (1980, with Walter Cronkite). He won an Emmy and a Peabody Award for his African documentary. The *Harper's* cover story by Sam Adams on the uncounted enemy provoked such interest that even the House subcommittee (the Pike committee) was formed to investigate the allegations.

He joined CBS in 1976, and began thinking about making a documentary in the fall of 1980 on the uncounted enemy.

First, he did an extensive investigation into the Pike committee findings and had many talks with Sam Adams, who had interviewed in the neighborhood of three hundred people for his own investigations. Then he read and reviewed the writings of Tom Powers about Richard Helms, and the book by Nguen Cao Ky, the former ambassador of Vietnam, and Johnson's book, *The Vantage Point,* and a book by

Westy's former aid, Chandler, and he decided to present the idea to CBS for a documentary.

He met with the heads of CBS in January 1981, and in January 1982 the documentary provoked the history that we are now living.

I wonder if he's sorry he ever heard of Westmoreland.

It's obvious watching Westmoreland that he has no regret at having started this suit. At least, not visibly. He sits there proudly, day after day.

Cheryl said at lunch today that she thinks Westmoreland is hard of hearing. I think she's right—he doesn't seem to flinch at anything.

I think he probably may be hard of hearing, but also is afflicted with total tunnel vision. He doesn't seem to internalize any of the evidence against him. Either that, or he feels so confident in being the general that it doesn't matter what is said.

I really can't figure him out.

Mrs. Westmoreland seems to be more alone these days. There are no wives keeping her company while their husbands are playing witness. She seems to be buried more and more in her needlework, looking up only occasionally. She still dresses well—she is wearing her green and red outfit today.

The symphony of Boies's questions and Crile's answers fills the rest of the day.

Why did you use some material and not others? Who would appear on camera—who would not? Why wouldn't Colonel Barry Williams allow you to photograph him? What about Bernie Gattozzi? What are their present jobs?

Both Williams and Gattozzi are still deeply ingrained in our government, but it came out that both would appear as witnesses for the defense.

Boies whipped out a five-page document of notes Crile took of an interview with Williams. We, the jury, got a copy.

A lot of interesting statements were introduced. Williams was present at the National Intelligence Order of Battle Conferences before and after the Tet offensive.

Yes, MACV indeed had a ceiling on the infiltration of enemy numbers that would be admitted.

Williams was present at the Pentagon hearings when the arbitrary reductions in figures of enemy were done.

Williams believed SD were an integral part of the Vietcong militia. They inflicted a great many injuries on our soldiers . . .

The only reason they were taken out of the Order of Battle was to keep the ceiling below 300,000 enemy.

I think it was Williams, but someone focused a lot on Graham, claiming he was the man responsible for the major cuts.

As the antiwar movement strengthened in the United States, pressure seemed to mount on the military in Vietnam to make it appear that we were winning . . .

Crile mentioned others who told him personally that there indeed was a ceiling on the numbers of enemy that the general would allow to be reported: McChristian, Hawkins, Godding, Colonel Hamscher, Williams, even Komer and Carver, and of course Meechem.

God, why did Westmoreland ever let himself be dragged through this courtroom if indeed this is all true? Crile sounds convincing.

We had a break.

No one mentioned a thing about the trial in the jury room. It's like we go in there and we're there for a party. Books, magazines, newspapers, needlework, and talk, talk, talk. The jury room looked a mess today. The old Christmas stockings and tinsel looked faded. I felt very fat. I ate too much the last couple of weeks—too many parties. I decided I wouldn't eat lunch today. I went into the john and locked the door and did some stretch exercises to try to wake up. I would have splashed some cold water on my face, but I didn't want to ruin my makeup.

When we got back into the courtroom, we were met with mounds of paper. Documents, exhibits—evidence.

I remember a passage here and there—the humorous or the human-type statements are what linger in my mind.

One document mentioned that Davidson's (Westy's J2) flying circus included Graham and Charlie Morris—and something about McNamara being a statistical nut. So MACV played a statistical ball-game! They gave him what he wanted.

According to my recollection of McNamara, he didn't seem to swallow their numbers. At least that's what I think he said. I don't know what I think anymore. I'd like to read over some of these courtroom transcripts to refresh my memory.

Meechem became a major focus. We got to read some of the letters he wrote home to his wife. He wrote a letter a day to Dorothy. He numbered them.

We read numbers 212, 213, 223, 230, and 231. Then 304, 213, 223, etc.

I woke up. The letters were real. Meechem referred to personal family problems and episodes obviously in answer to Dorothy's letters.

He was a good writer—fluent, to the point, yet colorful. He had good, legible handwriting—on the bold side. He dwelled on para-

graphs pertaining to his experiences in Vietnam and his job as Order of
Battle analyst. The latter were the passages we were referred to.

Boies's voice never missed a beat: "Would you please turn to page
three, the third paragraph, the paragraph that starts with 'When I
went'—do you have that? Mr. Crile, could you please read that paragraph into the record?"

George would obligingly read between coughs. I devoured the
whole letter.

They were a hell of a lot more interesting than reviewing infiltration
data and counting SD and SSD.

Meechem talked about the weather, which hit in the hundreds, the
swimming pool, which was empty for days in the midst of this, because of the ineptness of the manpower there; the open drain; the rockets at night; the fighting all around them. I got more of a feeling of
what was going on there in Vietnam this afternoon—through Meechem's letters—than I have in three months, other than an occasional
tangent that Westmoreland was allowed to speak about.

Apparently, there were a lot of people in Saigon. Meechem talked
about traffic jams with coolies and bicycles and cars. He talked about
trying to find a book, in a bookstore, that Dorothy had mentioned to
him. His child's teeth problem, children's growing problems, and
things Dorothy was dealing with alone came to life. The vases he
found, and the thwarted social appointments because things came up
with his job.

"We had to work into the night . . . you should have seen the antics
my people and I had to go through with our computer calculations. . . . We started with the answers and plugged in all sorts of
figures . . . and we continue to win the war. . . ."

"We are winning the war and I can prove it—we worked all day on
figures to show it. Having received sufficient and adequate guidance
from my leaders."

The letters we saw were filled with statements like this. They covered a few months—mainly after the Tet offensive.

In June 1968, he wrote: "DIA Types were here trying to pry the
truth from my sealed lips—they smell a rat and can't find where to
look for it."

A final letter in July, just before Meechem left Vietnam, said something to the effect that "I had a talk with a CICV director. I told him
about the coverup figures—now my conscience is clear."

He went on about the meaning, or the value of a conscience, if it
could be relieved so easily.

A lot of his writing gave real insight into this human being—he was an idealist, floundering in a pragmatist's world. He didn't wear the suit very well. He sounded tormented.

When things were wrong, it bothered him. You could tell by other passages he wrote. There was a sequence where he criticized his wife on her use of the past tense in her writing.

He was correct—her use was off—but who the hell cared? She had written him 294 letters. I wanted to hit him over the head. Obviously, she did too. They are now divorced.

But regardless—Meechem said what was on his mind, and I had to respect him a lot for that.

We were given our lunch break.

Cheryl and I walked and walked. She had to return a Christmas gift, I had to pick up a tape. We had a quick lunch.

The waiter took our order as soon as we sat down. Our lunch, after a near public scene, arrived a half hour later.

When we got back to the jury room, they were already filing into the courtroom.

I was in a rotten mood.

We were back on documents. Crile was still on the stand.

Boies: "Did you have this document in your possession when you made your documentary, Mr. Crile?"

"Yes I did!"

There were others. One particular document was headed, October 11, 1967—Paul V. Walsh, acting Department Director of Economic Research (or Resources?) to George Carver, SAVA (reviewing MACV numbers).

"I have received the draft statement and as seen from my office I must rank it as one of the greatest snow jobs since Potemkin constructed his village—CIA not to be associated either directly or indirectly with this briefing . . ."

It included statements such as "purposeful deception by MACV . . ."

"This briefing and similar fictions . . ."

"CIA following along with MACV would be falling into a deceptive trap . . ."

The accusations—the evidence flowed.

Crile was allowed to go into monologues, though structured, with Boies interrupting to clarify points.

We heard more about Gains Hawkins and Sam Adams, who Danny Graham thought was a "mental case."

We heard more about the tactics of the Vietcong—the mental war.

Though the North Vietnamese lost Tet militarily, they won politically, a whole psychological thing.

Crile, when talking about the Tet offensive, mentioned that in the middle of Tet, Westmoreland requested 200,000 more men.

I looked over at the plaintiff's table, and Mr. Burt and Westmoreland and the other lawyers were shaking their heads and chuckling at something.

In hindsight, I think they are very analytical people.

I know—I think we, the jury know—that was a figure of speech on Crile's side. Westmoreland had requested the men before Tet in anticipation of such a happening.

But militarily—courtroom-wise—one must not use figures of speech.

Real time is of utmost importance. The testimony became tedious. Not that it was that boring, but I was tired—I wanted to go to sleep. I was actually fighting not to.

More documents were laid in front of me, and my vision was blurred. I did things like shake my head, rock in my seat—tried to study the spectators. I even counted the bricks in the outside wall I could see through the window.

Crile was only repeating points he had made before. How credible he believed Sam Adams—why Hawkins was so important in his estimation.

Suddenly, out of nowhere, Boies announced he was finished questioning.

Out of nowhere I woke up—a break—then, surprise of surprises.

We were dismissed for the day. It was only 3:30—I mean 3:37, to be exact.

We were to return tomorrow at ten, but it would be a short day. How short, we don't know yet. But . . .

It never ceases to amaze me: I was planning on going home as fast as I could and sneak in a nap before dinner, and suddenly I was so wide awake I could have run the Boston Marathon, and I almost did.

I bought dinner, drove Cheryl home, found a parking space that was good for tomorrow, too.

Inside the apartment, I made dinner, worked on the school budget, and prepared for tomorrow.

Forecast: Freezing rain; sleet; maybe a lot of snow!

I hoped we would be let out early so that I could beat the storm.

January 4, 1985

The weather people don't know what they're talking about. It's five in the evening and it hasn't started to do anything yet. Not that I'm upset about it, but it would be nice to be able to rely on an accurate report.

I wonder if the weather people tamper with their statistics and re-ports the way that MACV seems to have. Perhaps this world is one huge conspiracy—to keep real information from the public.

I'm beginning to hate myself. I feel like I'm becoming cynical.

I was thumbing through *The New York Times* this morning at break-fast at home, and I did something I haven't done up until now—I read the article on the Westmoreland case.

The judge's words, like a guard sitting on my shoulder, screamed in my ears—*don't do it!* Don't let yourself be influenced by anyone—do not watch TV reports—do not read the newspapers, especially edito-rialized versions. Discuss the case with no one!

As tough—and I mean tough—as that has been, I have heeded those warnings and my only release has been this diary. So I read the article. I was surprised to see how lengthy and accurate it was. It was reported by M. A. Farber. I wondered which one of the reporters he was—he took down good notes. In fact, he was a hell of a lot more thorough than I, in many respects. I read it over again and realized—yes, it sounded more accurate because of exact names and titles and positions that he included. Actually, the positions and data—such as that Meechem was thirty-seven at the time he was in Vietnam—were basically irrelevant to the evidence (the only thing that we had to take into consideration).

He included passages from Meechem's letters that I had not remem-bered. I was speed-reading those things while Boies and Crile were talking—no wonder I missed them.

One passage in particular hit me. After reading the article, I realize that I had forgotten it.

"I'm not talking about confusion and inefficiency, which, to a cer-tain extent are products of all wars," he wrote, "but about muddle-headed thinking, cover-your-ass orders, lies and outright foolishness on the very highest levels."

I reread my own passages, written yesterday, and realized I had pretty much written the same things, more candidly. Now I could see why it was a good idea to not read anything or listen to anything someone else reports. We all indeed see things our own way, and after all, I was on the jury. I had to form my own opinion.

When I went to get on the subway this morning, I picked up the *Daily News* to read on the train. Not being in the middle of any book right now, I wanted something to occupy my time. As I read through the pages, big bold headlines caught my eye: TRY TO SCORE AGAINST WESTY WITH LETTERMAN. The article was a half column long. I fig-ured, What the hell—as long as I already read the *Times* article, I may as well give the *Daily News* equal time. All the column stated was that Meechem's letters were introduced today.

Westmoreland has sued, charging that the show was inaccurate and that Meechem had signed an affidavit on October 3, 1983, saying, "It was my dislike for my job that I was expressing in my letters and my occasionally flip reaction to the events of the day. The rhetoric . . . is exaggerated and does not reflect my calm judgment on the events of the time."

I was in a state of shock. Yes indeed, we were told about that affidavit—it wasn't even in evidence—but in my mind, no one sends over three hundred letters saying the same thing—lies, lies, gargantuan lies, coverup and so forth—and not mean at least some of it. I realized this article had a Westmoreland slant and the other perhaps a CBS slant, though I believed the *Times* article accurate.

Could it be we see and hear what we want to? I didn't believe that I really had a predisposition to any of the parties, but the way I saw the evidence, it certainly looked like there was a coverup of some sort—maybe not a coverup as much as a misguidance, or whatever. It was obvious they—MACV, Westmoreland side—have even said they were sensitive about the press. Westy had given us his long, emotional speech.

"Of course I was sensitive to the press—my men fought hard, etc., etc."

I tended to agree with Meechem after hearing Westy, and especially Graham.

Muddle-headed thinking—cover your ass—orders. Outright foolishness on the very highest levels.

I could buy that after meeting the characters involved: the egos, the club—

I got into the jury room about twenty minutes early, with some coffee. I started to chat with the other jurors. Groups within the group, of course, have formed. Kate, the grandmother, seems to gravitate toward Carmen and Jean. Eileen and Linda and Randy and Richard usually pal around playing cards. There are a lot of loners in the group. Harold usually sits in the corner reading his paper. He's a nice man. He's very pleasant, but he doesn't seem to mingle with anyone. He lunches alone, so do Myron and Phil and Lili. They pretty much keep to themselves.

Anyhow, out of the clear blue, Loretta says, "I don't think I can stand another minute of listening to Crile. He talks too much, I can't understand a word he says." Jean and Kate jumped in, in agreement.

Kate said outright she didn't like Crile or believe him. They all jumped in about the letters. I don't believe those letters. How did CBS get them? Those people making documentaries will do anything to get a story.

I butted in: "You mean you don't believe those letters? You mean you think that CBS made them up?"

"Oh no!" Jean answered. "I don't think they made them up, but he was young and lonesome at the time, and Meechem is a complainer—he just exaggerated. You could even see how he looked when they interviewed him on camera. He didn't want any part of CBS—he even signed that affidavit—he even said that he exaggerated and that those letters didn't reflect his true feelings."

Kate chimed in: "Most of the letters were about his family, the children's teeth—" She went on about the part where Meechem criticized his wife's misuse of parts of speech.

"I don't like Meechem. He deserves to be divorced," she added.

"Kate," I said. "Whether you like the man or not is irrelevant—but he was there, writing every day. Every single day he mentions something about how many lies, and the coverups."

"Oh no!" Kate attacked. "There is only a sentence here and there. Most of the letters had to do with his daily life and his trips and his family."

I didn't have time to answer—we were called into the courtroom.

Dear God, deliberations are going to be tough. I wonder what the others think?

Actually, this short conversation only made me more aware of my *own* opinions.

As I looked into the room, I noticed there were about ten copies of the *Daily News* scattered about. I only saw two copies of *The New York Times*.

The spectator seats were half empty. Crile was still on the witness stand. He still had a box of Kleenex next to him. But it was now Burt who was reexamining the witness.

He was low-key, but is he disorganized!

He hands the witness a document. "Turn to page thirty-five."

Crile says there is no page 35 in this copy. Burt goes to the table to look for another copy.

Finally, Boies says, "Here, let the witness use my copy."

Burt takes it from Boies—no thank you—and marches it up to Crile and takes Crile's copy and proceeds to start his examination.

Boies looks up in annoyance and says, "Mr. Burt, I wanted to expedite matters and allow the witness time to read over the pages for context, but now I don't have a copy."

Mr. Burt hands Mr. Boies the copy he just took from Crile.

Boies says, "But this doesn't have a page thirty-five." Out of exasperation, he just sat down and Burt blundered on.

It was nothing of consequence.

Burt brought up the Pike committee again—apparently, there were some numbers or statements that Allen had downplayed at the hearings. He had penciled in accurate numbers, doubling a MACV report of numbers. In the Pike hearings he had claimed the penciling meant nothing.

Crile claimed that when he had spoken to Allen about this, Allen claimed he had been taken aside by some higher-up in the CIA and told to answer as narrowly as possible—to not open up more questions.

Burt produced another document: I love the titles of these things— who the hell dreams them up? They'll never hit the best-seller list!

"Report of the Conference to Standardize Methods for Developing and Presenting Statistics on Order of Battle Infiltration Trends and Estimates."

Turn to page five, please, and Burt continues, without taking a breath, to read: "'Enemy losses, the conference also agreed on the use of a wounded in action (WIA) to killed in action (KIA) ratio of 1.5 to 1.' Do you see that, Mr. Crile?"

Crile hadn't even had time to flip to page five yet, which I could well understand—the title alone took up two pages.

Anyhow, Crile found it. Burt badgered him with: Why didn't you read this evidence? This statistic was out long before you produced that document. You purposefully tried to mislead the public with the ratio you used in the document.

Crile read it and simply said, "I'd heard a lot of ratios."

Burt said, "But this one was the official ratio."

Crile answered, "I stand corrected."

We had a break. We filed back to the jury room.

"What is the ratio?" asked one juror. Five people all proceeded to answer at once, and they were all completely different.

We all got a chuckle out of that one. Everyone seemed in a daze. No one was certain what day of the week it felt like. It was supposed to be a short day—how short? Will we have lunch?

We were called back into the courtroom. Boies was now on a re-question or reexamine or cross-examine—who the hell could keep track of the terms.

Boies went about showing all the various statistics that had floated around.

Gattozzi, the gains-and-losses analyst who worked with the statistics all the time, claimed it was 3 wounded to 1 killed.

Another statistic was 8 to 1; 2 or 3 to 1; 100 to 35.

Wasn't it Benjamin Disraeli who said: "There are three kinds of lies: lies, damnable lies, and statistics!"?

Crile then talked about why everyone catered to MACV. At the Honolulu conference it was decided to give MACV—the men in the field—a totally free hand at estimating the enemy.

After all, they were in the field—they should know!

Boies turned to the judge as he smoothed down his navy basket-weave tie and announced: "I'm finished questioning, Your Honor!"

We were dismissed for the day. It was eleven forty-five.

Joy! Joy!

Back to my other life, in the country!

January 5, 1985

Beautiful blue sky—about two inches of glistening snow on the ground. A fire in the wood-burning stove, with a pot of hot mulled cider on top.

Leslie and Tracy are up for the weekend. It should be fun.

January 6, 1985

The weekend was wonderful. We bought a VCR. We rented *The Big Chill, Sophie's Choice, Forty-eight Hours, Vacation, Stripes,* and *Broadway Danny Rose.*

When we weren't watching a movie, we were tramping around in the snow or eating. I did very little work.

But who cares? The girls were a lot of fun. Tracy's on a vacation from school; Leslie doesn't go back to college for another week or so.

This kind of weekend has become more and more rare.

The weather all weekend has been beautiful—though Friday night was a horror of a storm.

January 7, 1985

The words of my philosophical father ring in my ears today. One of his favorite sayings is: "An inconvenience is an unexpected adventure."

No wonder New York City is such an adventure. My first adventure came this morning as I entered, or rather tried to enter, the subway stairs at 77th Street. Throngs of people were blocking my way.

Warnings were called out: No subway—walk up to 86th Street.

It only took a couple of steps for me to realize that walking with these throngs was like trudging along in the Exodus. There were so many bodies one couldn't sidestep.

So I turned around and headed to 59th Street. It was pleasant out, and I figured the exercise would do me good.

Making these tactical maneuvers made me feel like a maneuver statistician, an analytical traffic psychologist!

Perhaps a bus might come along going downtown that I could jump on.

The way people walk to work in New York City is like a mini marathon.

People of all kinds of shapes and sizes pace along at a gait worthy of a race. Headphones, briefcases, swinging arms—all behaving like they will be first at the finish line.

I thought about Tracy after her Mazola race in the park. She said you don't compete with the throngs—you pick out someone a little ahead of you and you race with him or her.

I picked out a stately woman in a mink coat about sixty-five years old, wearing Nike sneakers. No matter how I tried, I couldn't catch up with her.

Suddenly I caught a glimpse of a bus saying CITY HALL.

I ran to the stop on the next block and jumped on. The problem was that the bus was so crowded, I couldn't get off the first step; nor could the doors close completely behind me. My purse was hanging out.

The bus took off. I held on to both side poles for dear life.

The next stop was 59th Street, and I quickly escaped. Never deposited my token. I caught an express train and made it to court with five minutes to spare.

My father-in-law told me that Westmoreland was to take the stand today. He heard it on 1010 WINS.

He was wrong. Ira Klein was in his place.

Ira Klein was the film editor who worked on *The Uncounted Enemy.*

It was quite obvious he didn't like Crile. Klein had his day in court.

I was shocked when Klein gave his age as thirty-three—he looked like he was twenty-three. He had dark, wavy hair. He was neatly dressed in a gray suit and red tie. He sat forward in his seat, playing with a pen in his hand, his elbows on his knees. He looked like he was sitting watching a ball game.

His answers were short. He added little else to what was asked of him—except on one occasion, when the judge reminded him just to answer the questions.

His testimony was interesting because it was new. We heard about *The Uncounted Enemy* from a film editor's point of view.

He had worked on other documentaries—mostly short, not more than twenty minutes in length.

When George Crile approached him with the job of working on *The Uncounted Enemy*, he was excited about it because of its length. It would be a challenging project.

That was in December 1980.

In January 1981, he learned that Crile still needed to do some interviews before this project would get final approval. They were completed at the end of March 1981, and Klein began his editing in April.

This type of interview and film is called a talking head film.

Ira Klein hired an assistant, Phyllis Hurwitz. It was her job to extract the pieces of film George Crile wanted to use from the interviews. She used a transcript that had been marked by Crile.

The jury was given parts of the transcript she used.

I noticed three or four new faces among the spectators. They stood out because they were new and didn't look like they were the typical reporters who frequent this trial. I thought perhaps they were friends of Ira Klein's. They looked around the same age and could possibly fit into the film set.

Burt got smart today. He waited until all the jurors got copies of the transcript before he began reading.

It was the section of film from the Hawkins interviews. The portion to be used read as follows: ". . . there was never any reluctance on my part to tell Sam or anybody else who had a need to know that these figures were crap. They were history—they weren't . . . they weren't worth anything."

A sentence just preceding this statement was left out; it read: "Now, prior to this, when we had the old figures that we inherited from the South Vietnamese forces . . ."

This bothered Klein a lot. Klein also said that he had taken Crile aside and told Crile that he thought Adams was obsessed. Did Crile trust his opinion?

Crile just answered, "I know," and never said another word about it.

Ira Klein's job was also to review stock footage of the Vietnam War. Some of it came from CBS, some from the government, and some from third-world film production houses.

Crile told Klein he didn't want Adams present while they were editing even though Klein told Crile he needed his assistance there.

We were certainly hearing about a different side of Crile.

There was an elaborate commotion while the plaintiff's lawyers dragged a contraption across the courtroom. Burt had his boys set up an easel. On it was a big blank pad on which he said he wanted to write the sequence down for the jury to follow.

He may possibly have the most horrible handwriting I've ever seen in my life. He scribbled two illegible sentences on an uphill slant. He never repeated the sentences. I had no idea what he had just scrawled out, and he was already on to another topic.

I looked at Richard, the foreman. He looked at me and just shrugged—but in such a resigned way, like, Oh, I can't read Greek either.

We got a brief lesson on film editing and sound sync as Klein answered questions posed by Burt.

We heard about the dailies, the rushes, the long hours of Crile, Klein, and Adams working together, and then how Klein and Crile disagreed over how scenes should be edited. Somehow, Burt got it in there that George Allen had sat in on one of the screenings, and it was after that that he had a second film interview.

Klein apparently went to one of their supervisors and complained that he didn't like how Crile was doing this documentary. He was told to stay out of it—not to get involved.

There was a viewing sometime in December, when a new president was taking over CBS's news department. Klein told how he was instructed by Crile to lower the sound in the middle of one of Westmoreland's statements. It was the section of historic film of Westmoreland giving a report to the American newsmen.

Westmoreland said that the infiltration had reached five or six thousand a month. The sound was lowered when Westy added, "But they have the capacity of stepping up."

There were also some statements that Klein claimed Adams made to him—something about the premise of the film being wrong, we have to come clean. It never was clarified when Adams said this or in what context. I think it was purported to have been said in February, after the film was aired. I'm not even sure if it was said.

We were dismissed for lunch. Cheryl, David, and I went to Chinatown. I nearly fell over a couple of cases of fish that were sitting in the middle of the sidewalk.

Being a fish lover and recalling the twenty-pound swordfish I bought for twenty dollars at the Fulton Street fish market, I got all excited.

One box had five-pound red snappers. There were three black kids all telling me what a great buy. I could get them for five dollars a fish—they'd pack them in ice for me.

I told them to let me get lunch and I'd buy it on the way back. I jokingly said to Cheryl and David at lunch that the fish had probably fallen off the back of a truck.

I had to laugh at myself on the way back when all the cases of fish were still sitting there and the three black kids were nowhere in sight.

When we got back from lunch, Boies was examining Klein.

He began: "Mr. Klein, would it be fair to say that you had a difficult personal relationship during part of your editing job with Mr. Crile?"

"Yes, that's fair," answered Klein.

"Would it be fair to say that you had several uncomplimentary terms for Mr. Crile? That you couldn't stand to look at him?"

There were objections and overrulings, but the bottom line was that Klein called Crile a social pervert, and he believed Crile was devious and slimy.

There was another accusation that Klein had called Mr. Alba, the researcher, a homosexual.

Boy, was this getting juicy—it was beginning to sound like an afternoon soap opera.

I looked at the transcripts of Klein's deposition; it was three inches thick. Klein had refused to talk to any of the defense attorneys at all, but he had met with the plaintiff's attorney's at least twenty times.

Klein got to defend himself on the accusation of Mr. Alba that he had made, saying that he, Klein, when trying to fix up Mr. Alba with one of the secretaries at CBS, was told by her that he's a nice guy and all that, but he's gay. So, thank you, but no thanks.

Boies began referring to the book *A Matter of Honor* by Don Kowet that was written about the documentary. Apparently, Klein had quite eagerly given the writer his opinions of Crile and Adams and the parties involved.

Boies asked Klein if he had read any of the transcripts of Crile's interviews. He hadn't. Had he gone on any interviews with Crile? He hadn't.

Klein had never interviewed anyone, never written an article—he wasn't aware of any notes that Crile or Adams took. He knew about Adams's chronology, but he'd never read it. He never read any CIA documents, never saw any Order of Battle documents. He never heard of the Pike committee, never knew about its results. He didn't know about SD or SSD or any officers who believed there was a deception.

In short, the guy sounded like sour grapes.

The judge had him write on a piece of paper when the problems with Crile began. We were not allowed to see it, but the judge and the lawyers seemed to suppress a humorous reaction to it.

There was a spell when Klein didn't work for CBS.

At our break, the jurors conjectured that Crile probably had had him fired. I was surprised when Loretta, the one who keeps saying Crile talks too much—she can't understand him—said to me: "I don't know about this guy. He doesn't seem as professional as Crile, or as intelligent."

More of the same after our break, and then we were dismissed. No Westmoreland today. I couldn't wait to go home to tell my father-in-law you can't believe everything you hear on the news.

When we got to the subway platform, the local train was waiting and I jumped on.

Five minutes later the motorman announced this was becoming an express—there had been an injury on the local track at 23rd Street.

When we got to 59th Street, he announced that the train would continue to be an express up to 125th Street, and promptly closed the doors before I could get off.

Here we go again! I got off at 86th Street and walked ten blocks home, remembering the words that started off my day.

An impossible DECISION

Getting to court this morning was like clockwork. I even had time for breakfast. It was also deceptively bright outside, and when the wind gusted, you had to hold on to something not to blow away.

It was a day that one stayed awake. When we got into the courtroom, we were told that it would be a short session.

Everyone gave summaries.

Burt summarized his case and rested.

Judge Leval summarized his points and gave the floor to Mr. Boies.

Then Boies gave the defense summary.

Burt's summary: You saw the broadcast. You saw from the evidence that General Westmoreland did not deliberately deceive his superiors on the size of the enemy.

Look at all the documents we saw. Remember in particular the memo of May 19, 1967, where the higher numbers were briefed.

Admiral Sharp *was* present at the briefing.

You saw the view graphs.

You heard about SNIE 14.3–67 at the Langley conference, where everyone was briefed and agreed on numbers. Documents don't lie.

You saw eighteen witnesses. You heard eighteen men tell you General Westmoreland never deceived anybody. Men may forget, but documents don't.

When Boies took the floor, he picked up on the documents-don't-lie theory.

You saw that there was, indeed, a command position on infiltration figures and enemy strength figures.

That was General Westmoreland's position—he was MACV.

The position was developed by General Westmoreland—he was the one who dropped SD and SSD from the Order of Battle.

You heard Morris and Godding and even Westmoreland himself tell us that they were politically motivated about reporting enemy strength figures.

You heard McChristian himself condemn what General Westmoreland did as being improper.

We all knew there was a debate, but we see now that it was a debate that was not honest. There were falsities in the estimates.

You heard Rostow and McNamara tell you that they were totally unaware that there were any political considerations.

You saw Meechem's letters, documents—they don't lie. The West Point textbook, the Pike committee findings, and Ky's book, Thomas Powers's book.

The plaintiff has failed to prove that the broadcast was false.

You see that CBS, at the time it did its broadcast, did not believe it was false.

The defense will take the floor to prove to you that, indeed, the documentary was accurate. Thank you.

The judge reminded us that we must keep an open mind. We can certainly go back critically and observe the evidence we've heard, but we must not allow ourselves to come to concrete conclusions. Keep our minds open, even when we must go in to deliberate.

We were read two depositions today—one of Joseph Zigmund, who was the head producer at CBS until he retired February 1, 1982, after twenty years with CBS, and one by Dwain Gatterdam, who worked in the CIA, in charge of the Near East, Southeast Asia. Both men were retired and lived at a considerable distance, hence one of the defense attorneys sat in the witness stand and read the deposition answers while Boies asked the questions.

The judge instructed us that this was just as though the real person were sitting on the witness stand. The witnesses had been under oath when their depositions were taken. Mr. C. was merely being an actor, but the words were those of the witnesses.

We began with Joseph Zigmund, who apparently had asked George Crile to allow him to work on *The Uncounted Enemy* with Crile.

Zigmund had nothing but praise for George Crile, calling him a man of the highest integrity—a tireless worker, absolutely thorough—and he went on with the superlatives. He said he would be proud to be a part of anything that George Crile worked on.

He, of course, was asked many questions about Ira Klein. He never gave unqualified praise about him, but he didn't have anything horrible to say about him, either.

He said Klein had been working long hours on his editing and he was worn out, tired. He had no objections when Joe Fackovec came in to complete the editing toward the end of the making of the broadcast.

He was asked if he knew of any problems among the people working on the documentary or if he knew that George Allen had a second screened interview.

Zigmund said that when he returned from a vacation, he had heard all of these things from Ira Klein.

Zigmund was surprised by the second film interview with Allen. He didn't see anything wrong with the first interview. In fact, he said the second one was almost identical—nothing basically different, except that it went more smoothly. In other words, as I understood him to say, it was no big deal.

Zigmund said that on a broadcast of this magnitude, everyone was a watchdog on everyone else. They all were well aware of the allegations that they were making, and everyone did a lot of research to make sure of the accuracy because they were quite aware of the possibility of a libel suit against them.

He again stated that he had the utmost regard for George Crile's work and accuracy.

Zigmund's deposition was completed. We were given a short break.

When we got back into the courtroom, we heard Gatterdam's deposition.

He had been with the CIA for twenty-four years, was assigned to Near East, Southeast Asia during the years we are concerned with, and had worked at times with Sam Adams.

Nothing but praise for Adams. (Those who have testified in favor of Sam Adams have had good words and suggestions of genius.) "One of the best analysts around."

Gatterdam said he was quite willing to give an affidavit because he felt it was important for the truth to come out.

MACV had ignored a lot of evidence on the size of the enemy they were fighting.

Gatterdam wanted to support Sam. "I had a commitment" he said.

He felt that SNIE 14.3–67 downplayed the enemy quantifications, and that it didn't give the reader an accurate feeling of what we were up against.

Gatterdam felt that Adams's methodology was sound and that his own research had confirmed Sam's findings. He also claimed several MACV officers had admitted the same thing to him.

Gatterdam believed that CIA had figures of 150,000–200,000 more enemy than MACV was reporting—and that included main force troops as well as SD and SSD, which MACV had dropped from its calculations.

Gatterdam also believed that there was an arbitrary ceiling of 300,000 set by MACV. He believed that MACV was trying to show progress.

According to Gatterdam, the enemy was moving into Vietnam steadily on an average of 20,000 a month from September 1967 through January 1968. They were lying low, preparing for the Tet offensive. While this was happening, MACV was interpreting the silence as a winding down of enemy strength. (I'm rephrasing this, but the meaning's the same.)

I noticed while Mr. C. was reading the depositions and turning pages that a lot of words were blacked out.

I assumed this went along with the type of testimony we heard in the courtroom.

Often we have heard "I move to strike that segment from the record—it's irrelevant" from one lawyer or the other.

However, the fact remains that we, the jury, usually get to hear these off-the-record comments.

I noticed the judge and the lawyers following along in their unmarked transcripts, amused at a point or two. I also noticed that CIA types have a way of answering things. They rarely say yes. It's always, "That is correct," or, "That is a correct statement."

The judge interrupted to remind us here and there when we should disregard an opinion because the witness had no way of knowing that statement as a fact. For instance, Gatterdam was not at one particular meeting, so he could not testify that Graham had a fight or that MACV really had a ceiling on enemy strength or that the CIA committee caved in at the Saigon meeting.

This testimony took place for another half hour or so, and we were then dismissed for the day, with Judge Leval's usual warnings to talk to no one, read nothing, return at ten in the morning.

I'm beginning to feel at home in the city. The need to use up every spare minute—shopping or taking in the sights—is disappearing. I just wanted to get on a subway and go home.

I was back at my father-in-law's by one forty-five. I puttered around for an hour or so. I looked out the window. It was magnificent out— what was I doing inside? In a few short weeks I would be back in the country, teaching, selling houses, and removed from this rich city.

I bundled up and walked to the Metropolitan Museum, stopping on the way in art galleries up Madison Avenue.

I had a wonderful afternoon. I didn't go to see anything in particular—I just wanted to get the feel of the museum. I walked along until a painting caught my eye. I learned new names, saw new things. I also learned some new things about some of my old favorites.

January 9, 1985

Today was a strange day. It was one of the days that are out of sync.

Bob was leaving on a business trip to California. The only way I can describe the morning is stilted. He'll be gone till Sunday. I'll miss him.

I heard on the news that there was a water-main break at 88th Street, between Park and Lexington. The radio claimed that it did not interfere with the subways, but already becoming savvy to the city, I was anxious.

As soon as I got to the train station, a packed train pulled up—the sardine express. I stood back on the platform. As the train pulled out of the station, another was ten feet behind. I got on it. We crawled all the way down to Foley Square. According to all the reports that I heard—from the motormen and the jurors—that's how transportation was all morning. Trains were backed up so badly that it was just one huge train stretched from one end of the city to the other. It took about forty minutes for the usual fifteen-minute ride.

The day in court was boring. I'd been eagerly looking forward to the defense taking the stand—anxious to see Mr. Boies flap his wings.

Instead, we had six witnesses—all on videotape, or a reading of their depositions.

When I look back on the day for an impression of what happened, the only thing that comes to mind is my discomfort.

I found new ways of sitting in the jury box. I longed to put my feet up on the partition in front of me but stopped myself for fear of making a spectacle of myself.

I can vividly remember studying the spot on the floor in front of me and visualizing how easily I could really lie down there. In my contortions, at one point I got my knee caught in between the arm and the back of the chair. I had to wait till they changed videotapes to extract myself.

Nothing new was introduced today. The witnesses merely echoed what we've been hearing right along.

I guess it was important for the defense to have these witnesses testify. But if only they were in the flesh. Real words, facial expressions, tones of voices can never be replaced by the reading of a deposition.

The judge started off the day with warnings and things to disregard and cautions of what is evidence and truth and state of mind.

He threw a curve at me when he went into a whole dissertation: The fact that MACV had not included SD and SSD in their Order of Battle was not at issue here. Nor was the fact that they did not count the infiltration numbers, etc., the same way the CIA did.

What was at issue was whether they were dishonest. That really narrows the spectrum.

In fact, I feel we are sitting on the verge of an impossible decision.

When we had a break, I sorted through all the folders of notes I've taken in court. The notes fill three folders so far, and it took me almost an hour just to put them in proper sequence. A couple of other jurors had the same problem, but most didn't seem to.

I keep my notes by the day, arranging about ten pages a day one side—double-spaced—with my personal thoughts scribbled in between lines.

I noticed that a couple of other jurors kept all their notes in the same pad and numbered the pages. Richard is up to page 264, and every line is neatly written—like a long novel. Some of the jurors hardly wrote anything.

I found three pages of notes under the table, and when I looked at them, I froze.

The formations on the page looked like they came from outer space. I was unable to decipher one single word. The writing looked backhand and mirror image. The juror they belong to is kind of strange. He can't remember what he had for breakfast this morning. He can't decide what door he is going to leave the room by—in spite of the fact there is only one.

Both Myron and I brought our cameras today to take pictures of the jury—our job away from home must have a record of some sort.

I finished off a roll of film and took it to the Fotomat place around the corner at lunchtime. I had it back when we left court tonight. The pictures came out all right. So much so that I bought another role of film to capture the head shots that I missed today. If I can't have fun in the courtroom, I can at least try behind the scenes.

The defense introduced James P. Johnson of Colorado by deposition.

He was on the Pike committee. He had nothing but praise for the committee—Greg Rushford, the main researcher in the Tet investigation, was tenacious and thorough.

Sam Adams as a witness—they agreed with his findings.

MACV deliberately manipulated the figures of enemy strength to misguide the public, the press, and the Congress.

The documents they were supplied were irrefutable proof that there was a conspiracy—Westmoreland and General Wheeler were involved. He reiterated this fact several times. He even implicated Bunker, adding that no one knew how high the conspiracy went. He also mentioned General Abrams's name in this.

Then we had David C. Morgan's deposition. He had worked in the intelligence field—Order of Battle estimates, deputy chief.

He said there was a low morale in that department, a factor for him leaving the army early.

He said he smiles when he thinks about Colonel Hawkins. Morgan respected him—he was a workaholic.

He talked about the changing of numbers of enemy strength. He felt uncomfortable about that. He also had to tell men underneath him to discount accurate figures, and he hated that job. He talked about paper a lot—a lot of paper—how much?—a lot.

Morgan was asked to appear on camera, but said he waffled in the decision, ending it with a bargain: You really don't need me—you need Hawkins. I'll get in touch with him and Parkins. They will be much more valuable to you. If they won't speak, then I will.

Apparently, Hawkins will come in the flesh. I'm looking forward to hearing him.

According to Morgan, the numbers of enemy came from higher up—not the analysts in the field, the way they should have. He was disturbed by this. It was improper.

We saw a tape of Marshall Lynn, Order of Battle analyst—a MACV intelligence officer. This was an interview by CBS. We could only evaluate it on the state of mind issue.

The guy looked all right—clean-cut, glasses, in his early forties, and sincere. He seemed to have a sense of humor about him, and a resolved nature. He said it was his first big job.

He said that these things troubled him, but he was scheduled to leave South Vietnam within a month's time—he was not about to make waves or get involved, but they shook him up.

Cook the figures, he was told. He was young and enthusiastic, but it disturbed him. He said: "I scratched my head and asked, 'What's going on here?'"

For the most part, things were on the up and up, but one or two incidents disturbed him. For no reason at all, he was told to lower his figures by twenty-five percent.

He talked about the infiltration analysts becoming cynical, making statements such as: "When Westy needs more troops, we say there are twenty thousand infiltrators coming down the trails.

"When Westy wants to prove we are winning the war, we have five thousand infiltrators a month."

The battalions of enemy are marked on the map, but we can't recognize them.

"Why not?" asked Mike Wallace.

"Catch-22," was Lynn's curt answer. Lynn said he really didn't know what was happening when he was there. But when he got back to the States and heard smatterings of the news—he put two and two together. He knew they were making a mistake when he was over there, but didn't do anything about it.

When the video machine went off, Mr. Dorsen got up to explain to us that the battalions on the map were not official because there was no corroborated evidence. It was only a NSA indication.

As we recall, MACV, who followed the traditional methods of analysis, only counted enemies that they could prove with two documents. NSA, being with the CIA, would count anyone they had an inkling of.

Personally, I would have. (That's irrelevant—don't even think it, that's not at issue.)

Mr. Burt wasn't here all day today—he disappeared yesterday.

Adams hasn't been around, either—first time ever.

Boies said something about the maps showing the official Order of Battle.

Judge Leval warned us not to listen to anybody. He even said, "You are asked to partake in an impossible mental exercise." Lynn's interview was to be taken on solely as the state of mind issue.

Judge Leval went into a lengthy discussion on the hearsay issue, stating that even lawyers have difficulty with this court ruling.

Hearsay is any evidence we hear from anyone who was not present at the act in question. We then saw Colonel George Hamscher on video. We are to view him only on the state of mind issue. The words that stand out in my mind when I think back on Hamscher are "a group grope to fake."

Hamscher said that his carefully developed product—the enemy infiltration analysis, which he carefully developed—was used, abused, and misused.

He said that there was a ceiling on enemy-strength figures. The idea struck him as very, very bad.

Dishonest? Yes!

Hawkins was tortured because he saw his carefully developed product discredited, Hamscher said. MACV started with a total and worked backward. Godding, he said, had bad feelings about the numbers.

Hamscher said that Graham was the developer of the figures. He was the professional. He worked up his own formulas.

He was the specialist—there were no experts.

They met in a small room in the Pentagon. I'm not proud of what happened, he added. We went over Order of Battle strengths. We tried to reconstruct them so that they wouldn't go over a certain ceiling— though *ceiling* is not the proper term.

He likened the process to bargaining for a used car.

Then the television interview of Hamscher ended. His deposition was read. The deposition was taken under oath. I wondered to myself how differently I would talk on camera or under oath without a camera.

He said much of the same thing. He lost points with some of the women on the jury when he used the analogy of a fur coat or a fake fur coat—he said they both keep you warm.

So, what's the difference?

We gave the real figures, and we gave the fake figures. There was no real difference in the outcome.

Kate, Norma, and Loretta didn't think so.

He likened the disagreement between MACV and the CIA to a catfight.

I could see the importance of analogies when I heard the views of the other jurors—some identified with one thing, others with another.

This guy talked in terms identifiable to the average person. In spite of the fact that he was on camera and had his deposition read, he was reaching some people.

But it was still nothing like flesh and blood.

Hamscher's testimony was read for a long time after lunch.

In fact, there was so much material from Hamscher that the jurors were annoyed—to use an acceptable term—that he wasn't here in public.

He said things like: "There were truths, but half truths . . . I assumed a semipious pose . . . Godding made several phone calls to Davidson while we were at the SNIE conference—to get us a little more (he called it) negotiating room. Yes, the term *ceiling* was used."

Westmoreland couldn't live with a figure higher than 300,000.

We got to use 333,000, because equal numbers looked okay—they didn't have the same psychological barrier that 334,000 had. Yes, we discussed the numbers this way.

When they all had to go to the side bar during the afternoon, all the jurors started talking about the judge.

He had his hair cut at lunchtime. I said I thought he took a shower. When we had a break and the jurors quizzed the court clerk, it turned out I was right: shower, no hair cut.

I had to wonder how my students discuss my various hairstyles when I'm in school. I took a few moments to think about my real job. The judge told us we would not be in court on Friday. That means I teach.

It seems like an eternity ago that I was there.

It seemed like Hamscher was the witness forever. But he said a lot of things. For one, he talked about Peterson. He really respected the guy and very much wanted to work for him. We had seen Peterson a long time ago. He had appeared in the flesh as a witness for the plaintiff. I can remember liking him, also.

He seemed honest and straightforward. The fact that Hamscher mentioned Peterson above some of the others impressed me. I thought of Hamscher as having integrity and good judgment. (Like I do, of course.)

Hamscher said he felt like he became a whore—defining a whore as someone who will do just about anything just to please. In the process, he felt that he prostituted his own integrity.

We heard a lot of confessions along that line today—men sounding like they were in the confessional.

These things—lying about enemy strengths—have haunted them all these years, as they put it. Good men were killed because of it.

It was falsification of intelligence data. We saw a taped interview of Mr. Hovey, who was an intelligence analyst stationed in Saigon at the time in question.

His big claim to fame was that he had predicted Tet. No one seemed to listen. He said, "All hell is about to break loose in South Vietnam. They are going to hit the cities. The guerrillas are coming out of the jungles—we should prepare for it." Again, he warned them in late 1967.

"Be prepared—there's an impending large-scale enemy attack, the likes of which have not been seen in South Vietnam!"

"I remember on my ride back from MACV feeling, I did all I could—I told them, it's off my back.

"We had volumes of material—so overwhelming. I knew from my experience with the Vietnamese—if they say something, they'll do it.

"By God, they told us what they're going to do."

Next, Richard McArthur, a MACV guerrilla analyst, appeared on the video screen. He looked like he must have been ten years old when he was at MACV in 1967—he didn't look thirty. But as he spoke, a concerned, forceful, solid type person appeared.

He was not only concerned, but he was articulate—when he spoke and described things, they came to life.

He described helicopter rides in pea-soup fog and going as far as five miles down on enemy roads, not knowing if you'd be shot at.

He said this was his introduction to Vietnam. He had inherited the job of analyzing the guerrilla strength, and when he went into the jungles and the different corps areas, he was hearing from one captain after another that someone was changing the numbers on his intelligence reports.

One field advisor showed McArthur copies of his reports, then he showed him a copy of MACV's Order of Battle summary, and his numbers appeared there cut by half. He had reported 500—they listed 250! He was disturbed, to say the least.

He talked about his roommate, who was killed in the Tet offensive—trying to get to work. His figures were being tossed around and battered like a sack of potatoes. "I had a certain amount of sanctity for those figures, I worked hard on them—they were accurate. Instead they were being massacred, slaughtered, faked!"

He was advised to go on a vacation, a little R&R after his roommate was killed. So he went, and when he came back, he found his charts that he kept his guerrilla list on. Someone had changed all his figures to exactly half of what they were. "I had 70,000 to 90,000 guerrillas, and they had been reduced to exactly 40,000. I exploded!"

When he complained, a superior told him to "lie a little" and he said, "I won't."

"Shortly after, I was transferred out from the analyst section to Order of Battle, out in the field."

This testimony really got me feeling down. This guy sounded sincere. We could only evaluate it on the state of mind issue—but, God, if I were CBS, I would have every reason to believe this witness. I felt a lot like crying.

I had a date to meet my friends Jeanne and Tom Cassidy. Tom was sick and couldn't join us, so Jeanne and I went for drinks and a light snack. We had a good talk.

I left her at about eight-thirty and decided it was still early, so I walked the three blocks to Grand Central to take the subway.

There were about twenty-five or thirty people on the platform, a far cry from the rush hour crowd. But I felt no concern. It seemed like forever. No train in sight.

I looked up at the people around me. Other than two middle-aged black women waiting for the express, I realized I was the only other woman. As I looked around again, I realized that none of the other people looked like what you'd probably term desirable types—in fact, I froze as I realized the situation. There was a middle-aged, shabbily dressed black man in heavy conversation with himself. And a de-ranged-looking man wearing a skullcap and rags walked past me, carrying a large brown plastic garbage bag.

Suddenly, right behind me, he smashed the bag against the pole. Its contents scattered everywhere. I could have gotten an Academy Award for my performance.

I casually walked about fifteen feet away and slowly turned around as though I was preoccupied. When I turned around, I saw the man hopping around like a monkey playing with his garbage, and I was frightened when I saw the way he was watching me. My skin started to crawl, except that out of nowhere two Guardian Angels appeared. It was like a stage drama.

I'd seen them on TV and heard a lot about them but had never seen one in the flesh.

Quite frankly, if it weren't for the red berets with GUARDIAN ANGEL printed across them, with all those medals and badges, I'd probably have been afraid of them, too.

But I knew what they stood for, and I did feel comfortable knowing they were around.

The thought of writing a letter to their leader, Sliwa, crossed my mind.

A train pulled in and the rest of the trip home was uneventful. Thank God.

January 10, 1985

The day was starting off fantastically—no broken car windows, no stolen radio, and I even got into a parking lot today.

We saw the conclusion of the McArthur tapes. Bad records followed him because of his "I won't lie" episode. Finally, an understanding officer hand-carried good reports and placed them personally in his permanent files. There are a lot of good people in the military—that is the message I got—in spite of the unfortunate falsification of documents.

I like McArthur. I felt he was straightforward, right-on, a real sensitive person. In short, he appeared together.

Then we had a deposition read. Mr. C., from the defense, read, and Boies questioned. I was a little annoyed. I couldn't believe we were to experience another day like yesterday.

But it wasn't.

Thomas N. Becker, a former intelligence analyst, somehow got through to me. I could hear *him* speaking through this actor on the witness chair. Becker's testimony touched me a great deal.

"When I first got to Vietnam," Becker said, "I thought we had a good chance to win the war. But after a while, reading documents and such, I realized we had understated the enemy—in size, and scope and determination. We were fighting a military war—it was really a political war.

"Everything in Europe is very neat—so many tanks, etc.—the military likes neat units."

(This has been my suspicion.)

"But here in Vietnam, we had punji sticks—holes in the ground [booby traps, sharpened sticks at the bottom of large holes]. Things swinging out of trees."

The way he described these things—chills ran up my spine. We were talking about a real bad war. All we've talked about in court so far are numbers—SD, SSD, numbers. But this officer made it clear that the numbers represented people—enemy.

They were excellent organizers—that was one of their strengths. The SD and SSD were the ones that our men encountered most, not regular forces. These SD and SSD inflicted well over half the wounds to our forces.

I looked over at Westmoreland and froze in my seat. All I could think of was that rendition of "Silent Night" by Simon and Garfunkel: "Silent Night" plays clearly in the foreground while you hear a horrible news report behind.

I'm hearing words here, read by an actor: wounds, punji sticks, hand grenades, lies.

Westmoreland is sitting before me with a grin on his face. I try to interpret it.

Is it a nervous reaction? Is it disbelief? Is it real? Could this man hear?

I became upset. I had my eyes glued on the general while the deposition was read.

Becker sounded knowledgeable. He described the political situation, how radio stations were taken over, who ruled the towns. I learned for the first time that SD were the people (our enemies) in the unfriendly areas controlled by the Vietcong. The SSD were their counterparts in the friendly, or South Vietnamese, zones.

No study had ever been made of how many women comprised these groups, but people of all ages participated.

He had nothing but high praise for Sam Adams, calling him one of the best. He'd go one step beyond, he'd go to the source, he looked all over for infiltrators, he was a true researcher—is how Becker characterized him.

Next, we saw Sam Adams on the video screen, being interviewed by Mike Wallace (who, I hear, is being dismissed from the hospital this weekend). Sam Adams and me—we, the jury. We have been sitting opposite each other for three months now. I have watched his countenance—I've watched him look up at the jurors. The whites of his eyes become the most prominent feature. I've seen his handwriting, and I've looked at his clothes, watched his manners. He usually is buried in note-taking. He has a very serious presence.

This man on the video monitor was someone else. When he talked and moved and thought in front of you, he turned into another entity.

Then the tape went off, and he was called to the stand in the flesh.

As I've said, I've watched him for three months. For three months I've heard all kinds of characterizations—from a mental case to a genius. I've seen the serious frown daily, and the occasional smile break out. By far, of any of the people who have taken the stand thus far, Sam Adams is the most real.

As he approached the stand and took the oath, it was evident that he was nervous. Even in the opening statements it was evident. But it was real, and when he relaxed, he was real. It was hard to believe that this guy was capable of any kind of untruth—even trying to disguise his shyness at being a witness.

He was beguiling, to say the least. When he was asked a question, he took it so seriously—his face would contort into all kinds of positions. You could read his thought process. He sounded so different from George Crile that I momentarily questioned the partnership.

George Crile: I do believe him to be credible, but he's a controlled individual. Everything about him is neat and proper. He appears to me to weigh things and take pains to be proper.

Sam Adams is—he doesn't stop to think what's right and wrong, he just does it—like a little boy who was taught this is right and this is wrong. He seems like the type who doesn't look for the gray areas.

I'm sure Crile was attracted to the bare honesty and Sam Adams to the properness. Sam Adams just blurts it all out in plain English—just like Carver said. Sam tends to be impulsive, while George Crile has learned the use of euphemisms.

Sam Adams was born in the same town I was born in—Bridgeport, Connecticut. But his schooling was elsewhere, via Harvard Law School and ending in Washington, where he mentioned some CIA school. He said he learned how to trail people and do things that spies do.

The two guys from the CIA were there again. The other jurors told me during the break that they were rolling their eyes and covering their heads with their hands, seeming to be all embarrassed and upset at a lot of the things Sam said.

Adams told us things like how he identified Russian planes flying into the Congo, how he kept track of Che Guevara.

He said, "There were a group of bad guys in Angola, the country next door," (he was in the Congo) and he told us how he figured out how many of them there were, and he arrived at 3,000. "We knew when they were going to enter the country and we had a guy there counting them for the CIA. They counted 3,012." So, he said, he was close.

I guess so. The two CIA guys turned a deep shade of red.

When he got the job to analyze Vietcong morale, all he had to do was to walk around a partition to another desk.

When Boies said, "It sounds like you liked your job," Sam said, "Yeah, I did. The CIA is a good place to work."

He gave his testimony like he was telling the story for the first time.

He looked at us—all of us in the jury—talking to each one of us like he was telling us the story when we bumped into him at the water fountain outside our office.

"You know, I got to Vietnam, so this guy, his name was Travis King—he was a big, long, tall Texan, and he was going to drive me out to the various provinces, and he took me to one of the hospitals. Ya know, so I said—'Hey, Travis, why are ya driving so fast?' He was doing like sixty miles per hour on these roads, you know. They weren't so great, and he said to me, 'I'm trying to get through before

the Vietcong can set up an ambush.' And then we got to this here
hospital and a Dr. Lowe—that's L-O-W-E—from Utah led me around
from bed to bed—all around the hospital, and you know, it was horrible—injuries. They were mostly to the legs—lost feet, lost legs—
most of the casualties were around the legs—other things, too, but I
asked, 'Hey, how come these guys are getting these injuries?' So they
told me there were the mines and booby traps. You know, these are
the things that the SD sets up. They take a hand grenade and they tie a
string around the pin, and then they take the string and lay it across a
trail and then maybe they pile some leaves around it, and then these
soldiers come marching down the trail—you know, the good guys, our
guys, and—"

And he continued with a description of some of these booby traps—
holes in the ground, stakes at the bottom.

He told us about an interpreter he had. He said: "She was really
good, but there was a slight problem—she didn't speak English."

Everyone laughed. But he added, "But she could speak French, and
I can write French, so we could at least communicate. You know, I'd
write things and this—oh, you know what I mean."

He told us about a Chieu-Hoi center—it was a defector center. He
said that there was a large file on each defector, and there had been
about a hundred over the last four months, so he said he looked over
these files. Then he went to the MACV Order of Battle listing, and
they only listed one 160 Vietcong in this area.

"So I said to myself—I scratched my head, and I said, 'How can
this be?' In the next three months, you know—it just couldn't be."

Bullets were still flying around.

He said he went into Binh Dinh. He found 50,000 SD and guerrillas—maybe, he said, some regulars too, but he didn't think so.
Anyhow, when he checked MACV's Order of Battle, he said they had
4,600 enemy listed.

When he was asked if this kind of discrepancy was nationwide,
Adams said no. He had gone into other provinces and the figures were
close to the true reality—but there were a few others like Binh Dinh.

I think he said the only categories that he worked on were the irregulars (guerrillas and SD).

He gave us a lesson. He said he used to teach this at that school in
Washington—before guys were coming out here to Vietnam, they'd
take these courses on the enemy in Vietnam.

There were the Vietcong regulars—they were the guys who wore
uniforms and carried rifles and could march in formation—if you
wanted, and they belonged to divisions or regiments.

Then there was the administrative services—they were MACV types, the intelligence and officers, and stuff like that. Then you had the guerrilla militia—the Vietcong guerrillas and the SD militia, and then the political cadre—or the infrastructure. Those were the Communist Party members, like the Vietcong police and the tax collectors and the postal services and things like that.

Adams said he figured there were probably around 300,000 irregulars.

He said he talked to a lot of other guys—John T. Moore, George Allen—a lot of guys were coming up with figures like these.

We again saw the charts that were taken to the Langley conference in August 1967, the view graphs—of the previous estimates and the revised estimates. Both came up with the same figures. The previous estimate chart listed a total of 297,800; the revised, a grand total of 298,000.

Sam Adams was at the Saigon conference. He said that one day when they went in, there were these papers in front of everyone's chair from the CIA, and they said—if you agree to drop the SD, MACV will let them have 15,000 more guerrillas.

Carver's response was, "I can't believe they put this in writing."

George Allen accused Sam of selling the CIA down the river. Sam said he had left the conference early, and this was all a shock to him.

Carver had caved in to MACV.

On the day after the Tet offensive, Adams sent a letter to Carver, his boss, saying the department is a monument of deceit, and he wanted no part of it. He went and worked for I'm not sure whom, but Ron Smith became his new boss.

We were dismissed until Monday at ten.

January 13, 1965

It was a good weekend. I got a lot done—went for a long ride on Saturday, previewed a house up in Beekman—a seven-bedroom historic house that was listed as a potential bed-and-breakfast inn.

I can't get the place out of my head. I even told Bob about it on the phone—asked him to give thought to us running a bed-and-breakfast inn.

He did think, and is a lot more cautious than I am. But when I showed him the photos I took, he was intrigued.

I know he'd love to play lord of the manor—as long as he wouldn't have to do any work. He made it clear it would be my baby.

I daydreamed about the place all weekend.

Court tomorrow.

January 14, 1985

Met Loretta outside the Greek restaurant. She joined me for breakfast. She's a nice girl—girl? She told me she's forty-six years old and has four children. I nearly dropped my teeth. She has a beautiful, young face, beautiful coloring, and she bleaches her hair blond. A blond afro on the high bronze complexion certainly is a striking contrast. She told me she has really enjoyed listening to Adams.

"I never expected him to sound like that," she said. "He's so lively when he talks and expressive, and you can really understand what he's telling you. I love it when he says the good guys and the bad guys. I know who he's talking about. And you can tell he's intelligent. Crile—he was intelligent, you could tell, but I didn't understand what the heck he was talking about."

When we got to the jury room, I handed out the photos, and we were called in shortly after. It was a heavy day—about twenty pages of notes. The most ever.

For one thing, I really wanted to get down everything Sam Adams said, and then when we saw the documentary in full—from the beginning to the end. I wanted to capture all I could, to really get the full import of the sequences.

I know that we'll be able to ask for the script in deliberation, but I wanted to have it in my notes, to be able to review it for myself.

We had never seen the broadcast run straight through, and I marvel at the work that went into the continuity.

After seeing all of the unedited interviews and pieces of historic film, I enjoyed watching the cuts and editing. Ira did a good job.

Cuts from super-closeups of helicopters to zooms out into the brush, hearing Wallace's voice over the sound, and then cut to him interviewing or talking. The whole broadcast was smooth, direct—the message came across quite clearly, especially after our three-and-a-half-month education.

I felt Crile did a damn good job. The documentary really could be award material.

I tried very hard to look at this thing with a completely open mind. In fact, I tried to tell myself to watch it as if I were General Westmoreland.

I guess I wasn't too successful at doing that. When it was all over, I felt that the film merely suggested the possibility of General Westmoreland being implicated in this coverup. But the evidence certainly led you to believe he could have been. Danny Graham was the one who many pointed their fingers at. But he, too, had a chance to deny the charges.

The problem was that Danny Graham wasn't convincing, and General Westmoreland hung himself. He said the same things on TV that he has in court. I think that watching himself on the TV monitor was a shock to him.

The bottom line was: He was concerned about the press. A lot of them were.

I also had to remember in what sequence I was seeing the film.

Sam Adams gave testimony for at least an hour this morning.

He told us where he was when Tet broke out. He was safe in Washington, on the seventh floor of CIA headquarters. All hell was breaking loose. He started a cable, something about counting who the enemy was.

One officer finally told him: "Forget about sending the cable to Saigon. Let them fight off the Indians first, then worry about counting them."

He told horror stories about how commando units led the attacks and how the political cadre and secret self-defense executed 3,000 South Vietnamese officials. The Vietcong secret police were the real bad guys.

After it was all over, Sam's figures of enemy strength were pretty much confirmed through captured enemy documents and interrogation of prisoners.

We heard about safe houses, where enemy ammo was stored, about the assault youth, who, Sam said, were not boy scouts.

The day after Tet, he left SAVA (Special Assistance for Vietnam Affairs) and went to the South Vietnam branch and worked for Ron Smith, who told Sam, no way could the enemy have carried out that offensive with the few numbers MACV carried on their Order of Battle.

Sam explained how the Tet offensive worked and how long it lasted.

The first big wave lasted two weeks. But the total Tet offensive went on for four months.

Prior to Tet, we were reporting 200 American soldiers killed in action a week. At the beginning of Tet, we had 400 of our soldiers killed each week. It stayed at about 400 in March, peaking at about 600 in the first week of May, even though it had gone down to 350 in April. By August, it had leveled off at 200 again.

Sam said that he concluded in March 1968 that the enemy Order of

Battle should have read 500,000–600,000—that number having been reconfirmed over and over again. Adams named almost a dozen other people who shared his views.

Sam said that the same intelligence data were available to MACV as to the CIA.

He talked about Colonel Hawkins again. Apparently, they have become good friends. Sam had had Thanksgiving dinner at Hawkins's home in West Point, Mississippi, where he now owns a home for the aged.

Hawkins really unbared his soul to Sam and confided in him that he was indeed under a ceiling with his MACV Order of Battle numbers.

Hawkins told Adams that Westmoreland had said several times to him, "What will I tell the press? What will I tell Congress? What will I tell the President?"

Adams said that he had written to the CIA inspector general asking if these statements are true—is there a violation of the military code of justice?

Adams felt he was witnessing one of the biggest scandals in military history. He made three copies of the documents on a Xerox machine. He buried one set in a plastic bag and wooden box on his farm. He hid another set in his attic. He took a third set to, I believe, Paul McCloskey.

Anyhow, he truly believed that these documents would be destroyed by MACV, and no concrete evidence of any of this taking place would be documented.

I can see how the plaintiff has been accusing Sam of being paranoid. On the other hand, maybe he did have just cause! After he wrote his article for *Harper's* and the Pike committee did its investigations, Sam began seriously writing a book, for which he has a contract with Norton.

Sam Adams claimed he had interviewed almost three hundred people. He told many stories of how one person confirmed another's story—and it went on and on. He told about the reading he did—investigative reading reports from *The New York Times* and *The Washington Post,* anything he could get his hands on from that period.

He talked about how Johnson, on March 30, 1968, made a speech deciding to change his policy on Vietnam and not to run for President that November.

Adams began working on the documentary in late 1980, but full-time from January 7, 1981, to July 1981, then late August to the date of the airing, January 23, 1982. But he said the documentary was not the end of the story.

We had a break.

When we returned at noon, we saw the broadcast from beginning to end. We had a luncheon break and saw the completion of the broadcast. Then Sam gave some closing words. It was interesting to see the broadcast from beginning to end. The continuity of all the garble we've seen was refreshing.

In the beginning we saw the historic cuts with Mike Wallace's voice on an overcut. He laid the premise, the foundations, of the broadcast.

General Westmoreland "may well have been" involved in a conscious deception. Those words rang in my ears.

Something about a conspiracy to alter documents: Well, we've heard those allegations. I guess we have to go over the evidence. Those words were strange!

The Pike committee believed there was alteration of documents, a ceiling. *They believed!* That's fair—no cause for a libel suit! Besides, the Pike committee was engaged in a pretty heavy investigation.

We saw cuts of Johnson announcing to an audience, "We are strong! We are winning the war," and we heard applause. Then a voice saying, "We spent 150 billion dollars and 12 years—and 50,000 dead."

How could we have lost the war?

Johnson placed his confidence in one man: General Westmoreland. He was the first real hero since Eisenhower.

Then there were more pictures of Westy and LBJ over the body counts.

Then we went to Sam Adams, who was saying, "So I asked who are we fighting?" Boies stopped the tape and started quizzing Adams. "Where did you get who we were fighting?"

Sam mentioned a whole lot of people: Goldberg, who was one of the wise men Johnson relied on; Chandler, some guy who wrote a book; several of the other analysts; and even Bobby Kennedy asked that the night after Tet.

The documentary continued on about the crossover point, when the enemy couldn't replace its casualties.

We saw Westmoreland addressing Congress in April 1967. He showed them figures indicating that we were winning the war.

The documentary goes on to say that while he was addressing Congress, his men found evidence of more enemy—agreeing with the CIA figures.

GIs found underground tunnels with records and documents showing that there was a far larger enemy.

I marveled at how few words are actually stated in the documentary—with pictures verifying the words.

Also, I marveled at how many months it took them to tell us the same thing in court.

Had in fact the plaintiff proved to me otherwise yet?

Then we saw Westmoreland being interviewed by Mike Wallace. Saying: the information was unreliable. There was some man called Adams who claimed we were underestimating the enemy, but we were there on the ground.

We saw Adams, then McChristian, Westy's J2. We heard "political bombshell"! We heard other allegations.

Then the takes of Westmoreland listening to Mike Wallace's question, licking his lips—it did look bad, especially when Mr. Boies stopped the tape to question Sam Adams on a point.

There was General Westmoreland on the TV monitor—with his tongue sticking out! It looked like a cartoon.

Adams answering Boies's questions very seriously. Boies posing serious questions, and you'd look at the TV monitor, and there's Westy's tongue sticking out.

No one else appeared to see the humor, nor did any of the jurors comment afterward. I'm positive it was not intentional.

But if Boies—subconsciously—ever wanted to get a message across, he did it!

Boies finished questioning Adams and turned the tape back on.

Westmoreland was still talking. He was saying, "I was suspicious of these figures—these estimates. You get into these hamlets—you have young boys, old people, they didn't have any military capabilities of consequence."

The tape stopped and Boies asked Adams to comment.

There was nothing, I thought to myself, that was new here. Westmoreland and all his friends here in court told us the same thing over and over again—we heard the SD was not at issue, they have no capabilities, archaic weapons.

Then Sam Adams's words broke into my train of thought. He was telling us that in Europe during the Second World War, three percent of those wounded had injuries from mines and booby traps.

In Vietnam, thirty-three percent of the wounds were from these sources.

He went on to mention several other people we have heard from who believed that the SD belonged in the Order of Battle. Then we saw Hawkins and McChristian and comments from them and then heard Adams's opinion in person.

We heard more from McChristian. The war not only affects the people on the battlefield . . .

Then at one point, CBS answers that it believes it was at this point General Westmoreland started to suppress figures and alter reports.

Hmmm—*believe* is not the same thing as stating a fact.

We heard from George Allen—Hawkins again. We heard the old-figures-are-crap sequence.

When Adams was asked to address this, he answered: Hawkins told him that the old figures were crap—the new South Vietnamese figures are crap—the old MACV figures were crap—and the new MACV figures were crap.

The only figures that weren't crap were the figures that he couldn't report!

We continued watching the documentary and we heard all the same allegations capsulized.

Everything had been addressed in court already. We were finally let out for lunch at one-ten. Be back by two twenty-five, be prompt, please.

I hadn't had time to launder Bob's shirts—besides, they were becoming worn, so I ran down to one of the bargain places near here that he refuses to go to, and I bought a bunch of shirts.

This act alone saved me one week of guilt. No time—no laundry.

The war was continuing when we arrived back from our lunch break.

Same allegations: Remove the SD to enable lower enemy Order of Battle figures. Adams talked about that.

We heard Allen say they ambushed our troops.

Westy said they had no offensive capability.

Adams: You count them when they're dead—why not when they're alive?

Allen: It was a civil war.

Westy: Stop it, Mike. It's a nonissue. The facts prove I was right.

Then Hamscher—the group grope issue. Westy, when asked about cutting of figures: I didn't get involved in this personally! (That statement hit me.)

Adams was quizzed on something, and he talked about the Saigon conference.

We saw films of Saigon burning—McArthur accusing; we saw Meechem, Graham—

Graham is a _____ I'm trying to think of a good euphemism . . .

We saw more, but that's all I can remember. The day ended with Sam Adams giving his premise, telling us how great he thought George Crile was and leaving us with the thoughts Boies posed.

Why were you so obsessed with this?

I was there—I liked the CIA. He went on: We never lost a war before. Here we are, this big nation fighting the little one—how could we have lost it? There was never an adequate investigation.

But Adams went to visit the Vietnam Monument—58,022 names carved in granite. After suicides and accidents, 45,000 were killed in combat! As an analyst, he asked how many were killed by people not listed in the Order of Battle?

Return Wednesday at ten.

Tomorrow is a holiday—Martin Luther King's birthday. Adams's answer to Boies on what we could have done if we knew the real figures stayed in my mind. We could have withdrawn and saved a lot of lives. Or else we could have fought with a lot more troops, and probably—he didn't say so, but I assume—saved lives!

In all, it was a heavy day, even in the jury room. I locked the men's room door behind me. The women's john was occupied—no big deal, we use the men's room all the time. But when I went to leave, I couldn't open the door. The lock was jammed—I couldn't even turn it. Having a touch of claustrophobia didn't help—I almost panicked.

But all's well that ends well. I finally got out—to the cheers of the other jurors!

LET THE EVIDENCE SPEAK FOR ITSELF

January 15, 1985

It's cold. The wind-chill factor, according to my classes today, is five degrees Fahrenheit in the country at one forty-five in the afternoon. The day was difficult.

I taught—or tried to. Three out of my six classes were very undisciplined. The first grade was a horror. They didn't want to do anything. The two sixth-grade classes were so busy flirting and being eleven-year-olds going on sixteen that I thought I'd lose my mind.

I knew my job as an art teacher was demanding, but today reminded me just how demanding! Nothing like a sabbatical to make one focus on reality.

How many more years will I have the energy or the patience to do what I've been doing?

That country inn is looking better and better. I spent the last few days pushing a pencil around—how economically feasible is it? What do I want?

I drove into New York City, found a parking space, and met Bob coming into the building at exactly the same time.

We brought our bags upstairs and then went around the corner for a hamburger. We talked a lot. We discussed the logistics of my bed-and-breakfast idea.

If you want to do it, do it—but I want no part of it, was Bob's response. In the past I probably would have just dropped it—another pipedream. But it encompasses everything I like. I love to entertain, decorate, manage, plan. I love antiques and have toyed with opening up a shop.

I'm going to go for it. I could see Bob trying to suppress his smile when I said, "I know you're dying to play lord of the manor. I can see you coming up on weekends, playing host, as long as someone else does the work—me!"

He's right—his niche is his business. Fortunately, he can always stay with his father if he has to during the week. In fact, as I told him, the crazy hours he drives—6:00 A.M. to 10:00 P.M.—some nights I think I'd feel a lot better knowing he wasn't taking ten years off his life with the commute.

January 16, 1985

Court today may have taken the prize for being boring. Weren't you at the 1967 Honolulu conference? Mr. Dorsen started right in—no good mornings, no greeting the jury.

It went on and on—I tried to follow what was transpiring in the courtroom.

Cross-examination is tough: questions, answers, objections, side-bar trips.

There isn't the same continuity as straight testimony.

Dorsen was a lot calmer than I'd seen him lately. I was also delighted to see he allowed some time to answer. No accusing fingers pointing. But we still had a lot of the shuffling of papers for the correct document. And the wrong pages—and where are you reading from?

He gave Adams one document. Adams just said, "I can't read—it's all black," and held it up for us to see.

Then he got another document, later on in the day. Again, "I can't read this, it's all white," he held it up to show us and shrugged.

At another point he was asked to review a document from which half the words were missing.

The plaintiff asked him to read it aloud. When Mr. Boies held it up for us to see, it looked like one of those treasure maps you see that someone tried to piece together with gaping holes in the pages.

So the reading went something like: The MACV dele_____

some and _____ July—Order of _____ seems as though _____ etc., etc.

I thought to myself, This is typical of the plaintiff's counsel. When I got into the jury room for a break, I heard a few of the other jurors:

Adams is doing this on purpose—he could read that. Crile tried to pull the same thing. They're doing this just for effect—they're trying to make Dorsen look bad.

I couldn't believe what I was hearing, but I bit my tongue. I figured, Save the fight for deliberations. Let the evidence speak for itself.

One of the most difficult tasks I have in this trial is keeping my mouth shut. Keeping my opinions to myself is not my forte. (A lot of my friends will verify that.)

Dorsen touched on a few points today, but the main event that he spent most of the afternoon on was who was at the NIE conference at Langley in August 1967.

It was terribly difficult today to follow what transpired. There were three or four points that Mr. Dorsen cross-examined Sam Adams on. Mostly, Sam came right back with quite logical answers. He never once appeared to me to be flustered or trying to skirt an issue.

He seems like a basically straightforward, intelligent being. He has no airs about him.

He sits in the witness chair just like that—take me or leave me. Here are my answers.

His code of dress speaks the same way. His uniform seems to be a herringbone jacket—well worn—button-down shirt, low-key tie and khaki pants. I've never seen him in anything else—except for the time I bumped into him and George Crile coming to court. Sam wore a ski parka over his uniform. Even on the documentary he was wearing the same uniform. He's well built, a hair on the stocky side.

I kept watching his hands today. They're big—big, with knobby knuckles.

At one point today, Mr. Dorsen said in reference to some incident that Sam said he didn't recall, "Isn't it true, Mr. Adams, that all you've done for the past seven years is investigate this issue that the trial is about? Shouldn't you know that?"

Sam answered: "No, that's not true, sir. I have a 250-acre farm in Virginia."

Looking at his hands, I believe he works that farm personally.

From a distance, across the courtroom, I found it hard to believe Sam was anywhere near the fifty-one years old that he claimed.

He still appears younger than his years. A good deep voice that fluctuates in key, depending on the subject. When he's asked to talk about himself, it has a higher, shyer sound. When he speaks about army tactics—Order of Battle, etc.—it is quite deep and authoritative.

Apparently, there was some preliminary study on the size of the irregular forces. A document noted that the existence of the study surfaced in February 1967. This changed the tone of the Honolulu conference in February 1967 that we've heard so much about.

Sam's answer was, Yes, the existence of the study surfaced—we heard it was in the works. We didn't see it until sometime in March of '67 (I believe the size of the irregular forces had been changed to 198,000).

Apparently, Bobby Layton was the principal drafter of SNIE 14.3–67. "Didn't Mr. Layton take your views into account when he was drafting the Order of Battle?" Dorsen asked. Apparently, he did.

This got a lot of play, because Sam Adams has been testifying against the accuracy of that document.

There was a whole session in the courtroom on a few documents that our side had obtained. They were enemy documents that Dorsen found memos on from Sam to someone else, asking them to verify if they were falsifications.

Adams explained to us how he got documents. He said he never saw originals. POWs were captured and their documents were seized and given to a translator, who, in turn, would forward a translated copy to Adams in Washington.

He said two of these documents had similarly reported numbers, and he wanted them verified. Occasionally, the enemy would make up falsifications, making sure the documents were captured.

Things such as the enemy were going to strike at point A at 3:00 P.M. Sunday. But in reality they would be planning a strike at point B at 2:00 P.M. on a different day.

He said there was a Mr. Suc—he was a very bright Vietnamese at the Combined Documentary Exploitation Center. Sam would verify stuff with him to see if it was genuine. Adams kept trying to talk about a third confiscated document that he said was the best document we ever got. It broke down guerrillas into provinces and . . . He never got a chance to tell us any more. Dorsen didn't want him to. Even the judge stopped him.

I'm anxious to read his book when it finally gets published—and this is all over—to find out more.

Dorsen asked him to read paragraphs of the manuscript into the record. Dorsen, of course, picked sentences apart.

There had been a cable that George Allen sent to Carver at the Saigon conference. Sam has claimed he never knew about this cable and was shocked and upset when he returned to Washington and found out that the CIA had caved in to MACV.

According to his manuscript, it wasn't that cut-and-dried, and perhaps he did know what the outcome of the Saigon conference was before he ever got back to Washington.

I listened to these passages—as the artist I am, and as a writer: the poetic license that I myself have taken for the continuity of my work.

What I heard in these passages was a good story.

Now as I'm writing this, I looked back over my diary. My God, if I was ever called on the stand to verify every line—sequence and word—I'd probably be in a lot of trouble. However, the basics are here, seen through my eyes. Isn't that one of the issues in this trial? The defense's state of mind? It's seen through their eyes—in that context, a lot of what we've been hearing is quite acceptable.

Dorsen got back to the captured documents and asked, "Wouldn't the enemy inflate their numbers of soldiers to get more money?"

Sam looked at him, puzzled, and innocently asked, "For what?"

Dorsen said, "For more money—more soldiers—you get more money to pay them?"

Adams looked shocked. "The guerrillas don't get paid."

Dorsen said, "For more rice—more people to feed—more rice rations!"

Sam matter-of-factly blurted out, "They eat locally."

The courtroom fell into hysterics.

Dorsen brought up the *Meet the Press* interview segment when Westmoreland was asked about infiltration numbers that Crile allegedly cut.

Westmoreland's answer: five to six thousand a month—the part obliterated: "But they have the capability of increasing . . ."

Sam's simple answer was: "In retrospect, it made no difference in the context of the film. I thought it was excellent—the film was accurate."

When Dorsen tried to continue on this line, Sam said, "Hey, I wasn't the editor—I didn't make that film, but I did think it was accurate." A trace of unhappiness crossed Crile's face.

We had a sequence on the crossover point and what it meant. Adams explained that the crossover point was when the communist losses exceeded their input. But he explained that this never really happened, except momentarily. They always had more resources from North Vietnam.

When we broke for lunch, David couldn't stop talking about the crossover-point issue. It was like a light bulb went off in his head. He said: "There could never have been a crossover point in this war. They were always able to get guys from North Vietnam, Cambodia, all around. That whole premise was a lot of bullshit—Westy knew there wasn't a crossover point." David went on and on all during lunch. We got back from lunch and filed right back into the courtroom.

We heard about Hawkins some more. Was *he* at *that* Langley conference? Sam said there were several sessions. He was at all, or at least most.

We heard all about them. At one point Sam said he wasn't sure if Graham was there or not—he doesn't personally remember seeing him—but Colonel Barry Williams and Colonel Hamscher both told Sam that he was. Even though Graham said under oath that he was not there.

Adams even told of anecdotes others had told him. This was rather important because Graham has been accused of arbitrarily cutting enemy figures at this conference.

The documentary stated that five men met in a long narrow room in the Pentagon and placed Graham there, I believe.

Dorsen asked: "Is it not true, Mr. Adams, that Graham is a person you don't forget?" Everyone in court laughed.

We heard about the conference—who was there, who wasn't—we heard the same questions asked over and over again, and the same exact answers from Adams, without deviating one word.

"I knew Barry Williams was there, and I knew Hamscher was there, and both of them acknowledge that the other was there, and they both thought Danny Graham was there, and I verified it with Kelly Robinson, who said he drove around Washington with Graham and even told of a situation where Graham left his briefcase in the car. I know two other people were there, and I thought it was Godding and Hawkins, but I know now that Hawkins couldn't have been there because of documents that I now have and I'm still trying to figure out who those other two people were."

We heard this answer seven or eight times.

Then Dorsen read from Sam's deposition, taken some time ago. The same exact question and Sam's same exact answer—I mean word for word—that we have just heard eight times.

I was shaking my head to myself. I couldn't believe I was being subjected to this.

Anyhow, Sam confessed that he's given up trying to find the answer to that one—who the other guys were.

Dorsen brought up the blue sheet. Apparently, on the blue sheet

Crile had written that Godding, Hawkins, and Graham were at this meeting. The documentary never stated that.

Sam squelched him quickly with the fact that the documentary was at issue, not the blue sheet.

I couldn't believe I was hearing about the blue sheet again. I heard an echo of a growl that didn't escape this time.

We were back into the Langley conference. Sam ended a long session of questions and answers with a statement that someone at the clean-up session at the Pike committee meeting had made to him.

The clean-up session, he explained, was when a few people stayed behind to get the documents in order and the deletions in proper form and so forth. But this person had asked Sam: Have we gone beyond the bounds of responsible dishonesty?

The session ran beyond a reasonable length. We got out long after five. I had everyone sitting home waiting for me to arrive with dinner.

When I turned the doorknob at six forty-five to find no table set and everyone glued to the TV, I knew it was the first sign of a difficult evening. When everyone finally was seated and the very first words out of Tracy's mouth were, "Why did you make the fish this way? I don't like it that way," I may have overreacted a little. The fact was, it was the perfect ending to a difficult day.

January 17, 1985

It had snowed heavily when I looked out the windows at six forty-five in the morning. The cars were covered with about four or five inches of it—all you could hear were the sounds of shovels and spinning car tires.

I decided it wasn't worth the hassle of driving downtown, especially since alternate-side-of-the-street parking was being suspended.

The subway was a nightmare. One train pulled out of the station just as I moved through the turnstile. The next train came twenty minutes later. By then so many people were on the platform waiting that I was afraid to move, lest I fall onto the tracks.

The train that finally arrived was the sardine express, but having become wise to the ways of the city, I pushed on.

I arrived in the jury room with five minutes to spare. A couple of people were missing. Kate was one. She has to take the PATH train over from Rockland County. One time she said she missed a train because she couldn't reach the step. She was at the back end of the platform and there was no one around to boost her perky little frame onto the train. She's only five feet tall.

We joked about Kate being lost in the snow, unable to reach the step of the train. Everyone added tales of the morning's difficulties. By ten-fifteen we were all accounted for, and filed into the courtroom.

The judge informed us it was to be a short and unusual day. We would have a longer morning break than usual. We would get about a half hour and be allowed to use the cafeteria in the building to grab a bite to eat, and then we would be dismissed at two-thirty.

Dorsen started right in about the little room in the Pentagon meeting. We heard the exact same answer from Sam again—the one he repeated eight times yesterday and that Dorsen had read from Sam's deposition.

"Isn't it true," Mr. Dorsen asked, "that the meeting never took place and that CBS made up the whole sequence?

"Which of your superiors did you tell at CBS that Hawkins and Godding were not at this meeting?"

Sam Adams looked at him, puzzled. "Which of my superiors did I tell at CBS that Hawkins and Godding—what do you mean, sir?"

"Well, it says here in the blue sheet that Hawkins, Godding, and Graham were at the meeting in the little room in the Pentagon."

The judge interrupted the questioning and addressed the jury at length about the blue sheet, reminding us that the document was not evidence. We were not allowed to consider it as evidence—the broadcast is at issue; the only reason we are allowed to listen to anything about the blue sheet is to acknowledge its existence.

The broadcast stated that five of General Westmoreland's men met in a little room in the Pentagon and arbitrarily slashed enemy strength figures. Dorsen was trying to prove that none of the people in the room, if the meeting ever existed, were Westmoreland's men.

Danny Graham, under oath, swore he was not there, Hamscher was technically from CINCPAC not MACV, and Williams was from the DIA.

Adams went on about the fact that even though the two men were from different agencies, they were under orders to accept MACV's command position. There had been an agreement at, I believe, the Honolulu conference that MACV was responsible for counting Order of Battle.

Adams told us that he had read Admiral Sharp's book on the Vietnam War. (Sharp was CINCPAC at the time.) Sharp claimed that General Westmoreland and he had divided up the war in half and that Sharp would be in charge of air and navy attacking North Vietnam and

Westmoreland would control the war in the south. Sharp would defer to Westy on whatever he considered the enemy.

Dorsen brought out an exhibit from April 1981 that allegedly was a conversation that Crile had with Bernie Gattozzi. Dorsen was trying to say Gattozzi had a bad memory and didn't even remember what went on at that computer base incident.

Dorsen offered one paragraph of the conversation between Gattozzi and Crile into evidence. He had Sam read it out loud. Gattozzi said he had a blank on the computer data base issue.

Boies stood up and asked the judge if Adams could read the rest of the document to himself for content purposes.

The judge granted permission.

Adams is not a master of disguise. He obediently continued reading, expression intent. Frowns—you could see his head move along the lines he was reading. Suddenly he looked up, his mouth dropped open, and he blurted out, "But it says here that—"

"No! No! No! That's not in evidence." The judge had to speak quickly over Adams's voice.

This whole procedure is frustrating—it takes so long for the story to unravel. It must be frustrating as hell to be up on the stand, accused of certain things, and to see something right in your hand that proves your side and not be able to say it.

Dorsen hit on a few other things. A memo Sam wrote about questioning who exactly to count in the SD. Then we got back to the Colonel Hawkins statement—that General Westmoreland had said to Hawkins, "What am I going to tell the press? What am I going to tell the Congress? What am I going to tell the President?"

"Wasn't that an innocuous statement that General Westmoreland made?" Sam disagreed and said it was anything but. Dorsen accused Sam of not even putting it into his memo.

Sam talked at length about the fact the statement was so incriminating that he didn't want to jeopardize Colonel Hawkins. He said he ran around like Paul Revere telling everybody who would listen to him.

I could picture this. Military documents and memos speak in veiled tongues.

I recalled Carver and his reference to his own strong messages as being written in purple prose. The first thing Carver was alleged to say about MACV's notes left in front of everyone's chair at this Honolulu conference—if you drop the SD, we'll give you 15,000 more guerrillas—was: "I can't believe they put it in writing!"

No. I believed Sam Adams not placing a hearsay in a memo. I again reminded myself that the statement is hearsay—I don't believe it's in evidence.

Sam said he had been suspicious that MACV was cooking the books, and that statement convinced him it was true.

We got our half-hour break. The short lunch. We could use the cafeteria on the sixth floor. This was big doings—forbidden territory.

All the jurors acted like children let out for recess. We climbed the stairs and found our way.

A Garden of Eden it is not. The line was chaotic. All those genteel people I've been watching daily in the spectator's bench acted like hungry animals. There was one cashier and a line bulging with people waiting for hot lunches—or carrying a meager Dannon yogurt, as I was. It took twenty minutes to get out of line and another five minutes to get downstairs.

The guy behind me in line was one of the CIA men who sits in court when someone of very high clearance takes the stand.

He told me it's like this all the time, even in the morning.

When we got back into the courtroom, I wanted to slip a note to the judge thanking him for making the cafeteria off-limits to the jurors.

They talked more about infiltration.

Would 60,000 or 70,000 a month be out of the realm of possibility? Sam said 60,000 wouldn't be, but he doubted 70,000.

Sam talked about a phone conversation with a former analyst in which the analyst wouldn't talk but would say yes or no to questions. Sam said the analyst confirmed that there were 100,000 unreported infiltrators before Tet. Sam explained how these infiltrators were kept in reserve and would act as replacements.

We heard about some high-ranking officials touring around MACV headquarters, and they couldn't see anything wrong.

Sam told us they were taken around by Danny Graham, who never let them out of his sight.

There were snickers in the courtroom.

Dorsen offered a document, and almost as quickly Boies got up to say, "No objection!" It was obvious from the reaction of all the lawyers at the defendants' table they were delighted and shocked that the plaintiff was using it. I made a note of it—exhibit 713. We should ask to see it at deliberation.

I was surprised to hear all the mentions of the Ellsberg trial. Apparently, a lot of these papers and issues were tied up with the Ellsberg dealings or the Pentagon Papers issue.

This is blowing my mind. The Pike committee, now the Pentagon

Papers and Daniel Ellsberg—all this has been presented to us amidst a lot of side-bar trips.

I'm beginning to wonder how serious an allegation we are indeed dealing with at this trial.

When Dorsen posed the question to Sam Adams: "Did it ever occur to you that all these people were lying?" Sam said, of course—you always wonder.

The Uncounted Enemy was a valuable document—it told the story for the first time.

The problem with the Vietnam War was there was never an investigation. It was the first war this big country ever lost, and it was to this little bitsy country.

I tried not to think about the trial at all over the weekend.

But every time I woke up, I was dreaming of some strange land.

One time I was watching Westy riding in a jeep: He was waving to his men to spread out—they were under cross-fire. It was hot—damn hot—there were flies, and it was sweaty. The occasional wind only blew choking dust, then it got very humid.

I lay in bed that morning trying to imagine what it was like to be in Vietnam fighting that ugly war.

I read the first paragraph or two in *The New York Times* on the proceedings of Thursday's courtroom—CBS—Westmoreland. The writer said that Sam Adams was not nearly as composed as he was under straight examination.

I thought quite the contrary.

The same old story—the blind men describing the elephant. I didn't read any further.

It snowed on and off most of the weekend. The sun came out in short spells and made the countryside seem magical. Looking out our windows—we can't see the road—I felt snowbound. A lot was happening on TV.

The preliminary inaugural activities: I wondered what our troops were *really* doing down in Nicaragua. With all the reports in the papers, I can't help but read between the lines and wonder if fifteen years from now some of the activities taking place in Nicaragua now won't be brought up in some trial.

The famine in Africa, a few assorted plane crashes, Lebanon—the news filled the weekend in between watching movies on our new toy, the VCR.

Then, of course, the climax of all—Super Bowl Sunday.

We enjoyed a four-foot hero sandwich with some friends and returned to New York City.

It's bitter cold—about six degrees Fahrenheit. They say it will be like this all week. Before we went to sleep, I asked Bob to make out a list of the order of command and what responsibility each commander holds with his title.

So many titles are thrown out at us and I'm never sure who is higher, a colonel or a major.

He not only wrote out the list but gave me the emblems for each.

I looked up the division and company and the other breakdowns of an army in the dictionary. I have a lot of memorizing to do, but I think it helped to put all of these characters in order.

I had dragged my reluctant partner up to see the country inn on Saturday.

It is good to see things a second and a third time. I still believe that it has potential, though, in spite of the obvious work the place needs.

We talked ourselves to sleep about it.

January 21, 1985

In my sleep I was trying to wrap my feet under more blankets when the clock radio went off. The first words the radio announced was that the wind-chill factor is twenty-five below zero. It was something like two degrees Fahrenheit.

I had my doubts about the car starting, but it did. It took a long time for the temperature needle to even budge. Bob had to go up to White Plains, so he drove me to court. Thank God. When I passed my subway station, the throngs of people emerging from underground told the horror story I would have had to face if I hadn't had a ride. I wondered how the other jurors were doing.

One by one, everyone arrived but Kate. I had stopped for some terrible coffee from the machine in the canteen downstairs. As the wait extended, the coffee tasted better. Our jury room was almost as cold as outside—we all sat bundled up until Pat, the court clerk, gave us a portable heater.

David brought in another jigsaw puzzle last week—a painting by Monet. It was a tough one, and sat for days in the same unfinished condition. I decided to tackle it. The room was quiet—everyone into his own thing. The newspapers got well read today. So did assorted periodicals and paperbacks.

We heard various versions of Super Bowl Sunday and snowy weekend activities. Finally, at eleven forty-five Kate walked through the door to a hearty cheer. Five minutes later, we were in the courtroom.

I couldn't believe how many diehard reporters were there in spite of the cold. The courtroom had no heat. Some of the spectators were wrapped in shawls. Absolutely everyone had on a coat—except for the attorneys and the plaintiff and the defendants.

Somehow they all managed to appear above these basic human discomforts. I sat on my hands every chance I got.

The judge gave us our morning greeting and expressed elaborate appreciations for the commitment we, the jury, have displayed.

Mr. Dorsen started right in, as usual—no preliminaries.

"We were on the testimony that you gave at the Ellsberg trials, Mr. Adams, when we left off on Thursday. Could you please turn to page 14774 and read at . . ."

We were back in court. Back to Order of Battle—back to whom to count, who laid mines, who should be considered worthy of being listed in the Order of Battle.

When did you first hear of the study that the CIIED was doing?

We heard all about the post-Tet analysis of pre-Tet infiltration. The bottom line was that the infiltration *was* greater than previously believed. They—whoever did the study—went through raw data collected by MACV. In so doing they discovered that the reports MACV had given were way too low.

How much was way too low?

I started to daydream. I looked out at the spectators. Mrs. Westmoreland was there doing her needlework. Sitting next to her was Sam Adams's son, and I think his daughter was next to him.

That kind of blows my mind. It's like one big happy family in the courtroom—not that everyone looks particularly friendly with each other, but there seems to be a social civilness, which in itself is rather interesting. Sam Adams said today that he'd never met Westmoreland until this trial.

I wondered what these men in front of me felt. Is this how civil people carry on? If so, it made me feel good. Civilized people *can* carry on civilized disagreements. It's not the person but his action that is in question.

My thoughts were interrupted by Sam Adams saying: "CIA originally felt the poor reporting could have been an honest mistake, but after going over the raw data and the infiltration reports, they came to believe it was done on purpose." He went on to say that there had been many reports, which analysts had tried to get through, that were turned back.

He explained how the CIA was not equipped to do studies prior to Tet because there was no one appointed to work on them, but after Tet they had started their own intelligence investigation.

There was a session on the testimony Sam Adams gave at the Pike committee hearings again. Boies started to stand up, but changed his mind. There was a moment of silence, and Sam Adams said, "Could you rephrase that question?"

The judge said, "Sustained," and laughed. It took a moment, but then everyone laughed.

It's the usual place for the attorneys to ask that question. The question was reworded.

Sam was very serious today. It seems that his sense of humor was asleep—like most of us in the courtroom. *Preoccupied* is a better word.

The courtroom was so uncomfortable that no one seemed to care what was going on. How to stay warm was the main issue.

After several other lines of questioning, Mr. Dorsen turned to the judge and asked, "Is this a good time to break for lunch?"

"Very!" was Judge Leval's single-word answer. It seemed to be received with enthusiasm by everyone.

I had a sandwich left over from our Super Bowl hero. Most of us stayed in, but a couple of the jurors went out to fight the elements.

Those of us left behind decided to go down to the canteen to purchase assorted sodas and soups from the machines. What a fiasco! The change machine wasn't working—half the machines were swallowing money and not giving out their products. No attendant was around, and Carmen cut her finger on the coffee machine. Kate and Jean played nurse with napkins and we all walked back up three flights of stairs. Even the elevators weren't working.

When we were called back into the courtroom, Mr. Dorsen began with the statement: "Mr. Adams, it's true, is it not, that this whole trial issue has made a lot of money for you?" He continued with allegations that it was just more material for the book he's been writing.

He has been paid by CBS on a *per diem* basis since September 13, 1982. Sam claimed it's only amounted to about twelve thousand dollars, and he hasn't billed them for a lot of his expenses.

Dorsen pried further: What hotels have you stayed at? How much have you gotten for your book, and on and on.

When all was said and done, it didn't sound like Sam was living high on the hog from this money, except for occasionally staying at a couple of big hotels.

We heard about an hour of discussion on the killed-to-wounded ratio. It sounded as statistical as it did a few weeks ago.

So many formulas were used that it was difficult to follow who used what, when, and how accurate it was.

Dorsen brought up testimony from the Ellsberg trial again. All I could gather from the questioning was that some of the same issues we have been talking about for months here had also been issues in the Ellsberg trial.

In the jury room this morning, Eileen was reading a new book she had just picked up, *The Falcon and the Snowman*. In the middle of one page, she stopped and said, "Guys, you won't believe this," and she read aloud a paragraph that included the names of a couple of the very people we've seen in this courtroom. When she was finished, she and I just looked at each other with a glazed stare and shook our heads. Neither of us said a word, and went back to our respective things.

All the while I was doing the jigsaw puzzle, I couldn't get my mind off of it all. How big a thing are we involved in? My balloon of blissful ignorance was slowly deflating. I kept telling myself, The evidence—only the evidence that we've heard in this courtroom is at issue here. I realized what a perfect candidate I had been for this trial—absolutely no preconceived ideas about anything.

We heard about the dislike between McChristian and Davidson. "Isn't it true that McChristian loathed General Davidson?" asked Dorsen.

I watched the judge read the document with controlled amusement. I believe they were Sam Adams's notes. Through further questioning we learned that McChristian was contemptuous of Danny Graham as well.

It all gets down to the nitty-gritty—who likes whom, and who doesn't like what.

We heard more about the papers and documents that Sam Adams removed from the files.

He made copies of anything he believed incriminating and buried them in some plastic bags inside a wooden nailed box. He marked three trees with red thumbtacks so he could find them.

I looked over at his kids and they were smothering embarrassed laughs, trying hard not to look at their father.

We've heard from time to time accusations that Sam Adams was obsessed with this whole issue.

I could picture him with a lantern, waiting till dark, digging a hole in the woods.

He told us there was about two square feet of papers. He must have been busy.

He hid some in his house and gave a large pile to Congressman Paul McCloskey in 1973.

Dorsen said, "Why did you do this? Did you believe you would be executed?" "No," Sam said. "I never felt that. I wanted the documents preserved. I was afraid they'd be destroyed by the CIA."

Dorsen read a lot of the Pike committee testimony. He accused Sam of saying that there was a conspiracy—a bunch of villains sitting around a table conspiring with each other.

Sam said he didn't characterize it that way at all. He was more comfortable viewing it as a tragic event.

"I've been on this story for so long—I've begun to have a sympathy with the people involved in it."

I read him loud and clear on that statement. I think I feel the same way after three and a half months. Sam elaborated on the arbitrary cuts and the massive infiltration that the White House was totally unaware of.

The end result of the Pike committee findings was that they agreed that the intelligence reporting prior to the Tet offensive was not issued with logical intelligence data, but with political concerns.

Sam went on to say that he didn't believe that General Westmoreland fully communicated with his superiors. Adams said it's conceivable that the orders came from higher up to downplay the strength of the enemy for political purposes, but that it had to have been General Westmoreland's decision to keep the ceiling at 300,000, or, in Westmoreland's own words, within the parameters of the May 1967 Order of Battle numbers, which was really saying under 300,000.

Westy also characterized the SD as being a nonmilitary threat.

The very men who were gathering the infiltration data told of their reports being squelched—not accepted—arbitrarily cut. Their statistics were falsified.

Regardless of the fact that there may have been pressures on Westmoreland from high up (which would be a whole new story that needs investigation), Sam felt that Westmoreland was still responsible. If any of the men under him were the ones responsible for the cuts and blacking reports, then Westmoreland would still be responsible because of the idea that a man in his position should only appoint trustworthy people. By the same token, his superiors were also responsible for him, Westmoreland.

I could envision the bleak picture of deliberating this issue with the other jurors.

Dorsen completed his cross-examination.

Boies had Sam elaborate on a few of his answers and we were dismissed. Return tomorrow at ten.

Getting dressed to go out into this weather is a major production. Boots, gloves, scarf, hat—I was finally on the subway.

It's a pleasure to get on at this end, the first stop for the local. I took my usual seat—middle of the last car—and pulled out my book for the ride home.

I was so preoccupied with the courtroom today that I don't believe I read a word, and I even had to go back to retrieve my groceries when I got home. I had stopped to buy vegetables and coffee for dinner then paid for them and left the grocery store without them.

I even forgot tonight was our concert night. At seven forty-five, Bob and I were fighting the wind all the way to the Museum concert series.

I felt like I was back in the courtroom when I was seated. I found myself in the first row in the balcony, with a wooden partition in front. Unfortunately, the concert seats don't swivel.

Half the audience was absent and the maestro announced that there were several substitutes for the concert. Therefore, some of the pieces were changed. We would be hearing Haydn's "Farewell" Symphony and the conductor explained the story behind it.

In employment of Prince Austerum, Haydn was being overworked. His musicians were longing to be with their families, so Haydn's way of telling his good patron that a vacation was in order was to write the selection with musicians dropping out along the way and leaving the stage till only the conductor and one violinist were left—and then the lights go out.

It was delightful and humorous.

The conductor had mentioned Haydn's Surprise Symphony. All the while the Farewell Symphony played all I could think about was the "big surprise."

The Tet offensive.

Today in court, David Palma's book, *Readings in Current Military History,* was brought up again—the textbook we've heard so much about that was used to educate cadets at West Point.

Apparently, it was taken out of circulation at some point because the author had stated that the Tet offensive was the biggest surprise since Pearl Harbor.

January 22, 1985

We spent probably half the day in the jury room today. There were a lot of objections and trips to the side bar in between.

The objections today were different. I could tell that one lawyer didn't want the other lawyer to present certain documents, and vice versa. They would have lengthy jovial discussions at the side bar. It was more like a test of will—an exercise in debating. There was more to the documents than the usual.

I became curious.

The exhibits that seem to provoke so many questions are exhibits 311 and 1781, and 1782 also, I believe. I know those numbers by heart already. Three hundred eleven is the testimony from the House select subcommittee, better known as the Pike committee, and the 1781 series is testimony from the Ellsberg trial.

Perhaps I am overreacting. I am becoming quite sensitive about my apathetic attitude toward the doings of governments and men who didn't enter into my immediate daily doings in the past.

This trial has made me start thinking about a lot of things. The names and faces that were so far removed in the past—merely faces that passed across my TV set—were just that.

But now, having seen some of the highest military and government officials sit less than ten feet away from me, I have developed a strong interest in them.

I've seen them as real people—flesh and blood and idiosyncracies: their body language, their nervous movements.

Until the other night, when Bob gave me a lesson in chain of command, I had no idea what responsible positions these people held.

Sam Adams was being cross-examined most of the day. It was the same thing over and over. At times I think Dorsen hit on some points. I am still convinced Adams was for real and telling the truth, but I felt he was getting tired. He just wasn't as quick.

I met my friend Dorothy for lunch—after a session with the telephones.

The courthouse looks magnificent from the outside—stoic Grecian pillars, wide marble steps, gargoyles, revolving doors, polished stone floors.

But the elevators never work, the food is the worst—the canteen is a joke—and you can't use a telephone. If it's not some big-shot lawyer berating his secretary for fifteen minutes, it's a reporter calling in a story. I ended up going outside and down the street, standing in fifteen-mile-an-hour winds calling Dorothy to tell her I was free.

Though she teaches at Pace, a mere three blocks from the courthouse, we have only been able to coordinate a lunch once before in the last three and a half months. Her schedule is flexible, but my lunch break is erratic.

Anyhow, it was fun. We chatted and planned our next lunch. The rest of the afternoon was the same tedium. Suddenly, Sam Adams was excused. He stepped down from the witness stand to giggles and titters from everyone. Even the judge had said, "Okay, you're free now!"

George Allen took the stand.

George Allen had been Sam Adams's boss. We've been hearing about George Allen—the dean of Vietnam, the most well versed man in the world on Indochina, student of Vietnamese ways for over seventeen years.

As most of the witnesses who have preceded him, he is not at all what I expected.

He is short. He joined the navy on his seventeenth birthday and fought in the Second World War. He graduated from the University of Utah—a political science major, and studied international relations. He went to Washington, D.C., with the specific idea of working in intelligence—the rest is history. We know him as Carver's deputy. SAVA's dynasty—the man who was the maven on Vietnam. His voice had a hoarse grasping sound. But I learned how well he could sound effective.

When he raised his voice or became agitated, he never sounded out of control—he just let you know he meant business.

His suit is too dark for his complexion. It is a deep navy pinstripe; the darkness swallows him up. His face is long, with rectangular glasses that I think looked too pointed for his countenance. But he is answering the questions posed to him with authority and poise.

His credentials were impressive; he'd even been involved in arms negotiations with the Russians. In spite of all the credentials, he seemed approachable. I liked him.

We heard the same things from him that we've been hearing for the last fourteen weeks. But he added new insights. He spoke in more detail. One could tell from his testimony that for one, he knew the Vietnamese very well, and secondly, that he respected them. He spoke of an enemy, but he added qualities about these people that reminded you they, too, were humans.

He respected Sam Adams. He spoke of him in such glowing terms that it was touching. Allen said: "I wished I had the courage of my convictions the way that Sam has had for his."

He was called to the stand very late in the day. I was certain the attorney had him scheduled for right after lunch, but they were so busy examining Adams—and cross-examining and reexamining him—that Sam hadn't left the witness stand until after four.

We were finally dismissed at five-fifteen. Because the jury comes from such diverse areas, that extra fifteen minutes or half hour makes all the difference in the world. Even staying in the city, I didn't get home until six-fifteen. Kate told me she got home at eight-thirty. The other jurors had their stories too.

Cheryl had invited Bob and me to see *Brighton Beach Memoirs*. Her boyfriend is property manager for the theater. Tuesdays he could get us cast seats. When we arrived at the stage door entrance, he was waiting for us and we got the fifty-dollar backstage tour.

The play was delightful, and when it was over, Cheryl and Bill met us for dinner in a little out-of-the-way French restaurant, where they were welcomed like family. We closed up the restaurant with coffee and anisette and were home in bed by one-thirty. It was a perfect day—the dream of what life would be like in the city.

January 23, 1985

At first I thought it was my imagination, but when I turned around to see what was happening, I was looking into the eyes of a sexual pervert. The train was crowded, but not the usual sardine express. He was an average-looking businessman—well dressed, moustache, had on a hat and a tweed overcoat. But the frightened gaze that stared back at me told me it was no accident—he knew what he was doing. He had purposefully been pressing his genitals against my body.

I wasn't in the mood for this.

I gave him a "get the hell out of here" look, and he obediently turned around. I went back to my book.

George Allen was on the stand. Boies was doing the questioning. We had heard it all before, but this was from the horse's mouth.

Today Allen was wearing a gray suit, white shirt, brick-colored tie—small print. He looked good—his attire was much more flattering than what he wore yesterday. We heard more about the Vietnamese, what the leaders themselves had told Allen.

He explained things in straightforward terms. He brought it down to basics.

He told us that the Vietnamese military in this war were organized much like our Revolutionary army. Every community had its militia. All males from fifteen to forty-nine were required to be in the militia. They made it work. They recruited people. By and large, Allen claimed that he had seen reports that estimated the SD militia was responsible for forty percent of our soldiers' wounds.

We heard a lot about SNIE 14.3–67, the document of Order of Battle that supposedly had been worked on for a long time. The Order of Battle conference, where everyone was to sit down and put on paper what the official numbers were. In spite of all the hullabaloo, George Allen felt that SNIE 14.3–67 was a farce. MACV heavy-handed everyone to use their figures. We heard all the intimate details of how this came to be.

We were told this portion of testimony supports the truthfulness of the case for the defense. Then Boies proceeded along another line of questioning, to establish state of mind.

I tried to write all this down, but wondered how I'd get it all straight for deliberations.

Allen called the SNIE document the mistake of the century. It was totally misleading. They played games with semantics. I myself have noticed this game since the trial began.

Allen said: "My own professional integrity had been compromised on the altar of political expediency and for public relations."

We heard Allen's version of how he believed the SD should have been quantified—he thought more in terms of paramilitary than non-military. We saw more cables.

Mike Wallace has been here the last couple of days. He looks better—a lot better. More color, and he seems to be more social.

In fact, everyone seems to be more social lately. The jury has been punchy. The jury room has become rather raucous. The moment we're let out of the courtroom, the ribbing and joking starts. How are you sitting in your seat? I saw you falling asleep. And on and on. When the door shuts behind us on our break lately, everyone just lets down his hair. I mentioned this to David at lunch. He agreed, but with reservations. I'm beginning to realize that David is a very exacting person. I guess it goes along with his occupation—a genetic researcher would be exacting. "What do you mean? Everyone isn't acting that way." There is no such thing as a general statement with David.

If you ever thought that you were a well-balanced person, capable of making clear, logical assessments of what is transpiring around you, get on a jury.

I'm beginning to toy with the idea of analysis. I'm beginning to wonder if my judgment is sound. Something happens in front of me, and I truly believe I know what I heard, and understand what I heard, until I go into the jury room.

It's the blind men and the elephant story each time.

How can so few people assess one situation in so many different ways? But there are things that we have agreed on, and learning that we have noticed some of the same things about the people in the courtroom unifies us.

One of the lawyers for the defense picks his face. This has distracted me for a long time, but I never made mention of it. Come to find out the four card players in our group refer to him as Face Picker.

He gets into these contorted positions, his head perpendicular to his body, and frowns and picks at imaginary hairs. When I look at him, all I can think of is Chagall's painting "The Poet"—the man sitting with his legs crossed and his head on upside down.

"Colonel Hawkins told me during a break at the August NIE conference that he was told to stay with the figure 300,000," said George Allen. We were back in the courtroom.

"I told Adams," George Allen continued, "we compromised the integrity of the agency—those estimates were dishonest."

George Allen doesn't mince words.

"This prostitution of the intelligence process was intolerable. I found it totally unacceptable. I told Adams that I wondered how I could continue my career in intelligence if things like this could occur."

I couldn't look at him anymore—he was too filled with emotion.

When the Tet offensive hit, Allen said, he had just completed briefing two high officials on the positive aspects of what was transpiring in Vietnam. We heard about his anguish and his subsequent trip to Vietnam in the midst of all this fighting. He had planned to go alone, but by the time he left—two weeks into Tet—an interagency group had formed, of which he was a member.

Allen said that after viewing what had and was transpiring, he estimated the enemy strength to be 400,000, not the 240,000 being reported by MACV.

Were the SD involved? Yes!

We heard controlled but emotional accounts of what happened. I reminded myself again—the Vietnam War is not on trial here.

Did CBS make false statements against General Westmoreland? Did it knowingly make false statements? Was General Westmoreland libeled?

We heard things like: dishonest estimate, MACV stonewalled, President Johnson was given an inaccurate assessment of the enemy. MACV had imposed a ceiling on enemy strength figures. Komer played an important role in public relations concerns. MACV robbed

Peter to pay Paul, always taking from one category and placing them in another. In fact, Allen sounded more emphatic than Sam Adams.

Allen even said he had personally attended the April 8 conference and challenged Danny Graham on his figures with: "Danny, you don't really believe what you're telling me—the SD is only comprised of old men and women, and that they have no place in the Order of Battle?"

Danny, Allen said, answered him rather curtly: "Of course I don't, but it's the command position!"

Allen added that the episode was one of the low points in his career.

Allen talked about the Pike committee hearings. He said that Colby himself had taken him for a ride before he was to testify.

Allen was told to be a good soldier, toe the line, don't make it look like the agency (meaning the CIA) is trying to make the military (MACV) look bad. He was instructed to be careful, to not elaborate, to not say too much.

Allen said he spoke in guarded tones at the hearing, where he was interrogated for five to six hours. Dorsen naturally insisted on reading some of this testimony into the record when he cross-examined Allen.

I got annoyed at this. Perhaps unjustifiably, since Dorsen was just doing his job. But I felt, after hearing Allen unburden his soul to us and practically confess that he was close to perjury at the Pike committee hearings, it seemed like a moot point—why waste our time? Allen himself had just told us what he was doing.

On the other hand, it's interesting how Allen can make a statement sound innocuous. If Allen did what he said he did—played a good soldier, toed the line—he did a good job. He was masterful at veiling allegations without actually lying.

At times like this, I realize one has to go with her gut feelings. Is this man a credible witness?

I think he is.

LESS IS MORE

From the moment I got up in the morning, I prayed I could make it through the day. I wasn't really sick, but a flushed face, chills, and queasy stomach stayed with me till well after I arrived back home in the country at nine in the evening.

I tried hard to be attentive. Dorsen was doing a fair job of trying to discredit the witness. Allen had just about bared his soul. I felt like I was sitting inside a confessional with him.

We heard much of the same thing we heard yesterday. It was typical cross-examination. Nowhere near as fluid as straight examination. There was a point here and there that Dorsen scored on.

On a couple of Allen's lengthy answers, he did say a thing or two that could easily have led into flaws in his testimony. But Dorsen is so conscious of his allotted time that he races from one subject to another.

Even when he makes a point, he doesn't spend the extra minute to emphasize it to the jury. Allen, in his enthusiasm to tell the truth, made a statement to the effect that the Order of Battle was much too low even in 1962.

We, the jury, are only concerned with 1967 and 1968. The defense has spent four months trying to convince us that the low Order of Battle count was a pre-Tet problem after McChristian's dismissal from the J2 office.

Sitting on this jury has been a good lesson in less is more—the less you say, the more convincing you are. I myself must learn the art of consolidating my words. One does not have to fill the air with explanations.

Upon reflecting on Allen's statement, I remembered the main point that the defense has been trying to make. The debate *has* gone on for a long time over the Order of Battle and how to count these enemy. The basic difference between CIA's way and MACV's way is that MACV needs two verifiers and CIA needs but one. The point is, was the debate in good faith? When we got into the jury room on a break, Kate and Jean couldn't stop talking about the fact that in 1962 the Order of Battle was too low. I tried to nonchalantly explain my interpretation, but it fell on deaf ears.

All of us are tired.

I even caught Mike Wallace putting his head on the table today. God knows, I wanted to do the same thing, but I have no table on which to lean.

I don't know how the judge does it. He not only seems tolerant of everyone's shortcomings, he stays on top of everything. He yells out "sustained" often before one of the attorneys stands up to object. He's been caught off guard. After all, he's not God—but he's pretty damn good. How he manages—keeping notes, truth of evidence received. When the plaintiffs can't find a document, the judge hands it to the witness. Today he corrected Dorsen when the latter asked if the information in the document was true.

Leval said, "Is the substance of the paragraph accurate?" Dorsen thanked him.

Allen's testimony included exactly what we've been hearing. The Order of Battle—the guerrillas, SD, SNIE 14.3–67. The Saigon conference, the Honolulu conference, the memos, the cables—you would think these witnesses had been sitting in course 101 on Order of Battle pre-Tet South Vietnam along with us. They know about everything that it has taken us four months to learn.

I have almost stopped taking notes. But I can't help but write down some of the statements Allen makes. He has the ability to talk in very understandable terms. I know the other jurors feel he has clarified a lot. He talks their language. But he also has a good command of the king's English. He emphasizes simple statements in the phrases I wrote down—I didn't want to forget them:

- SNIE 14.3–67 was a suspicious misrepresentation of what was agreed to at the Saigon conference.
- The Tet offensive was a tactical military disaster for the enemy.
- I did not follow the vicissitudes of the CIA and Pike committee relationship.
- In reference to the Pike committee versus the CIA: There was initially a serious adversary relationship. The whole purpose of the investigations was to assess the performance of the CIA.
- The enemy achieved its principal objective—which was a political one and a psychological one.
- The integrity of intelligence analysis was seriously jeopardized.

Allen had to address all the issues we've been hearing about for the last three and a half months.

Allen was Sam Adams's immediate boss at SAVA. Allen was George Carver's deputy. George Carver was head of the CIA desk on North Vietnam.

George Allen confirmed all of the allegations Sam Adams has made about what transpired back in 1967 and 1968 in Vietnam.

Allen also testified that SNIE 14.3–67 was not a good-faith document but a peripheral misrepresentation of the enemy-strength numbers—prepared to mislead the policymakers.

When Allen testified at the Pike committee hearings, which were designed specifically to investigate all the allegations we've been hearing in this trial, Allen played the good soldier. He went along with what his superiors had told him to do: Do not appear to be attacking the military to make the CIA look good; make them dig for it. That was what he was told.

Allen agreed to talk with George Crile before the documentary was made, and he was quite candid with Mr. Crile. He told him everything, held back nothing—but Allen was reticent about doing this on camera.

"I wanted to be loyal to the agency. They'd been good to me. I didn't want to air their dirty laundry and mine in public. I did not want to be used as a vehicle to attack the CIA.

"Before I was interviewed on camera, I told George Crile that I had to adhere to my oath of secrecy regarding classified information with the agency. I hoped that he wouldn't press me on the role of the CIA and its culpability with that dishonest estimate—meaning SNIE 14.3–67. Crile told me he was a journalist and couldn't make any promises to me until he'd seen all of the evidence. I was testy and

uncomfortable with Crile on the camera interviews. I was not yet prepared to confront my own personal involvements.

"When this litigation was initiated and I was called for depositions,
I lay awake nights. Distressed at all that had transpired before, I realized the time had finally come to stop being evasive and face up to the
fact that I had to say the 'whole truth' in spite of personal stress and
strain."

When Mr. Dorsen had George Allen take the oath—"I shall tell the
truth, the whole truth, and nothing but the truth"—Allen said he had
asked to take the oath again. "It was a symbolic gesture to me," he
said, "to remind myself that I am telling the whole truth this time."

He did. He told all. He even told of a campaign headed by Rostow
to make the American people and the Congress believe that we were
winning the war.

"It was a distorted and exaggerated campaign to head off mounting
public opposition to the Vietnam War."

Though Allen is now retired, he is still maintained by the CIA on a
per diem basis. Allen also gives lectures (we were not allowed to find
out where) on subjects such as the integrity of intelligence analysis. He
often leads these lectures off by showing *The Uncounted Enemy*.

Allen was finally dismissed.

As the day continued, I felt worse and worse. I joined Cheryl and
David for lunch, but all I had was a bowl of soup. I left them early on
the guise of some errands—the truth was I just wanted to get out into
the fresh air.

The courtroom was warmer this afternoon—just what I didn't want.
I spent the afternoon trying to stay awake and not throw up. The afternoon was long.

Our new witness was young and handsome and wholesome-looking.
Douglas Parry is now a lawyer, but he had been recruited by the CIA
from the University of Utah back in 1966.

He was active in the Mormon Church, the Boy Scouts, and a few
other things such as that. His testimony was straightforward and matter-of-fact. His story agreed with what we've heard from Sam Adams
and George Allen.

The judge interrupted him and asked him to please speak slower.
The court reporter had already interrupted three or four times, asking
Parry to repeat himself.

Parry apologetically acknowledged the judge's request with a simple, "Yes!"

The judge answered him with, "That's fine!"

One can measure the boredom among the spectators by the response to any sign of levity in the proceedings.

That statement was responded to like a 7 on a laugh-monitor scale of 1 to 10.

We were dismissed for the day at four. Other counsel sitting among the spectators were biting at the bit to get their cases out of the way (cases that Judge Leval was assigned to).

We have Fridays off as a rule now because the judge told us that he has other matters and litigations he must attend to.

The same cautions were restated. Speak to no one. Do not be influenced by anything you read in the papers.

When I arrived home in the country, the neighbor with whom I have an arrangement to watch the house and feed the cat intercepted me.

I was warned that the front door had blown open, and by the time he discovered it on Monday night, the house was like an iceberg. I was thankful that no pipes had frozen and everything was intact.

But I became upset when I found all of my plants dead. They hung like wilted lettuce leaves all over the house.

Some of these plants I had had for fifteen years—three of them were trees.

They somehow appeared as symbols of the neglect my home has been subjected to for the last three and a half months.

In spite of it all, Bob and I managed to have a pleasant night.

January 26, 1985

Things have been working out well in school. My substitute is conscientious, impulsive, and thorough. The kids like her a lot—she's kind to them, and patient. She does some nice projects with them.

We were in together today. I was thankful that my boss had arranged it this way. There was so much paperwork to get caught up on. Though I completed the budget for next year last week, as I was cleaning the storage closets out for the impending fire inspection, I kept discovering more materials I needed for next year.

With two people working the art department, it's hard to keep track of supplies. Report cards were also due, so we split up the classes to give each other free time to get these things done.

I found out today that her husband has been out of work for the last six months. I guess this jury duty has helped a lot of us. My substitute needed the money and distraction; my father-in-law was enjoying our company, and I was having ample time to reflect on my life. How much longer could I juggle all the things I've been trying to do?

Though I've been toying with leaving real estate, out of the clear blue people have approached me for property or houses.

I spent the weekend making arrangements to show 107 acres to a group of investors. That would be a nice little commission if I could make it work. There's a lot of research I have to do. That's nearly impossible while on jury duty.

I also spent the weekend trying to get my mind off the trial. But certain statements, certain words, echo in my mind.

When General Wheeler went as a part of the interagency group to South Vietnam during Tet, Allen was there with him, saw his reactions. Wheeler had no idea of the magnitude of the enemy. He was stunned.

That kept racing through my mind. Wheeler was chairman of the Joint Chiefs.

Allen told Crile that he was almost certain the Joint Chiefs were not adequately informed. When Tet hit, they had to come to Langley to be briefed. It was obvious they had no idea of the magnitude of the enemy. They, too, were stunned.

Certain facts, certain statements, stunned me all weekend.

January 28, 1985

There was an article in *The New York Times* this morning titled "Reporter's Notebook: CBS Jury Cautioned in Sharon Parallels." I scanned the article and realized it said nothing about the trial, but gave background information on the lawyers, which I read with interest. Dorsen, when he's not playing lawyer, reviews restaurants in Washington.

Mention was also made of the jurors—even an episode when Carmen got sick in the courtroom a few weeks ago. The paper said it was attributed to the chicken soup she had had for lunch. I didn't know that. I guess if you want to find things out, you have to read the papers.

Back in court, Parry was still on the stand. He said much of the same thing that we've been hearing from the defense.

He went on a little spiel about how he had been an idealist. This, he felt, was almost a prerequisite to maintaining the integrity of the CIA, the country, etc.

After SNIE 14.3–67 and MACV's behavior at the April 1968 conference: "I lost enthusiasm for the agency," he said. "Truth became political! I didn't want to be a part of it anymore—I wanted to leave. The CIA had caved in."

Dorsen cross-examined, then we had the next witness: John Dickersen.

He was examined by Mr. Mastro, one of the defense attorneys we have seen in court daily but never have heard speak. He, like Duker, is young. I'd put them both in their late twenties or early thirties. Both have a quiet, low-key, but controlled manner.

Both of them, when they take the lectern, greet the jury, as does Boies—a small common courtesy.

Dickersen is from Denver. He gave us his credentials—college, career, present employment, which is some kind of advisory work for his own company. He was with another company for a while, but they wanted to transfer him to New York City, and "I just didn't want to do that," he said. A few snickers could be heard.

The part of his career that we were most concerned with was his work as an intelligence analyst in the coalition branch in the American Embassy in Saigon between '65 and '67.

His main job was studying enemy logistical structure—where they got their supplies, food, weapons. He had to know the size of the enemy in order to ascertain how they fed and clothed themselves.

He talked about the strategic materials that flowed through Cambodia and Laos. He talked about the jungle borders, which were not easily defined. In the jungles you really wouldn't know if you had crossed over into another country, but these were just side points. All anyone in the courtroom is interested in is if the Order of Battle numbers were correct.

Was MACV attempting to deceive everyone, or did they just not know how to add?

Most of what Dickersen said was the same as the other defense witnesses said, except Dickersen said that he was pretty sure there was a conspiracy to hide the numbers from the CIA because they used to go to all of MACV's meetings and briefings: We were supposed to be a team. Then MACV cut us off. We were no longer included in their briefings.

It was twelve twenty-five. The judge dismissed us for lunch: You are to return at twenty to two.

When I got into the jury room, Richard, our foreman, and Pat, the court clerk, were doing a jig, chanting, twenty to two, twenty to two!

We returned at twenty to two and Paul McCloskey was called to the stand. He was examined by yet another attorney that we've seen but not heard, Michael Doyen (we've been calling him Pinocchio). He sits with a smile day in and day out: young, tall, dark hair, pleasant face.

Congressman McCloskey was elected to Congress in 1967 and ran for three terms. He was a Republican from California. He had written books—a text on the U.S. Constitution that the New York public schools use. He taught at a few universities, he had been in the navy, the marines, he was awarded a Purple Heart, a Navy Cross, a Silver Star. He taught counterinsurgency warfare to soldiers before they left for Vietnam.

The guy had been busy. He'd even attempted to run for President. He is probably around sixty years old, with a full head of dark gray hair. His tanned complexion and his full mane are his outstanding characteristics. He is a good-looking man.

He talked in a very low voice. You had to strain to hear it. The judge asked him more than once to speak into the microphone. It was still a strain. You were afraid to breathe lest you miss his words.

Shortly after he was elected to Congress, he went on a fact-finding mission to Vietnam. He went with another congressman and someone who had been affiliated with the CIA. He was there for eleven days.

He had been heavily briefed by MACV. They were most accommodating—they showed him charts and statistics and even gave him a booklet, which he had with him to show us.

The booklet was filled with the same misleading charts that the plaintiff has been telling us were used to brief the President and Congress in the fall of 1967.

McCloskey said that according to the briefings, we were winning the war, the enemy was running out of men. There was a light at the end of the tunnel.

When McCloskey went out into the field and spoke to the field commanders, the story was different. They each had stories of how many enemy they were reporting, yet when the monthly Order of Battle was published, their numbers were cut.

Three weeks after Congressman McCloskey returned to the States, the Tet offensive took place.

He confirmed a lot of what we've heard, but his testimony was interrupted a great deal. It was the same old legal proceedings. Was he giving us firsthand information or was it hearsay? Was McCloskey in a position to know?

During the many lengthy trips to the side bar, we in the jury amused ourselves by making bets on when Kate's grandchild would be born.

Loretta said February 23, Richard, February 19, I said February 27 at 10:30 and that it would be a girl. I didn't want to commit myself to morning or evening. Kate wrote down all of our predictions in her jury notes.

One of the questions the plaintiff's counsel was most concerned about McCloskey answering was his opinion about the SD. Should they be included in the Order of Battle?

Even the judge did a lengthy questioning. Before the judge let him answer, he gave the jury his typical lecture on state of mind: this man's opinion—it doesn't mean that his answer is the truth; we must judge his credibility. It was the same lecture we heard with Parry and Dickersen today. Finally, McCloskey was allowed to answer. "They have to be included for it to be an accurate Order of Battle." They *were* included at the local level.

McCloskey met Sam Adams at the Ellsberg trial concerning the Pentagon Papers. They were both called to testify.

A couple of days later, Sam Adams went to McCloskey's office and asked him to keep some papers for him in his safe. He was afraid something might happen to him or the papers and no one would ever know about what we are hearing at this trial.

I guess I was wrong. Sam Adams's papers and documents we've heard so much about were *not* a part of the Pentagon Papers.

In April 1975, McCloskey read three documents into the congressional record. They were the cables we've seen involving Komer, Abrams, and Westmoreland.

McCloskey felt that the Abrams cable was the key cable, the most damaging. McCloskey told us he was overwhelmed by the documents Sam Adams had shown him.

McCloskey could understand how MACV would try to hide information from the press. But to explain how they could leave out the most pertinent information from the NIE, he could not understand. That was formed to hide the true facts from the President. That would only extend the war.

Westmoreland is a master of disguise. He sits there stoically day after day. I'm not sure if it is my imagination or not, but he appeared shaken by McCloskey's testimony. On a couple of occasions, especially when McCloskey explained about why the SD belonged in the Order of Battle, he shook his head from side to side ever so slightly.

I wasn't sure how to read that motion—it was so unconscious. Was he disagreeing with McCloskey's views? Or was he saying to himself, I can't believe what I'm hearing.

I'm not sure how the other jurors reacted to McCloskey. I, personally, believed his testimony to be quite damaging to the plaintiff. His being a member of Congress and receiving the charts that we've already seen were misleading, for one—three weeks before Tet! I can imagine the shock.

Fly halfway around the world to see a war firsthand. Come home: Don't worry, guys, we're winning the war—and three weeks later, the enemy attacks! I'd be a little annoyed if I were he.

David thought something he said about not hearing the term *SD* was going to damage him. A couple of jurors discussed the fact that he wasn't really there in Vietnam; he was only on a visit.

Kate didn't like him: He's hiding something—why can't he speak up? I don't believe he gives lectures—he couldn't if he talks like that. I think he's lying, she said.

Dorsen cross-examined.

"Weren't you a leading opponent to the Vietnam War?

"You believed anyone capable of inflicting a wound should be counted in the Order of Battle? Do you believe seven-year-olds and old men should be in the Order of Battle?

"Did you only read those three cables? What else of those documents?"—and on and on.

Dorsen pulled out McCloskey's testimony from the Ellsberg trial. It was never identified to us, but I recognized the exhibit numbers.

McCloskey had said Sam Adams was afraid of being executed. "Is that what Sam told you?"

"No," McCloskey said. "He never said that. He said, 'Keep those documents in your safe—I'm afraid something will happen to them or me.'

"That was an interpretation on my part."

The paper this morning said that two attorneys from the CIA were there in the courtroom daily—just in case any top-secret stuff should fall out of a witness's mouth. It also said two of the attorneys with the defense were attorneys from CBS's insurance company. They didn't do any examining, but occasionally advised on proceedings.

The paper also mentioned Baron, who has done a lot of legwork and behind-the-scenes work for the defense lawyers. It talked glowingly of his trips all over the place to take depositions and work with witnesses. I wondered which one he was.

I brought in a picture of Chagall's "The Poet" to show the other jurors. They laughed and recognized the character right away. It looked like Baron.

I think I have a couple of the faces figured out, but I'm not sure.

Bob and I had dinner with a couple we haven't seen in ages. It was fun to see them again. We had a good, inexpensive meal and finished the evening at their house over some port.

He is an artist. We looked at all his latest work. I was jealous. I miss my studio. Ideas are flowing through my head. I can't even think about painting until this trial is over.

I came home depressed.

I was in bed before the late news.

January 29, 1985

I had to get to the car before 8:00 A.M. I didn't want another ticket. I honked my way downtown. I was really in a good mood. The sky was blue. The weather, all thirty-two degrees of it, felt like a heat wave after the frigid winds we've been experiencing lately, but everyone behind the wheel of a car today was crazy. Traffic was heavy. People, especially taxi drivers, were playing kamikaze pilots. I and Mendelssohn's Italian Symphony barreled down to Foley Square, negotiating the crazies with the skill of Andretti and my trusty horn.

I kept reminding myself to leave my car keys. Thursday I left my car in the garage without them. The parking attendants were rather civil about it (a major shock to me in New York City)—they didn't charge me the thirty-five-dollar warning fee that is plastered all over their walls. I wanted to accentuate my apologies of Thursday with a thank you, so I found a bakery down on West Broadway, where I purchased coffee cakes for them and, while at it, for the other jurors.

The bakery looked like it belonged in Europe. Cakes were exhibited on one side of the store and small tables were set up on the other. One lone man nonchalantly sitting there completed the picture. He had a foreign air about him. Well-dressed—casual trench coat and a nonchalant tie over an open collar. A hint of Nordic features and a savoir faire way about his posture.

I wouldn't have taken much notice of him, except he reminded me of my Uncle George. The woman behind the counter told me I was making her nervous. I guess because I was asking the price of this and that and wasn't really seeing what I had in mind. I apologized, asked her forgiveness, bought what I needed, and ran out to my illegally parked car.

The parking attendants were delighted with their treat, and so were the jurors. We were called into the courtroom at ten-twenty.

When I looked up at the stand to see the new witness, I froze in my seat. There sat a man who looked like the man from the bakery this morning. All that ran through my mind was, You never know who you're rubbing elbows with.

Ron Smith, CIA, Sam Adams's former boss, was now to give his testimony. His name had been mentioned rather often in the preceding weeks. I had already formed a visual picture of what Ron Smith looked like. The man sitting on the stand was not it.

Though none of his background hinted at a foreign background, there was an air about him that was. He didn't have an accent, but his speech pattern, or something about his enunciation, made me think so. Perhaps it was his heavy Russian studies background that came through.

We've been seeing one CIA-affiliated personality after another. To date, I have not observed any trait that would distinguish them from ordinary mortals. They possess a diversity of appearance that would defy putting them in a group. Carver, Allen, Dickersen, Adams, and Smith could not look more dissimilar.

Ron Smith was doing us a favor. He appeared slightly testy, but this emotion came and went. I was later told that he was recuperating from a medical ailment. That explained his behavior. He seemed to be quite eager to give testimony—but would suddenly appear to be totally disinterested. He had a petulant lower lip. He would tuck his head into his loose shirt collar to think. He never raised his voice. He didn't have to. He knew these documents by heart and was quite able to defend what he said. Dorsen's cross-examination had no effect. The whole issue with MACV's portrayal of the Order of Battle was a travesty. No intelligence justified the removal of the SD from the Order of Battle. Smith had organized the Order of Battle April conference at Langley. He was quite familiar with the numbers that CIA intelligence had estimated and the numbers that MACV was pushing for. They were about three hundred thousand away from each other.

Accusations of why this never came forth in documents flared, but Smith answered these, undaunted. Verbally, he believed they had reached an agreement, but those numbers never appeared after the conference.

The SNIE was a serious document—it was designed to brief the policymakers, the President himself. Smith had no other answer for its final draft other than that it was intended to mislead.

When we came back from lunch, Smith was gone. We were told he would complete his testimony tomorrow. In place, we had depositions read. All the jurors groaned.

Though we've been told depositions are as important as if a witness himself were on the stand, they are not the same.

They're like having someone read you a boring bedtime story with no emotion. The end result is you fall asleep.

John Moore, who worked in central intelligence on South Vietnam and also had impressive credentials, said the same thing that Ron Smith, Dickersen, and Allen all said—the only variation was the statement: "The absence of SD in the reports coming out of MACV was what was striking."

Colonel Cover's was the next deposition. He worked with MACV's J2. He said the same things that all of those for the defense have been saying. He elaborated more on the political cadre, telling stories about their role in the war. They sounded like mean bastards.

He sang the praises of Hawkins and McChristian—even more glowingly than we've heard to date, if that's possible (I can't wait to see these two gentlemen. I understand they will be appearing in the flesh). It seems as though the consensus among the jurors is the same. I've overheard some in conversation say they are not forming any opinions till these two appear.

We were dismissed after the last deposition, at three forty-five.

My friends who refinish expensive antique furniture were in town. We got a surprise phone call from them. They've been helping set up the annual antique show at the Armory. They wanted to meet us for dinner. I love this couple—they're always upbeat and can entertain me for an entire evening with stories of their escapades. Though we've been friends for over twenty years, dating back to college, we've all been busy with our own lives. Since they live in Massachusetts, we don't see them as regularly as we once did. In fact, it's been over a year. We accepted the invitation in spite of the fact I just wanted to go to sleep early tonight.

The evening was just as I expected—one laugh after the other. The stories were wonderful. We parted at nine-thirty. I was in bed by ten.

January 30, 1985

The young virtuoso was back in the subway. His violin vibrating off the dreary walls of the tunnels until I got onto the fourth train and read another chapter in my book, which is about Von Bülow and his trial. It's interesting to me, because the author gives elaborate descriptions of the court proceedings—pretrial, the deliberation. The same tedious procedure that we've been subjected to.

I've enjoyed the interesting fact of humanism in the courtroom: the reporters, daily sitting vigil; the air of carnival that somehow escapes;

the laughs here and there that break into the somberness. At one of these descriptions in the book, I stopped—I had to read it over again.

"This brought a laugh from the courtroom and the first smile to Von Bülow's face. Up until then, he had sat impassively, occasionally making a ticklike grimace—a thrusting out of his jaw and lower lip, followed by a clenching . . ."

When I got into the jury room, I showed that passage to Cheryl and asked her whom it brought to mind. She read it and looked at me and without hesitation said General Westmoreland.

My thoughts were confirmed. The observations that William Wright made of his subject couldn't have described ours better.

Ronald Lee Smith was back on the stand. That name did not belong to him. It bothered me. I thought it should be Hans Anderson or something like that.

He was being cross-examined by Dorsen today. Someone told me there had been a rift between the plaintiff's counsel. I wish I didn't hear that, but it also explained an attitude I've been observing. Burt is usually rude—he prances around his team giving orders, ignoring notes, etc. For the past couple of days he has been sitting meekly in his big green chair, which appears to swallow him up. He has been giving nervous little smiles to Dorsen and leans over when Murry says something to him. It's been so out of character that I began believing that I had mischaracterized him from the beginning.

In turn, Dorsen has lost a lot of his nervous mannerisms. He still appears high-strung, but he doesn't fix his tie as much or smooth his balding head as much as he had in the past.

Dorsen was really giving an impressive argument. However, facts are facts. Testimony is testimony—witnesses are credible or incredible. Dorsen's arguments were beginning to fall on deaf ears: mine.

"You can fool some of the people some of the time . . ."

Too much water under the bridge—I could see the holes in each attempt. There is something about the truth that rings out, like a trumpet.

I'm sure someone said it somewhere—something to the effect that if you tell the truth, you don't have to remember what you said. . . . These people were telling the truth. They were unburdening their souls. One by one, they said it. We heard testimony after testimony stating something to the effect that—I've been plagued for over seventeen years about this. For seventeen years I've kept my mouth shut. My conscience no longer can bear the burden. They all have stated that Sam Adams has been the only one who had the guts, the power of his convictions.

246   THE JUROR AND THE GENERAL

Smith, Adams's immediate boss, had nothing but praise for Adams—as we have heard from others. He was the best analyst around. He was dogged, determined—he . . .

The more I listened to this testimony, the more I believed I was watching history in progress. Sam Adams was being talked about by men who knew him—colleagues, men who were in the position to know. Sam Adams was a rarity—he was what we've envisioned our forefathers to be.

My husband had told me that one of the newspaper articles said that John Adams was some distant relative of Sam's.

I am certain that Sam was brought up to maintain the Adams good name—truth was his God.

Smith read over documents, studied others, identified those needing identifying. Dorsen quickly put them into evidence—why? I don't know, because from what I could ascertain, they were of no help to the plaintiff. The words that rang out from Ron Smith were: "Rampantly dishonest"—all these documents.

Like a crumpled piece of paper, Smith was thrown off the stand.

We now call Richard Kovar.

Kovar walked up the aisle of the courtroom, stood in the witness box, and was sworn in. Kovar: Reston, Virginia, CIA for over thirty-one years, University of Pittsburgh (it was interesting—all of the MACV witnesses graduated from the same places—West Point, Harvard, etc.).

Most of the defense witnesses have been from more diverse backgrounds—University of Utah, Tufts, Princeton.

Kovar did Chinese studies. He spent time in the Far East and Africa, did radio work and translating. I think he was the deputy director of intelligence at CIA during the years we are concerned with—1967 and 1968.

By now the names are old friends. He'd refer to Allen and Carver and Adams, of course—and Hawkins and Gattozzi, and I now knew whom he was talking about.

When he said Allen was known as Mr. Vietnam—I'd heard it before—I knew whom he meant.

Kovar said Sam Adams had a reputation before he hit Vietnam, when he was working in the Congo. He was known as that brilliant analyst: unusual character, inspired, fantastic writer, good reputation.

Sam Adams was highly regarded.

Baron was questioning Kovar. This was a first. For four months, this attorney has been sitting on the sidelines, his head drooping over his chair, picking at imaginary hairs.

Baron was terrific! He had poise—he was quick—he had presence. I was shocked. I admonished myself for all the characterizations I'd made of him. When he got the floor, he was a capable, competent figure.

Kovar was a face you wouldn't pick out of a crowd. He had salt and pepper, curly hair, gold-rimmed glasses, and unusual chinlines. He had to be in his late fifties or early sixties. But those chinlines intrigued me. There was a chinline an inch or two below his lips, then a real chin, then a set of double chins under that. I looked at his chins while he spoke of the drafts of SNIE, told us all sorts of things we've heard before, dwelled on the various drafts of the document in question–SNIE 14.3–67, the document meant to inform the President.

According to Kovar, it did not fulfill its purpose. Whole categories of people were removed. It was a misstatement.

As Kovar spoke, the mild-mannered witness before us slowly became emotional. Never in harsh terms, but you could feel his very soul boil up with controlled confession—his own: "I didn't have the courage of my convictions."

"Was Sam Adams a mental case, as some have professed?" asked Mr. Baron.

There was a moment of silence. Kovar looked up and quickly said, "In answer to your question, *no!*" He searched for words, then blurted out, "The trouble with Sam was, he wouldn't salute and he wouldn't shut up. A subordinate is not supposed to do this. That made people mad. He went after the director of intelligence himself."

Kovar went on in this vein, and we were quickly excused for lunch.

No one wants to hear emotional testimony—testimony is supposed to be given in the air of analytical logic. Though his delivery was logical, his words had been heavy. I noticed Sam's face turn red during this episode. Randy said he saw tears in his eyes.

I was unequivocally moved. How much do we have to hear to convince one that truth is truth?

I've been hearing testimony for four months now. I have reacted with every conceivable human emotion. I've felt sorry for this one, believed that one, questioned this one, but at this point—goddamnit—there was a conspiracy! Evidence and letters and words and everything were tangled up in my head. If anyone asked me to give a logical summation of what has transpired to date, I could not—but blazing across my brain was an answer.

Sam Adams has been right.

As quickly as the revelation hit me, just as quickly did my logical self protest. Evidence—look at all the evidence. The trial is not over.

You cannot form an opinion until after deliberation. But we are now hearing the defense—they've only had six witnesses to date. The other witnesses are on their side. We're in the bottom of the ninth inning. The judge has reminded us over and over again: The MACV figures are not the issue. The issue is—were they arrived at honestly?

Honesty is on trial here, not arithmetic—a war began going on in my head.

After lunch, Dorsen cross-examined Kovar. He wanted to discuss the drafts of SNIE. "Did you read the first draft? Did you read the final copy?" Kovar had said that the SD didn't appear in the final copy, and Dorsen was trying to prove that it did.

In actuality, SD did appear in the final copy. In paragraphs 35 and 36. In small print. The paragraph began with a sentence to the effect that the SD was difficult to count accurately and that it was insignificant.

Kovar was arguing that that was an absolute misstatement because they had incredible documentation of the SD and indeed had an impressive figure that could be verified.

Dorsen wasn't interested—all he was trying to do was to discredit Kovar by stating that the SD was indeed mentioned in the document. As could well be expected, his cross-examination was interspersed with several objections by the defendant's attorneys. Baron was the lawyer to state these objections.

If only he could see himself on camera. He has the most incredible facial expressions.

Dorsen would pose a question, its intent obvious and misleading. Before Baron got up to object, you could see the thought process on his face. Whaaatt?? His eyes would close in disbelief, his mouth would drop open. He'd blink a few times as if he were thinking, "Did I hear correctly?" Then he'd shake his head as the light bulbs flashed ON and would jump to his feet and yell, "Objection, Your Honor!"

Once on his feet, he was poised in front of a court of law. I got enormous pleasure out of watching Baron's countenance. It's so refreshing to see real people.

This scenario lasted another hour or so, and then Mr. Kovar was dismissed. The judge said thank you to the witness. I believe this is only the second or third time since the trial began that the judge has thanked a witness.

He did it with Leverone, who was a witness for the plaintiff. I had liked Leverone. I felt he was extremely straightforward. I was glad the judge had thanked him. I was glad he had thanked Kovar. He definitely deserved that courtesy.

Bernard Arthur Gattozzi was our next witness. The trouble was, he wasn't in the flesh—we heard another deposition. I had been anxious to see Gattozzi. He was the one who allegedly changed the data base on the computers under Graham's direct orders.

I had not formed any mental picture of Gattozzi, and I was unable to from his testimony. Half of the trouble with depositions are they are read from between blacked-out lines, sometimes pages.

In the courtroom you are able to hear a witness make a slip—go beyond the scope of the question. You hear the objections and see the side-bar conferences, and then you hear orders from the judge to disregard that statement.

Though the statement must be disregarded for hard evidence, it may often stay implanted in your brain, giving you the foundation of forming an opinion about a subject.

Gattozzi shed more light on the Parkins-being-fired-by-Morris incident. According to Gattozzi, it was definitely because of wanting to count actual enemy. More than MACV wanted to admit.

Gattozzi shed more light on the McArthur incident. When the young anaylst came back from R&R after his roommate was killed and returned to find out that someone had arbitrarily slashed all of his hard-worked-on numbers in half, Gattozzi said McArthur went off like a roman candle—subsequently being fired or removed with bad records to follow him.

In spite of the fact that Gattozzi wasn't here in the flesh, and in spite of the fact that we couldn't hear all of those intimate little slips of the tongue, Gattozzi was definitely more ammunition for the defense.

We were dismissed for the day. I got home as fast as I could and covered myself with an afghan and was dead to the world.

The ringing of the telephone jolted me awake—it was Bob. I was to meet him and his partner and his partner's wife, who was in town for the day, for dinner on Second Avenue. "Meet us there in twenty-five minutes."

With more reluctance than I can remember in years, I joined the party for a light dinner.

One of my favorite outings is dining out. But three days in a row kind of kills the glamour. I was really tired and am sure I was dull company. But the evening was pleasant. We lingered over our coffee and dessert, but we were still home before ten. I was in bed ten minutes later.

ARTFUL FILLIBUSTER

January 31, 1985

I awoke at three in the morning, feeling that if I didn't get to a toilet quickly, I would die. I got to the bathroom just in time. This scene was repeated again and again. I couldn't get back to sleep. Bob was snoring like a baby. The antique clock on the mantel was keeping time. Its beautiful clear chimes of the day sounded like Chinese torture at four.

I started thinking—about Sam Adams. I started to think about what I hadn't allowed myself to think about before. It's hard to put into words. But I suddenly felt like I had lead weights draped around me— I could not escape.

I was engaged in one of the most overwhelming experiences that an ordinary citizen could fall into. I sobbed myself to sleep.

Bob was showered, shaved, and dressed when he finally awakened me to get my stuff packed for him to take home for the weekend. He had a meeting at eight in White Plains; I was to meet him there after court today.

In my stupor, I tried to get it all straight—what train I should take, what number to call, what time.

I went back to sleep. The mantel clock rescued me at nine. Frantically, I got ready and was out the door by nine-thirty—the latest I have left to date. Fortunately, the trip to Foley Square went like clockwork, and at five after ten I was sitting composed in the courtroom.

Joseph C. Stumpf III was called to the stand. He is nice-looking—fortyish, well-dressed, and walks with assurance. While he was taking the oath, I heard Eileen, behind me, say, "He looks like a mouse." I almost lost it. He did. He had a pointed nose and a thick head of hair that dipped down over his forehead.

There the similarity ended. He gave more testimony, much on the same line that we've heard. All of a sudden I felt cold chills and thought that I could pass out. Fortunately, we got a break and I spent it in the ladies' room. When the court clerk called us back into the courtroom, I mentioned to him that I may suddenly run, not walk, back to that haven. He mentioned it to the judge and five minutes later the judge mentioned it out loud to the entire courtroom. I wanted to die.

I could envision the reporters running to telephone, "Juror sick." The judge never mentioned me by name or by number, but you could see the faces of the spectators searching our faces. I tried hard to dispell my nausea. The feeling remained all afternoon, but I never gave in to it.

To write what Joseph Stumpf said would be redundant. It was all incriminating for MACV: intolerable; frustrating; analysts disgusted; not an accurate portrayal; dishonest. He was dismissed. We heard surprise interim summaries.

Burt took the floor. He had his boys set up elaborate easels—with the order of command on one, and a blowup of an advertisement CBS had for the broadcast on the other.

Burt never referred to the order of command easel. But he went over each word of the ad with an imaginary magnifying glass.

Burt behaved like he had taken a course in drama. He'd stalk back and forth in front of us with a mean look on his face. He never took his eyes off *me*. I sat frozen in my chair. Why is he talking to me? Does he know I'm not buying this? Does he think he's convincing me? Does he know I feel sick?

He referred to the letter (memo) that George Crile sent to Mike Wallace, flipped it out of Murry's hand, and began reading it to *me*.

In a falsetto voice, he mimicked the writer: "We now have Westmoreland where we want him." I laughed. As quickly, I looked away. I could no longer keep my composure. Now Burt was mad. He raised his voice—he read further—I quickly went on one of my mental trips to enable me to maintain courtroom decorum. Boies gave his summation, and we then got our next witness.

Greg Rushford. He was the main investigator for the Pike committee hearings.

Greg Rushford was short. His hair looked like a bad toupee. He looked young. Maybe pushing it, he could be twenty-nine, though I knew he had to be older. He looked at us and the spectators in the courtroom like he was examining the skyscrapers of New York City for the first time.

His answers were, "Oh yes, sir," "No, sir," "Oh, by all means, sir."

There is a blaring difference between the witnesses we've had for the defense and the witnesses we've had for the plaintiff. The defense witnesses appear intelligent.

In spite of their credentials and officer status, the plaintiff's witnesses, for the most part, have had bad memories. I was very impressed with McNamara and Rostow and a couple of others. But to reuse the words that Crile used in describing Carver: "Sidestepping main issues with artful fillibuster" had been in widespread use.

I listened to Greg Rushford with interest.

The Pike committee was actually a House investigating subcommittee headed by Otis Pike. It apparently dealt with a lot of issues—Soviet invasion of Czechoslovakia, Cuba's Bay of Pigs, a coup in Portugal and Cyprus, the Mideast war, and the Tet offensive.

The Tet offensive was brought to the committee's attention by Sam Adams's article in *Harper's* magazine. His article was first sent to various authorities to shoot holes in. No one could.

Various people were called to testify. Rushford mentioned a lot of names: General Danny Graham was one. After Graham's testimony, one of the congressmen supposedly told Graham that he wanted to congratulate him: on the audacity to come to them with such outrageous testimony. Rushford said that Graham was, he believed, the highest ranking officer to appear before them. Westmoreland sent a letter.

The committee worked from May 1975 to February 1976. It was disbanded for lack of funds. But from what I gather, it heard a lot about the Tet offensive and the Order of Battle debate.

It was a most serious issue. In the middle of a war, the military was playing with numbers. It was an outrageous act. We lost the war in the midst of this.

A lot of people couldn't find their records to come and testify. Carver said he misplaced his documents. The CIA put out propaganda of sorts, stating no one affiliated with the CIA should speak to the committee without a P.R. person or a lawyer present. "Then you had no documents to support any testimony?" Dorsen accused.

"Oh no, sir, I had a lot of documents. I had about this much paper." Rushford spread his arms out.

We had an interruption in testimony. "Tell us in inches or feet, how much paper," said the judge.

"Oh, about four feet," Rushford answered.

Dorsen quickly added, "Do you know how many feet of documents we have for this trial, Mr. Rushford?"

An objection was sustained and we can only guess at the answer. Irrelevant.

Rushford said he believed it was a conspiracy. He mentioned some people and he said they were like Allen—they knew they did wrong, but they couldn't say it publicly.

A lot of decent people kept their silence. It was a shame.

Rushford even implicated Bill Bundy in a conspiracy to keep information from the press. They had found documents written by him with captions over certain statements: "Here's what we believe. Here's what you can tell the press."

Rushford said that the sentiment on the Pike committee was that the word *conspiracy* was accurate.

By now it was obvious that the plaintiff wanted this witness off the stand.

Dorsen made one final stab. He tried to show that Adams didn't like Westmoreland. "Oh no, sir—that's not true," Rushford spoke so innocently. "Sam Adams felt that General Westmoreland was an honorable, decent man who just happened to do something indecent. It was a tragedy—what happened. Sam Adams was charitable toward General Westmoreland—he felt sorry for him, but he didn't excuse the act."

No further questions, Your Honor—we were dismissed for the day. Return Monday morning at ten.

February 1, 1985

My feeling of sickness came in waves. One moment I wanted to be wrapped in a warm blanket on a soft bed, the next I felt fine.

All went according to schedule last night. I met my husband at the assigned spot, but had to kill a couple of hours around Grand Central Station because we got out of court early. I went to bed as soon as we got home. I woke up around two and had a repeat performance of the night before. This time Bob was up. He was trying to be cheerful. He was trying to make me laugh. So everyone gets sick. Don't go to work tomorrow. You can stay home and throw up all day. Look at all the fun you can have. Then he got tender and started whispering in my ear.

"What's happening at the trial, you can tell me."

I started to cry.

For four months, I haven't said a word. I've joked my way out of his interrogations. I've talked about everything else in the world to him, as if the courtroom proceedings were nonexistent. I broke down and told him all. When I was finished, I saw he had tears in his eyes.

He didn't say a word. We fell asleep.

I called in sick. I stayed in bed until almost one o'clock. By now the cat was frantic, so I got up and fed her. When I opened the curtains, the world was covered in snow—thick piles of snow on the ground, thick snowflakes floating straight down. It looked like a wonderland, a movie set. It didn't look real. There was no food in the house. I got dressed, made it down to the shopping center, and in less than an hour did a week's worth of errands.

The roads were fine, but the side roads were a nightmare. I managed to pull the car far enough into the driveway to get it off the unplowed side road. I had to carry all my bags up the two hundred feet to the house. This chore done, I went back to bed.

February 3, 1985

It was a lost weekend. It snowed all day Saturday. We ended up with almost ten inches. It was magnificent when the sun came out. I spent the weekend in and out of bed. About all I accomplished was to clear up all the dead plants from last week. It was really a chore—all three trees, several three-foot-high assorted jungle plants, and a dozen or so others. When this was completed, I went back to bed and before I knew it, it was time to return to the city to begin another week. I wondered what surprises this one would bring.

The sky was clear blue, not a trace of clouds. The sun was shimmering everywhere on the snow, on the ice-covered reservoirs. As the sun began to set, it took your breath away. It was spectacular. A Haydn concerto, a gorgeous evening, and an open road. Both Bob and I were transfixed by the setting.

As my mind wandered, I began to think about where it all began. "Bob, do you know what disturbs me a lot—aside from the obvious things. There have been statements here and there that grate at me."

"What's that?" he asked.

"When Danny Graham testified and was asked about the political cadre, he said something to the effect—oh, the man with the bullhorn, or, excuse me, I mean the white mice. And then, when Westmoreland was asked about the SD, he said something to the effect that it was like trying to count how many cockroaches you had in your kitchen."

"Yes, so?" he added impatiently.

"Well, that bothers me—these were people they were talking about, I mean."

He interrupted me. "They were enemy. What do you want from them? They were in a war zone, fighting a vicious enemy—how did you want them to look at the enemy? There'd have been something wrong with them if they didn't. It was the same for us in Korea. Listen, Pat, that's not your concern. Stop thinking about what it was like there—your only concern is what you hear as evidence in the courtroom."

I was silent.

"Am I not right? What has the judge told you?"

"Yes, yes, you're right," I said, and went back to watching the sunset.

February 4, 1985

The line of people waiting to get subway tokens spilled out into the street. I managed to squeeze my way past them and through the turnstile just as a train pulled in. Determined to get on this train, I barely did—the doors kept opening and shutting and finally we moved out of the station. I clung on for dear life at the next stop and was pushed even further into the train by the new crowd. This time we sat for a good five minutes. One of the trainmen was going up and down the train and shaking all the doors.

We had a repeat performance at the next stop with the trainman pushing his way into our car and yelling for all the people sitting down on one side to stand up—he had to fix some controls. This done, we moved on. At the next stop, an announcement came over the loudspeaker.

"Everyone off—disabled train." Obediently, the people left the cars. No one complained out loud. Like a bunch of robots, they all just lifted their books and newspapers and started to read—like nothing had happened.

I was learning something from all these New Yorkers. I wasn't sure what. I didn't even bother trying to cram into the next train, but the second one pulled in and I had no choice—the people behind me just shoved me on.

A young black woman in front of me turned around and snarled. I looked at her innocently and said, "I'm sorry, I was just pushed on myself."

"Well, you could have said you're sorry," she snarled, biting off words.

"I just did," I said. Everyone around us laughed. Thank God for humor.

Daniel Friedman took the stand. He was a veterans' counselor in Brooklyn and Staten Island. He was in Vietnam from November 1967 to November 1968. He was wounded twice—had received two Purple Hearts for wounds. His job in Vietnam had been as an armored reconnaissance specialist. He would go out and draw fire from the enemy. If the enemy was larger than what he and his men could handle, they would call for larger reinforcement units.

Boies was examining him, and Dorsen was objecting all over the place. Irrelevant—and how does this person know (beyond Mr. Friedman's realm)?

Boies crossly stated, "He was there, Your Honor."

The judge permitted the questioning. Friedman's main job as a witness was to emphasize the role of the SD and SSD. Daniel Friedman looked like an honest, straightforward, average individual—thick dark hair, thick moustache, late thirties, light blue polyester three-piece suit, a few extra pounds of girth, slight Brooklyn accent. He had been discharged honorably as a specialist fourth class. He seemed proud of his record and continued his testimony as a man of his rank, well aware that he was not of high official standing but that he had fulfilled his mission over there like a good soldier.

He had been on the front lines. He described the enemy—the SD, SSD, the villages. Some enemy were uniformed, most were not. The people they came most in contact with were the self-defense and secret self-defense.

Friedman said that the self-defense and local militia were one and the same. They were not regulars or guerrillas. The self-defense had regular jobs by day—farmers, barbers, merchants. At night they would lay mines and booby traps.

He and his troops would march through a secure area—a town considered friendly. The people would be standing by the roadside waving and begging. Our soldiers would throw them cigarettes and C-rations. At night or later on, when they would come marching back through that same town, they would be ambushed—fired upon, booby-trapped. When the smoke died down and our soldiers would recover bodies, they would recognize the very people who had waved to them as being the enemy who fired upon them. Our soldiers would find the bombs and traps that were made from the C-rations our boys had so generously shared.

He described free-fire zones as areas that were designated as unfriendly. Everyone was considered an enemy unless proved otherwise: "We were constantly warned about SD and SSD. Too many of my buddies went down by them." This last statement was objected to by the plaintiff and sustained and stricken from the record.

Friedman described the secret self-defense as Vietnamese who were thought to be friendly and in fact were not. He told stories of the Vietnamese who would work on the base as barbers or cooks.

The barber would set up a pole with a sign. Unbeknownst to our men, they would plant the sign next to ammunition dumps or petroleum storage areas. They would leave the poles up. Everyone assumed they would return the next day. Instead, rockets would fire at these spots at night, with utmost accuracy. The crucial spots were marked for the enemy by these poles. We heard stories of the cook disappearing and the whole mess hall exploding. This was the secret self-defense at work.

The self-defense sometimes had weapons, but more often planted mines. With the help of a hand grenade presented by the defense attorneys, he demonstrated how a booby trap could be made.

As Mr. Boies marched by the jury box with the hand grenade, I uttered the first words I have in court in four months. "You're not going to pull the pin, are you?" My concern seemed to be the same as that of the other jurors, and half the courtroom. There were a few moments of nervous comments and giggles.

No, Mr. Boies assured us, showing the bottom of the grenade to be empty. Mr. Friedman showed us how, by tying a fishing line to the cotter pin and straightening out the other end, the grenade could be buried with the fishing line stretched across a path and secured on the other side. An unsuspecting soldier would come along, trip the wire, and the grenade would catch the soldiers behind the leader.

No, the self-defense were not guerrillas—the guerrillas were set up in platoons or organized in regiments. They were from different locales. They carried food, which indicated they were on the move. When they were killed in combat, papers on their bodies would verify that they were from other locales. No, our men had no trouble identifying the difference between SD and guerrillas—there were several indications to tell us who was who. When our men made reports, they referred to SD or local militia or guerrillas.

Dorsen had a lot of objections throughout Friedman's testimony, but none of his objections or questioning changed Friedman's story.

When Boies asked him, "Weren't these civilians? You didn't want to kill these people, did you?" Friedman looked shocked. "They hampered our mission. We encountered them in every phase of our mission. They were hurting us."

Boies asked Friedman if it wouldn't have hurt his morale to know there were a hundred thousand more enemy out there.

Friedman looked shocked again. "No, sir! I would have felt better to have had more accurate information about the enemy I was fighting."

Mrs. Westmoreland didn't look well today. Her color was poor. She had had her hair cut—or she was wearing it differently—and it didn't appear as neat and trim as it usually does. There were a few new faces in the courtroom. These spectators have no idea how they stand out—a new face is something new to look at, in spite of the other hundred or so people there daily.

A new artist with a red sweater, thick gray beard, and red-rimmed glasses caught our attention. Every juror mentioned him when we had our break.

I thought Friedman was a good witness. Eileen said she thought he was the most damaging to the defense. She said that just proves it— they, the SD, were civilians—how could you shoot civilians?

When we got back from our lunch, H. Daniel Embree took the stand. He was from Starkville, Mississippi. He was married, had two children, and was an English professor at the University of Mississippi. He had been at West Point when Westmoreland was superintendent. He was in Vietnam from May 1966 until May 1967, when Westmoreland was COMUSMACV. He told us about his combat awards and Bronze Star, but mentioned a medal he had gotten for valor that he never wore because he didn't believe in it.

Professor Embree looked like a farmer or an individualist. He wore a corduroy jacket, light corduroy pants, a light pink-and-white-striped shirt and a very wide diagonally striped brown tie, with designs on alternate stripes.

Though his hair was dark brown, his thick grandpa's beard was long and gray. He had a country accent.

He had been stationed in Quang Tri province, the most northern province to the DMZ, bordered by Laos on the west and the South China Sea on the east.

He fought in the field for the year he was in Vietnam. Even when he was a captain, he was in the field. Embree's job was to tell us how bad the SD and SSD were. All through his military training he was cautioned about them. He had special training, as all soldiers heading for Vietnam did, on how to fight the guerrillas—watch out for boys, girls, taxi drivers, people on motorcycles.

He said his company was constantly on the move—their principal job was to protect and secure the countryside. They made continuous sweeps through villages. Embree said they saw combat more or less continually, with local militia, SD, and SSD—whatever you want to call them. They only engaged in battle with regular units—once a month or so. He said that the SD were responsible for fifty percent of their casualties. He lost at least, or on the average of, two men a day to mines or booby traps.

We got a lesson from him also on how a mine could be made out of a grenade. It took him fifteen minutes to give the same lesson that Friedman gave in one. I had to laugh. He was one of my people—a teacher, a professor. My pet peeve with some of the more illustrious of my profession is how complicated they like to make things sound.

Oh, it's simple, he said—anyone can learn how to make a booby trap out of this. He took the grenade out of Mr. Mastro's hand (the young attorney chosen to examine him). First, we got a history lesson: This is an older type of grenade. It was used in the Second World War, but it was common in Vietnam.

Then we got a physics lesson: It is called a pineapple fragmental grenade. You notice how the metal bulges out at these points like a pineapple would—and the metal is thinner here on these inside lines. That is designed to fragment when it explodes.

Then he demonstrated how the handle would fly off: Oh, he said, too bad—unfortunately, this has had the spring removed. Everyone in the courtroom reacted to that—even the judge.

Embree corrected himself: Fortunately, the explosives have been removed—unfortunately, the spring is missing.

He then took the wire Mastro just happened to have and was quite adept at setting it up for us and demonstrating exactly how easily the pin could be tripped by an unsuspecting foot along a jungle path. He verified pretty much the same things that Friedman verified. The SD were in Vietcong-controlled villages, the SSD in villages under our control. Guerrillas were organized in squads and platoons. They all were a big problem to our soldiers.

There was a big discussion on semantics. Dorsen didn't feel Embree was qualified—he was calling the guerrillas SDs and SSDs—where did you learn the term? How did you define them? Even the judge got in on the act—when all was said and done.

Embree said he was surprised that General Westmoreland didn't count the SD and SSD. They were fighting us. We were trying to fight them. I'm very surprised he didn't know what we were doing.

Dorsen tried to get his last word in. How much time did the SD spend on their job? They were not full-time soldiers.

Embree said it was not his business to theorize abstractly about them.

Well, Dorsen said, if we counted them, shouldn't we count people on our side who also just had ten minutes of training?

Embree answered, "There was no such person on our side with just ten minutes of training."

Still determined to get the last word in, Dorsen asked: "Isn't it true that you are here as a witness as a result of talking with Colonel Gains Hawkins and Sam Adams?"

We were dismissed for lunch. The jury shall return at quarter to two.

Pat, the court clerk, and Richard, the foreman, did their jig again in the jury room: a quarter to two, a quarter to two.

Joseph Fackovec was called to the stand. He was big—gray hair, brown jacket, expensive wool slacks, light shirt, no tie. He was nervous. He played with a paper clip while he was on the stand. I couldn't believe his nails when I spotted them. They were bitten down to the quick—every one!

He was the film editor who completed the editing of *The Uncounted Enemy* after the problem with Ira Klein. Fackovec had nothing but good things to say about George Crile.

He spoke of him as a man with a reputation for hard work and accuracy, very capable. Crile expected the same of those who worked for him.

Everyone knew there was a personality clash between Crile and Ira Klein—no one ever mentioned anything to Fackovec about the integrity of the broadcast. If there was any problem, you could always talk to George or to Andy Lack, the senior producer, or Stringer, the executive producer. They were always available. They'd always listen.

Crile never kept anyone out of the editing room—people were free to come and go. When there was a trip to the side bar, Mr. Fackovec stood up, and tried to bend his back; it was obvious he was in a lot of pain.

Mr. Boies offered him the opportunity to stand if he would be more comfortable. He said he probably couldn't get comfortable anywhere.

Burt had to cross-examine, of course. He was actually civil, though.

He tried to get Fackovec to say that sentences were cut up and interviews were taken out of context. He got nowhere. Fackovec said, "It's not my job to read all the interviews. My job is simply to read the transcript of the broadcast and edit the sound and the pictures."

"But weren't you interested to see what the full interview said?" gushed Burt.

"No," said Fackovec. "You're not going to read fifteen hundred pages of transcripts—for what? That's the producer's job."

Burt's parting statement was, "And you say you've been at CBS—was it thirty-three years?"

We had a break. Everyone was touched by Fackovec's testimony. Everyone felt badly that he was in such pain and thought that his appearance was a tribute to George Crile.

Joe Fackovec had such an imposing appearance, but he was so down-to-earth and simple with his answers, a lot of witnesses could take lessons from him.

When we got back into the courtroom, Burt began reading. Admissions of evidence CBS—he started right in, reading this stuff like it was the confessions of the accused. The judge interrupted to explain that this was simply a list of matters that CBS and the plaintiff had admitted were truths and not an issue.

The list was lengthy: issues like Mike Wallace had never read the Pike committee testimony; George Allen had an opportunity to be filmed twice; Adams also served as an associate producer. There were soft questions for sympathetic interviews and hard questions for adversary interviews. Westmoreland, Graham, and Rostow had particularly difficult lines of questioning. Crile wrote a letter to Westmoreland to get it on the record—Westmoreland seemed inept and stupid to him. This list was lengthy. Burt read it quickly, never really giving us a chance to absorb each allegation.

The judge instructed us when the reading was all over that we were not to judge anyone on the tone of an interview. CBS cannot be libeled for a harsh or sympathetic tone or for whom it chose to and not to interview or include in its programming.

The plaintiff must prove that CBS published false data, believing it was false, or was reckless as to the truth or falsity.

Next, Burt introduced a deposition and a taped phone conversation with Stringer, the executive producer of CBS's *The Uncounted Enemy*.

Number one: the statements were all out of context. Number two: Burt never differentiated between various phone conversations or two different depositions. He just sped from one statement to the next—in between blacked-out pages and segments. The gist of what I gathered was that Stringer was busy with a defense series that he was executive producer of. He mentioned that during the last month of the making of the documentary he didn't give it his total attention. He neglected George.

He also said he had a sneaking feeling at the end of the broadcast Westmoreland would cover for someone else. Do we really have the nerve to defy Washington?

One of Stringer's statements was: I thought Westy was a good general—I had no reason to believe he was honest or dishonest.

Then a later statement of his: I think that Westmoreland should have been fired years ago.

Burt gave another mini summation: Ask for this document when you deliberate, and so forth.

In rebuttal, Boies was quick to point out how confused the depositions and phone conversations by Stringer were. Boies emphasized his stronger statements were made after the completion of the documentary because of the lawsuit that General Westmoreland had introduced.

ONE LITTLE LIE

Colonel Donald W. Blascak was on the stand when we arrived in the courtroom.

He had a 1950s crew cut, wore a navy blue suit with red, white, and blue striped tie, and had an Ohio accent. He was tall and lanky and sat back in the witness chair with his legs crossed. He was still in the military, stationed in Frankfurt, Germany.

He had worked in the CIA along with Sam Adams, George Allen, and George Carver back in 1967–68. We heard all the lead-in questioning. His credentials took a half hour to relate.

I was surprised he could remember all the things he did in the last forty years.

He talked about the SD and the SSD—the guerrillas. He, too, told us how to make booby traps. He said that as the years went along, the SD's weapons became more sophisticated. When he was first in Vietnam in the early '60s, they were using homemade weapons. As time went on, they used the old French, Russian, and Chinese weapons. By the time he was there in the late '60s, the SD had access to U.S. and South Vietnamese weapons.

He likened the SD to the proverbial iceberg. You only saw the tip. When pressed to discuss the knowledge of the existence of the SD by everyone there, he likened it to this courtroom. He said, "I'm sure that there are people in this room totally unaware that construction is going on right behind this door." (He was referring to the renovations going on in the room adjacent to the jury room—all the jurors are very well aware of it.)

Blascak had definite opinions. The objections and the judge's warnings constantly reminded him to keep his own opinions to himself. But despite the courtroom protocol, we learned that Colonel Donald Blascak felt that SNIE 14.3–67 was corrupt—a carefully packaged lie. It was just a piece of paper that misinterpreted the enemy by at least two hundred thousand men.

Yes, he knew George Allen. He was the man who had spent slightly less time in Vietnam than Ho Chi Minh himself.

Yes, the SD did consist of young boys nine to twelve years old and old men above fighting age—but he likened the age dispersion to a normal curve with the majority falling into the fighting age range.

"Komer? Yes, I knew him. On either side of the ocean, it was hard to miss Mr. Komer." Everyone enjoyed that statement.

In spite of Blascak's drawl and laid-back manner, he was a feisty soul to deal with.

Dorsen quickly removed him from the stand. But not before Blascak, in a troubled crackling voice, attributed the impasse of reporting the true numbers to the policymakers to General Westmoreland. He stated—and did so with utmost sincerity—"this is very difficult for me to say."

Westmoreland, sitting at the plaintiff's table right in front of him, showed no emotion.

The rest of the afternoon was spent listening to Colonel Russell Cooley's deposition.

The afternoon was long—tedious and hot. The courtroom temperature must have been in the eighties, and all of us were dressed for the frigid weather outside—even the judge had commented on our sweaters and shawls.

One by one, the spectators sneaked out. The courtroom is always bursting at the seams with spectators, but after an hour into the deposition, I counted only seventeen diehards remaining. I looked around the jury box. All I saw were nodding heads and glazed eyes.

Finally, the judge interrupted and asked the attorneys if we couldn't have a break. The words were hardly out of his mouth and the jurors and spectators were standing up. Nervous laughter rang throughout the courtroom.

When we returned from our break, we saw Russell Cooley on the TV monitor. We were warned that these interviews, though containing a lot of the same testimony we will continue hearing in his deposition, could only be received on the state of mind of the defense because the interviews were not taken under oath.

He discussed Parkins being fired, his own role in CICV, plus Hawkins, Gattozzi, Fraboni, and McArthur, who worked with him; Morris, his big boss; Meechem, who took Parkins's place when he was fired.

He talked about the difficulty with the chain of command accepting their hard-worked-on figures for infiltration, which he numbered at at least 25,000 a month before Tet, and the shock of Tet and a lot more of the same things we've heard about time and time again.

Probably, the testimony he gave about Parkins being fired was the highlight of his testimony. He said their voices rang out all over the place—the walls being paper-thin. Before Parkins even emerged from Morris's office, the news had spread. Parkins was their boss, who went in to fight for the numbers that they had labored so hard over. It was a scene that stayed with him all the while he worked in Vietnam. There was no one you could complain to unless you wanted to be fired.

It was snowing when we got out of court today. The weather forecast is for seven to eight inches of snow and freezing rain before daybreak.

February 6, 1985

Alternate-side-of-the-street parking was suspended. My car was buried in snow, so I left it there. The subways were the usual nightmare, with the exception of the violinist, to whom I gave all my spare change. I was so grateful that he entertained us while we stared at the graffitied walls and the litter on the tracks.

Harold Boro was sick. He was suffering from all the symptoms I did last weekend. The nurse in the courthouse gave him a bottle of Kaopectate and a spoon. When we got into the courtroom, the judge acknowledged one of the jurors was ill and made it very clear that if he became too uncomfortable, he should not be bashful—raise your hand, get up and leave, if necessary—and he thanked us all for our dedication. It was a gracious gesture on his part. But having been in the position a few days ago, I knew how Harold felt. He'd probably faint before he raised his hand or got up.

General Joseph A. McChristian was called. He is one of the witnesses we've all been waiting for. As he made his way to the stand, I recognized him from the taped interviews we've seen. In spite of the fact that he was seventy years old and retired, he was still military.

He was all business. He spoke into the microphone, as though he were addressing a battalion. When he had taken the oath and was asked to spell his name and speak slowly, he did just that. He had been in the military for thirty-eight years, and we heard every minute detail of his experience.

He spoke proudly of his credentials, yet there was a definite humility about him. He had been a good soldier. He spoke of each position with utmost praise for the commander for whom he worked. He had done a few stints with Patton and General Keyes. He had fought throughout the European battles, as well as Korea and Vietnam. He was a self-taught intelligence officer. It appeared that he had been extremely successful.

The awards and medals he won are too numerous to mention here. But "ooohs" of admiration could be heard from the spectators. Unfortunately, the magnitude of those awards was lost on me (being naïve of military decorations). However, the human characteristics that emanated from him were not. This man won my respect.

He had a matter-of-fact manner, idealism, and dedication to his country that came forth unsurreptitiously. I recalled some of the descriptions that we've heard about him from others.

Sam Adams, for lack of a better word, described him as square. Colonel Hawkins had called him a prince, or a white knight. He appeared to be all these things.

We heard a firsthand account of all the testimony we've heard to date. He gave us a lesson in how to quantify the enemy—the duties of an intelligence officer.

We heard about the offices that he set up to perform more accurately the increasingly difficult job in Vietnam, and ultimately his leaving Vietnam and the circumstances surrounding his departure.

The most outstanding quality about his testimony to me was that he refused to point a finger or to lay blame on another. The more he testified, the more I accepted the glowing praise his colleagues had bestowed on him.

McChristian had been General Westmoreland's chief intelligence officer. In military terms, he was COMUSMACV's J2. He held this position from July 13, 1965, to June 1, 1967. When he left, he became chief of intelligence for the U.S. Army or, in military jargon, ACSE.

He explained that the J in J2 stood for Joint Chief of the army, navy, air force and marines, and that 2 stood for intelligence. General Westmoreland was the commander in Vietnam all the while he was there.

He described his job, one of whose main functions was Order of Battle. He described the role of Order of Battle as being able to describe the capabilities and vulnerability of the enemy.

The factors that had to be accounted for were: the enemy's strength, its composition, its disposition, its training, leadership, morale, logistics, and its weapons.

You had to get the very best picture of your enemy: the quantity and quality of your enemy.

He would collate this information and send it through a monthly Order of Battle, which was updated almost daily to everyone that would be concerned with this information. This included: DIA, CIA, NSA, SDI, the army, navy, air force, and marines, and intelligence officers. About five hundred copies were printed for this distribution. He talked about the Honolulu conference of February 7, 1967, where all the agencies agreed upon the categories that should be quantified. The categories included regulars, combat, maneuvers, combat support, administrative services, irregulars, guerrillas, SD, SSD, and the political infrastructures.

McChristian would debrief the chief of staff, who was General Rossen while McChristian held this office, and in turn General Rossen was to brief the commander, who was General Westmoreland.

McChristian was responsible for the inception of the office of CICV.

McChristian said that General Westmoreland's main mission was to help South Vietnam defend itself. As time went on, this mission became more and more complex—therefore necessitating the job of creating agencies such as CICV to better fulfill this mission.

He described one of the main functions of CICV as identifying things such as training centers of the enemy, ambush sights, hospitals, dates of combat, and so forth. He acknowledged that this had been a similar task in World War II.

They would have a large map with several overlays. Each overlay would have one of these concerns.

For example: a large celluloid map would be placed over the original with all ambush sites identified, then another with training centers, and another with hospitals. From these overlays, they could also see a pattern develop and therefore identify where and when the enemy was likely to attack.

McChristian spoke of Colonel Gains Hawkins, the chief Order of Battle analyst, with utmost respect. McChristian unequivocally acknowledged the importance of the SD to the enemy's strength. He said that the hamlet was the real battleground in this war.

He had brought along a bomb that the SD had used extensively. It was made from a beer can, and he demonstrated how it would be used. Then the difficult part of his testimony was drawn out of him.

The infamous meeting between General McChristian and General Westmoreland in May 1967 was finally told to us firsthand by McChristian. Allegations and characterizations of this meeting have been scattered throughout this trial. This meeting has been perhaps the whole crux of this litigation, or at least one of the main events.

Up until this point, it appears that everything in Vietnam was on the up and up. Everyone appeared to be doing their job and doing their best to do what had to be done. To be totally fair, perhaps the preceding months should be accounted for also.

General Westmoreland had been called back by President Johnson to give his account of the progress of the war. There's a light at the end of the tunnel; we have reached the crossover point; the enemy is not able to replace men as fast as he's losing them; and similar reports had been filed.

McChristian had been working on two major reports—RITZ and CORRAL. The RITZ report was a study of the irregular forces and the CORRAL study was about the Vietcong infrastructure, the political cadre.

Sometime between May 6 and May 10, 1967, the studies were completed, and McChristian had an unscheduled meeting with General Westmoreland about the results of the studies. He had a cable all written up with these results, which he believed were so significant that the cable should be sent off immediately to the policymakers. Before doing so, McChristian felt it was proper to alert General Westmoreland of their content.

The figures were double those that had been previously acknowledged.

"General Westmoreland read the cable and looked at me and said, 'If I send this cable, it will be a political bombshell.'" McChristian stated this with a combination of resolve and reluctance.

"Are you sure those were his exact words?" questioned Mr. Boies.

"Those words are burned into my memory," was McChristian's reluctant answer.

"Did General Westmoreland ever ask how you arrived at these figures?" asked Mr. Boies.

"General Westmoreland never asked for intelligence supporting the figures or the methodology used to arrive at these figures," answered McChristian.

"Did he ever ask for a briefing?" pressed Boies.

"General Westmoreland asked me to leave the cable with him. 'I want to go over it,' he said," answered General McChristian.

Questions and answers filled the hours. But the bottom line of McChristian's testimony was: In all my training in the army, it was emphasized there was no room for political concerns. A standard intelligence fact was to report it as you saw it. We worked on those studies for five months—periodically, General Westmoreland knew of our progress.

No, Westmoreland had said leave it with me. Let me go over it. The only concern he expressed was a political one. I even offered to go to Washington with it and explain it.

Through objections and side-bar meetings, his feelings about this were finally allowed. It would have been improper to hold back this kind of information.

We finally had a lunch break. Cheryl and I went to the Greek restaurant across the street, where we've met for breakfast. A couple of reporters were also lunching there. We safely stayed away from courtroom conversations.

Dorsen spent the afternoon cross-examining McChristian. Dorsen was unrelenting. McChristian was unbending. Here, in a court of law, under oath, he had no recourse but to be totally honest, in spite of the fact that he had utmost respect for those involved—he had to tell the truth.

"I had responsibility for timely, accurate, usable intelligence. The facts had to speak for themselves."

Interspersed with accusations and cross-examinations, another story evolved. I was surprised that Dorsen allowed it to come out. The night before McChristian was to leave Vietnam, there was a reception held in his honor. It was held at the embassy.

It had something to do with CIA. A Mr. Hart called General McChristian aside. There was a study you should have taken part in, he was told: We will let you read it, but you are to take no notes, and you are not allowed to tell anyone about it.

McChristian said that until he leaves Vietnam, he is still General Westmoreland's J2, and it is his responsibility to inform him—or they can tell him. (I'm not sure exactly how the sequence went—I'll have to make sure we get these transcripts during deliberations—but they ended up allowing McChristian to read the study.)

He said he was shocked when he read it. It kept going through his mind that he wouldn't do it this way. It had a lot to do with intelligence. It disturbed him a great deal.

Apparently, Komer had prepared it. The following day, General McChristian was scheduled to leave at noon. But McChristian went to Komer about the matter.

Komer's answer was, "Have a good trip home, Mac."

When McChristian went to General Westmoreland about the whole episode, General Westmoreland said, "Don't worry about it—I'll take care of it."

McChristian said he felt like he was kicked in the stomach.

Dorsen came back with statements that he had taken from Sam Adams's chronology, such as that McChristian loathed Davidson, and Komer.

McChristian refused to acknowledge these statements, saying he was hurt, yes, but it was out of his hands. He loathed no one.

McChristian said that he had never taken Davidson's place. He had no way of judging his capabilities. "I have no idea what he did or undid."

Dorsen had a series of hypothetical questions that McChristian refused to answer. There were a lot of side-bar trips.

During them, Eileen said she can't stand Crile.

Richard was clarifying points, but was totally noncommittal.

Kate was concerned because she had to reach her husband. Harold looked white, but said he was okay. Michael had a coughing fit, and Carmen gave him a Life Saver.

We all studied the spectators; they all studied us.

It was obvious the plaintiff's lawyers were checking us all out. And we were checking everybody back.

Michael thinks that one of the reporters in the third row is cute when she wears red. Richard thinks that one of the reporters in the second row on the other side of the courtroom is cute, but he admits she's a little fuzzy at this distance. I'm still trying to figure out which one is Farber, the reporter for *The New York Times*.

When we finally had to return to the business at hand, they were discussing a letter General Westmoreland sent to General McChristian.

There was some testimony about General Westmoreland saying to General McChristian that he believed that the conversation in his office of May 1967 was a private one between two West Pointers.

We were finally dismissed for the day.

Return at ten tomorrow morning.

February 7, 1985

It was clear and brisk, the kind of day that makes your face tingle. It took me about ten minutes to clear off my car. As I pulled out, I saw two cars fighting over the spot I had vacated. There were a lot of slippery spots, so people seemed to be driving sensibly.

I had a nice breakfast in my favorite spot and was in the jury room by nine-fifteen. The people who live the farthest away, as a rule, are the first to arrive. Eileen, who lives a six-block walk away, and Lili, who lives next door, in Chinatown, managed to get to the jury room as the clock hit ten!

George Crile was called to the witness stand by the defense. I couldn't imagine what else he could possibly say. He'd been on the stand for nine days with the plaintiff.

But I'm still learning about the protocol of courtroom procedure. Apparently, there are some subjects that can only be brought up by the plaintiff and others by the defense. I'll have to read a book on that.

Mr. Boies began with his usual smile and greetings and led Mr. Crile through a series of questions, mainly a clarification of who was responsible for what in the making of *The Uncounted Enemy*.

Then we got to view the infamous documentary again.

I think I know this thing by heart already—it begins with the music and a flag waving and a picture of a couple of soldiers. Westmoreland is superimposed over the flag, saluting. (On closer examination, it was President Johnson, hand on heart, and Westmoreland saluting.) Then the title comes on. *The Uncounted Enemy: A Vietnam Deception.*

Then you hear Mike Wallace's voice, with all the hoopla—"And yet we were told that we were winning the war." You see historic pictures of fighting and soldiers huddled under fire and you hear helicopters and guns going off. Suddenly the picture fades and an announcer's voice intones, "This is being brought to you by PERK."

The commercial for PERK is spieled off by a faceless announcer.

The courtroom fell to pieces. Even General Westmoreland dissolved in laughter. The monitors were quickly shut off, and lawyers for the defense were running all over the place looking for a copy of the documentary that had no commercials. They found another copy and the picture came on the monitors, but the sound would not. The video technician, who usually sleeps in the corner underneath all his controls, was now like a one-man band—racing from monitor to monitor, pulling plugs, switching wires. Still nothing. We were given a short break.

When we returned, the movie continued, with Mr. Boies stopping after each accusation—freezing the frame and posing questions to Mr. Crile to explain what evidence they had to suggest each allegation.

I learned a couple of new things. For one, the Pentagon Papers *did* play a role in this broadcast—much evidence apparently was enclosed in the papers about a conspiracy. They also used the Pike committee hearing notes.

We broke for lunch and my sister-in-law surprised me with a friend of hers and they took me for lunch. I suggested the Thomas Street Inn and we got a seat immediately—gave our order and chatted away. I looked at my watch and suddenly realized I had only thirty minutes left for lunch. No food was in sight, not even at the other tables.

People were walking out unfed. Apparently, there was a party downstairs being taken care of first. Poor planning. Don't these restaurants realize what lunch hour means?

Well, my soup finally came. It was good, in spite of the wait. Unfortunately, I had no time enjoy it. I left my surprise guests to finish their lunch in leisure and ran back to 40 Centre Street. One quick phone call determined that my date with a friend in Westchester was postponed. When I saw my sister-in-law back in the courtroom, there was no way I could tell her that I could drive her home and pick up Bob at the airport. Originally, she'd been planning to leave for a three-fifteen train to get home by six.

At our first recess, I slipped a note to the court bailiff asking him if it would be at all possible to get a message to her. He first had to give me a lecture. This was highly irregular and I must first alert the judge that there was someone in the courtroom who was related to me. I obliged, feeling like a second-grader being reprimanded by a veteran teacher. After the break, I saw the judge pass a note to counsel, and all the counsel turned around and searched out Juror 2, who sent the note.

"Once political concerns came into the picture, everything that followed after that was colored by this fact." George Crile was speaking. We were back to the tape, *The Uncounted Enemy,* the courtroom. We heard it all before—why was Boies subjecting us to this?

We saw more of the documentary. Now McArthur was on camera, stating that his numbers of infiltrators had been arbitrarily cut while he was on R&R after his roommate was killed.

Boies stopped the tape.

"And, Mr. Crile, can you tell me why you included this portion in the documentary? What evidence did you have to substantiate this segment?''

Mr. Crile spoke, as usual, after a pause. I was getting anxious about his pattern of speech. He is so controlled—he is so careful not to disrupt his image. He's asked a question, and instead of saying yes or no or whatever, he stops, looks down, looks up, thinks, and then says yes with an explanation or no with an explanation—or gives an explanation and then answers the question.

Another segment was shown. "And Mr. Crile," continued Boies, "why did you choose to include this segment of interview into the documentary?''

"As a reporter, it is not rare to meet up with whistle-blowers. But it is very rare to meet so many people who are pointing the fingers at themselves," Crile answered. We finally had a break.

I realized then why it was so important for the defense to continue with its case.

The more verbal jurors were chatting away. (He's lying—I can't stand Crile—he's hiding something—I agree with Ira Klein!)

I couldn't believe what I was hearing. At this stage of the game I was in a state of shock—I didn't say a word. I looked around the entire jury room and tried to take an evaluation.

Phil was buried in his book; Harold, in his newspaper. Harold hadn't said much, but at one point a week or so ago he mentioned that he was glad his son had been too young to go to Vietnam. He just missed it. He never said much, but he had made that one statement.

"If he had had to go there—I would have been shaking in my boots, especially after being on this trial and hearing how the Order of Battle was handled.''

That's all he ever said.

I found out today that he feeds the pigeons in the park at lunch. Some of the other jurors were teasing him that yesterday, when he was sick, the pigeons were chasing anybody with a red-and-black checkered hat.

After every session in court, Carmen spends time going over her notes. So does Lili, the Chinese girl.

After all these weeks, I was ashamed I didn't know some of the jurors as well as I'd like to. It *was* an extremely diverse group. Looking over the group, I realized the only ones who were truly verbal about their thoughts were the card players, and their reactions were mixed. They openly debated their opinions.

Eileen started talking: "I want to ask one thing—how important was this whole thing, the Order of Battle? Westmoreland says it wasn't that important. He was the general, in charge. I mean—is everybody getting carried away with this for nothing? How important was it? The general in charge is saying that the debate between CIA and MACV was nothing. He should have known—he was in control. Maybe this whole thing is a waste of time!''

A couple of the jurors at her end of the table got into a discussion with her. I couldn't hear it. But all I could think of was: Why did he sue? If the Order of Battle meant nothing and he was accused of screwing around with it, what *was* the issue? Why did he bother? It had to have meant something. CBS wouldn't have even bothered with the whole issue if it weren't something. They sounded, to me, like they had gone through the entire investigation that we are now forced to do. If they had done their homework like they appeared to have, won't we, in fact, come up with the same conclusions?

We've had testimony from the executive producers. Statements like ''we covered our asses'' have been put into evidence. Doesn't that mean that they did their own investigations?

We were called back into the courtroom. It was hot—I kept yawning.

Wallace was now interviewing Westmoreland on the tape. Wallace told Westmoreland that his men felt uncomfortable about it—cutting the figures—what they were doing with the Order of Battle. Westmoreland was biting back at Wallace, saying, ''Well, why didn't they come to me? No one ever told me they didn't like what they have been doing. Why weren't they forthright?''

In the meantime, we had seen Parkins get fired for fighting for the numbers his men had been presenting. McArthur was transferred, with a bad record. McChristian was removed from Vietnam. Anyone who complained about his role in this, or who tried to stay aboveboard, was removed.

I looked over at the plaintiff's table, and it looked like these men were sitting at a funeral. Dorsen was sitting with his head in his hands. Murry was staring straight ahead. Their female associate, who usually is bouncing here and there, was frozen in her seat. An elder attorney whom we've never heard from but who appears every day looked grim. The only ones who looked unaffected were Burt and Westmoreland.

Westy was jutting his chin out and Burt was sitting with a smile on his face, studying the jurors' faces.

The defense attorneys were oblivious of any of us. If they weren't engrossed in their own conversations, they were thumbing through files, getting ready for Boies's next questions.

Back to the screen. Westmoreland was telling Wallace: "I didn't do that! I didn't get involved in that personally." I heard Wallace saying, "It happened on your watch!"

The defense was well prepared. Giant easels were set up in front of us. In case we missed the words on the TV, we saw them on the giant visual aids. Boies was too short (though he's at least five feet ten) to comfortably flip the giant charts in front of us. They kept getting caught. But eventually, we could read them. We heard more words like *dishonest, prostitution, ashamed, critical event*! It all sounded like one long confession.

These men making confessions in front of me sounded so sincere. I couldn't believe that their anguish was in vain—where were my colleagues? Did they really believe this was a put-on? Maybe I was crazy.

Graham came on the screen. I think the jury's reaction to him was unanimous. The guy was an ass. The thing that really frightens me about him is that he's behind Reagan's defense program in space. I'm scared to death.

We saw him deny vehemently facts that even we have accepted as truth. Papers are put in front of him, and he'll argue that they don't exist. Every juror laughs at his credibility. His name is a safe joke.

Wallace showed Graham a cable and said, "Do you recognize this?" Graham looked at it and looked at it and then said, "Oh, yes— I recognize this. There were guys who wanted to put the SD into the Order of Battle and this cable is saying you shouldn't do that." Wallace said, "But the SD were in the Order of Battle since 1961, and you were trying to take them out."

Graham (Order of Battle authority) says: "Oh no, that's not true— they were never in the Order of Battle."

For four months we've been reading, seeing, reviewing documents that show the SD have been in the Order of Battle since before the French were in Vietnam.

But Danny Graham sat there like we were all crazy. We saw a segment—November 18, 1967, Westy with Johnson. Westy is telling Johnson that the enemy is running out of men. We saw a segment of December 1967—the same thing. We saw the Tet attack start—January 30, 1968. There was an objection by the plaintiff. Everything stopped.

Boies read pages, Crile read his papers, the court recorder closed his eyes. I caught him, and he caught me catch him. We laughed. The people at the defense table sat in quiet conversation. The people at the plaintiff's table did the same. The spectators looked restless. The jury whispered among themselves.

The judge looked up. Mr. Burt said, "Judge, there was an objection." The judge raised his eyebrows.

The courtroom broke into laughter. The objection was ruled upon, and we were dismissed for the day.

Return tomorrow—later than usual—at ten-thirty.

I drove Elaine to her home on Long Island. Thank God, I don't have to drive there every day. It took about an hour for a fifteen-mile ride. I saw her new kitchen. We went out for dinner, her husband and the two of us. They pointed me in the direction of La Guardia after dinner, and I surprised Bob at the exit gate. We had a nice trip home.

February 8, 1985

The good mood I awoke in was quickly squelched by Bob. Every time I turned around, he was biting orders at me. Finally, I blew up when he complained about the luggage I was taking home for the weekend. By the time I dropped him off at his office, we weren't speaking. I couldn't believe how bad his mood was—or mine, for that matter.

I met Cheryl for breakfast. She gave me a birthday gift—a Van Gogh art calendar. I was touched.

Court was the same as yesterday. The only thing new was a tape of a speech Robert Kennedy made one week after Tet. He was asking the same question so many have been asking. Who were we fighting? If so many enemy were killed in the Tet offensive and so many wounded, the numbers didn't add up.

It was too cold to go out for lunch. I bought an apple from the canteen machines and finished my book on Von Bülow.

Everyone surprised me with a birthday cake. When we got back into the courtroom, the judge made the announcement that it was Juror 2's birthday. He gave my name, and everyone wished me a happy birthday.

We saw the rest of The Uncounted Enemy. We heard more of Crile's explanation. Burt only asked one question of Crile when he had a chance to cross-examine. "Was it true that you said that the Tet offensive was an overwhelming victory for us?"

In Crile's usual fashion, he answered, saying that it was a disaster to morale. It was the point at which it broke our natural will—and on and on.

We were dismissed after the judge made an announcement that we would meet at eleven-thirty on Monday to accommodate one of the jurors.

David has been in a bind of late. He no longer has a job. The grant money for his research at Sloan-Kettering had run out. He can't collect unemployment while being on this jury. In fact, he hasn't even been able to file because of the hours court is in session. I was impressed by the understanding the judge had for his situation.

The judge spent ten minutes giving us warnings—do not speak to anyone about this trial, not even your family.

Immediately, a pang of guilt raced through my body. Had the judge heard me talk to Bob at four the other morning? Was my house bugged? We haven't said another word to each other about it. In fact, Bob never even answered me. He's refused so much as a comment.

I had wanted to share McChristian's testimony with him, but I didn't because, for one, he'd been away and I really didn't.know how to explain the effect it had on me. Joseph McChristian lived up to his given name. He told only the truth and tried desperately to avoid making judgments on others.

There are two Josephs in my life—my father and my father-in-law. Both men live by the same code that Joseph McChristian professed in court. I truly believe the names are a coincidence, but they started my train of thought. Both the Josephs in my life are religious men—my father goes to mass every day, my father-in-law, to temple.

Though both of their children hurt them deeply by marrying outside of their religion and not embracing their parents' beliefs, both men have bestowed nothing but love and goodwill upon the union, never making the other feel like an outsider.

These men not only believe in goodness and truth—they live it, in a very unobtrusive way. Their example has had far-reaching effects. In the lives that Bob and I live, we often witness unethical conduct.

Teaching is no problem; it is relatively easy to perform with highest integrity. But I have been hurt more than once in real estate. Bob has had similar disturbing experiences when he worked on Wall Street, and now in insurance. I've heard my father-in-law profess the merits of truth. There is no such thing as a little lie; if you tell the truth, you don't have to worry about your memory; and other such pithy quotations. His being a CPA, I've heard some of the situations that he had to refuse to get involved in.

My father's pharmaceutical profession put him in similar situations that I can remember as I was growing up.

As the weeks of testimony scrambled in my mind, an overwhelming thought seems the clearest to me: It was one little lie.

Something like Watergate, perhaps. The lie, or the embarrassing situation that was perpetrated, could have as easily been resolved.

Westmoreland wanted to win the Vietnam War so badly—he saw what he wanted to see: The enemy was quiet, things are looking up, there's a light at the end of the tunnel—he told that to the President. When his intelligence officers found evidence to the contrary, all he had to do was say, I was wrong.

I can well imagine his embarrassment, his trepidation, at facing that reality. So one little lie could save face.

But apparently Westmoreland, along with a lot of other people, many in high positions, never had that one simple fact embossed in their minds by a humble parent: "There is no such thing as a little lie!"

Is this the way it happened?

I don't believe that General Westmoreland is a dishonest person. He appears to be a proud man. He's had huge responsibilities, and regardless of how he handled them, I get the feeling from him that he did the best he knew how.

Perhaps the orders were from above.

Maybe the President himself told him—this is how I want you to report.

Maybe it is accepted—on these levels—that this is how to handle such matters.

But we are not living in the days of King Arthur. The days of hiding the facts from your subjects are no longer.

The wind was brutal. I was in the middle of Centre Street. My legs were moving forward, but I was standing still.

Randy, one of the other jurors, and Richard pulled me across the street.

Since we got out early and I was heading through Westchester, I offered them a ride home. We were literally blown to the garage where my car was, and we found ourselves finally on the FDR Drive.

Richard says it takes him an hour to get to court every day by subway. I couldn't believe it. We got into a whole discussion on the city traffic and mass transit. I live more than sixty miles from the city, and I can make it in under two hours. Of course I must always leave earlier to allow for unforeseen events. But I live fifty miles farther than Richard and Randy. We got into an exchange of ideas to improve the system.

I was supposed to pick Bob up in Westchester at six. I killed the time by waiting, reading, sorted out my briefcase. It was freezing, and the car was like an icebox. I went into a restaurant for a while to warm my blood again. I wondered what would happen when we finally met—we were at such odds this morning.

I received a cautious greeting and a laugh. We both made fun of our morning's behavior, and we were on our way home.

We exchanged the usual how-was-your-day conversation and then fell silent. The radio went on and we drove in silence. About fifteen miles down the road, Bob lowered the radio and began discussing his business trip. It disturbed him a great deal. He recounted one scenario in particular. "Pat, they were outright lying—they were distorting the truth," he blurted out.

I felt like I was back in the courtroom. "What do you mean?" I asked. "Was it veiling the true figures? I mean, could you say they were really telling the truth but stretching it? If you picked apart the statements they were using to influence these people, could you say that they were just stretching the facts and not actually making blatant misstatements?"

He interrupted me: "No! They were outright lying about the figures!!"

February 9, 1985

It's such a luxury to sleep late—not a care in the world! The cat did not agree. I got up and fed her and realized I had to get to the cleaners, the post office, and the bank. The day was spent on errands. We watched some third-rate movies from the video store. For my birthday, Bob gave me a Netsuke from a local antique store we deal with—it was a beauty. A lovely ivory carving of a fisherman. I told him I would think of him when I wear it, him being a fisherman too.

February 10, 1985

My real birthday. I spent it like a princess. Got up at noon, watched TV, read the Sunday *Times* from front to back. We went out for a nice dinner. Long Pond Inn—lovely setting. The owner bought us an after-dinner drink. Did some paperwork when we got home. Was in bed by ten-thirty.

February 11, 1985

We didn't have to be in court until eleven-thirty, so the pressure wasn't the usual Monday morning frenzy.

Bob had an appointment in White Plains, so he drove me to the station down county. I was at Grand Central by nine thirty-five. I killed an hour at the bookstore there and browsed in some of the other shops I'd been meaning to explore. Actually, it's kind of nice to have time to kill.

I was still an hour early when I got to Foley Square. Kate, Linda, and Randy were already there. They all come from quite a distance. They jumped on the goodies I'd baked.

Finally, all the jurors arrived. We shared our weekend accounts with each other and were called into court at eleven-forty.

Major Michael Dilley was called to the stand. He had been in the military for twenty years, all of which were spent in intelligence. He did security checks for individuals wishing to work for the government.

He had two tours in Vietnam—one from September '66 to September '67; the other, December '68 to December '69. The tour we were concerned with was from September '66 to September '67, when Major Dilley's job was to estimate the number of political cadre. He was quite adamant about the fact that he inherited a figure of 39,000 from the South Vietnamese. But around the spring of '67, they had a strongly documented estimate of 139,000. He talked about the project called CORRAL, which was instituted to study the political cadre.

We also heard of an ICEX Program, which was instituted to eliminate the political cadre by killing them. One section provided names of individuals in the infrastructure for targeting, Dilley told us. He told us that under McChristian, they were expected to come up with accurate, timely intelligence.

When Davidson came into the MACV J2 position, it seemed as though the opposite was expected. Suddenly the analysts were told to cut figures.

Colonel Gains Hawkins, the chief of Order of Battle MACV, came to the analysts personally and ordered them to arbitrarily cut their figures for political cadre, administrative services, and various other categories.

Objections rang out all over the place. Dilley said that no intelligence personnel understood the order, but of course we can't prove he was in a position to know that—so, we, the jury, are not allowed to hear it.

The day was one long side-bar meeting. We had a lot of time to chat in the jury box. Eileen grabbed a hold of the Netsuke I was wearing and got crazy—what are you doing wearing a Vietcong? Look, guys, it's a guerrilla—you can tell 'cause he's carrying food.

Loretta said some girl got a hold of her when she was coming up the steps of the courthouse. She gave her a business card. She told Loretta she wanted to get a group picture of all the Westmoreland jurors.

David gave me a birthday card—he called it the Gains Hawkins card because inside, it said, "Happy Birthday and all that crap!"

There are a few words that have been added to our lexicon—besides light at the end of the tunnel.

Objection—irrelevant—in words or in substance—your best estimate—and crap. Everyone's got a lot of mileage out of old Gains Hawkins's statement.

When Dilley's examination continued, we heard a lot more about the political cadre, their infrastructure. They were the Vietcong shadow government—they were pretty bad. They killed people who didn't agree with their politics. Though Dilley said he was positive his estimates were accurate, he and his men had to cut the figures. Colonel Gains Hawkins ordered them to. If they had four listed for a town, they'd cut the number to three. Apparently, there were a few in each area. We already know there were forty-four provinces—I'm not certain how many towns in each province, but I could see how the numbers could add up. The long and short of it was that Dilley's hard work was totally ignored, along with a lot of other men's. He said that his roommate, Marshall Lynn, was in charge of administrative services. He had been given the same instructions by Colonel Gains Hawkins that Dilley had. All the analysts did.

Cross-examination didn't change Major Dilley's story. Dorsen gave him several documents. Dilley carefully read each one, answering after each. No, this does not change my testimony.

On several occasions, Dilley wanted to explain what the document was and that it was not valid. No one—Dorsen, the judge, Boies— would allow him to elaborate. Just yes or no, Major Dilley. You could tell the witness was frustrated by the inability to set the record straight. However, he obliged and said no more.

Finally, the witness was dismissed. Now we will continue the reading of Colonel Cooley's deposition. All the jurors groaned. Everybody laughed—the judge, Westmoreland, Burt, even Boies. The judge said, "Why don't we take a short break?" There was nothing wrong with Colonel Cooley's deposition except that it was long. It looked like another inch of paper had to be read.

The jurors braced themselves with more of the calorie-laden cookies I brought in, and they wiped out Norma's butter cake. Loretta said, "If I'm going to be bored to death, I might as well enjoy myself and get fat." Everyone laughed. She already was a hefty lady.

We were called back into the courtroom. Everyone was grinning from ear to ear. The judge announced that we would be spared—we'll dismiss for the day now. You can go home and rest up and we'll complete Colonel Cooley's deposition tomorrow. It was four-fifteen.

My father-in-law was taking us out for my birthday. I had forsaken lunch and all the goodies in the jury room so that I could enjoy the evening out.

Bob came home about fifteen minutes after me. I could tell something was wrong the minute he came in the door. "I just came back from the police station," he snarled.

"Bob! What happened?" I asked, almost not wanting the answer.

"Why else do I go to the police station? The radio was stolen again!"

This makes the third time in seven months! "Where did you park the car this time?" I asked, almost accusingly.

"The Kinney Garage on Fifty-fourth Street," he yelled in angry frustration. "The policeman said to me when I told him it was in a garage, 'Was it the Kinney Garage? You're the third guy here in the last fifteen minutes from the same spot.'" The useless anger that we both felt, the frustration—I'm not even sure how to recount it. Someone has violated us again. We have $500 deductible insurance. All I could envision was the trip to the garage—get pictures taken of the damage, having to make time to get the car taken care of, which means losing time from work. Driving in silence four hours a day. Then Bob laid the clincher on me: "They broke into the glove compartment, also—they took the registration and the insurance papers and all of our tapes as well."

We went out to dinner in spite of it all. When my dish came, it wasn't what I'd ordered. By the time the waiter brought me my meal, Bob and my father-in-law were on their dessert. When the waiter cleared the table he dropped a few dishes, which splattered all over Bob and me. He gave us the address to send the cleaning bill to. We couldn't find a cab when we left the restaurant, so we walked home in spite of the brutal wind that came from nowhere.

It was the perfect ending to a rather imperfect day!

February 12, 1985

I didn't want to get up this morning. I kept going back to sleep. Even after I took my shower, I went back to bed to steal a couple more minutes next to Bob, who was sleeping like a baby. Finally, I couldn't ignore the mantel clock anymore. Those beautiful chimes rang loudly, along with Offenbach's "Can-Can" music. I made a mental note to call WNCN and complain about their choice of wake-up music.

When we got into the courtroom, the judge began the day with: "I have good news, and I have bad news. The good news is—we will have a short day. The bad news is we will begin with Colonel Cooley's deposition."

Boies asked the judge if he couldn't address the jury before he began. He smiled sheepishly, greeted us with good mornings, and apologized for the need to hear depositions read. He said that if it were at all possible, he would have the people here in person, but it is unfortunately not always possible. He asked us to please pay as close attention to the reading as we could because his testimony is important. It is the thread of continuity in the case he is trying to present. Listen in particular to Cooley's testimony in regard to the men who were affected. His story will lead in to the next witness we will be hearing.

We heard the reading of the transcript. It was completed in less than an hour. It was easier to digest at ten in the morning than it would have been at four in the afternoon. We were given a short break, and Colonel Gains B. Hawkins was called to the stand. Without looking at my fellow jurors, I could feel the excitement. We've been waiting for him.

A small, elderly man stood up in the courtroom and made his way to the witness chair. I wanted to jump out of my seat and help him walk more assuredly.

He was the witness who was going to make or break CBS's case. I got angry at myself for feeling partial to CBS. I quickly froze a blank look on my face and buried myself in my notes. I had taken a forbidden elevator this morning, on the other side of the courthouse. I had gone to the jury room on the first floor, where we have to sign in with our garage vouchers. It was very early and the elevator opened its doors, so I jumped on. The ones we're allowed to use never work, so I felt a bird in the hand—when it made its first stop and the doors opened, Baron got on with our new witness! I had tried to hide in the corner and make believe I wasn't there, but it's rather difficult to hide on a four-foot-square elevator. Especially when there are only three of you in it.

While Colonel Hawkins was taking the oath, I felt his eyes frozen on me. I desperately wanted to give him a sign, but couldn't. Relax— I'm not your enemy—I respect what I've heard about you so far. But that was short of treason. How much I hate my role. Being a juror is so very difficult.

Where are you from, Colonel Hawkins?

"West Point, Mississippi, sir."

"Are you retired, Colonel Hawkins?"

"Yes, sir—retired, sir—30 November 1970, sir."

"Could you give us some of your background?"

We heard a fifteen-minute-long sentence that the poor man raced through like he was racing a stopwatch. It was difficult to even understand him because of the Mississippi inflection. He stared right at us, motionless, frozen in one position while his voice raced on.

He made a statement or two in the monologue that was very funny. At one point, he said, "I had twenty-five years of duty and I got paid for twenty-nine years, thank God." Everyone laughed. Old Gains Hawkins never cracked a smile and raced on, hardly allowing us a second to enjoy his humor.

My heart sank. I almost broke out in a nervous sweat for him. "What was your job, Colonel, in Vietnam in 1966?"

"I was chief of Order of Battle branch, J2 section MACV staff. I reported to General McChristian, sir. I had one supervisor between me and General McChristian, but General McChristian asked me to report directly to him. It could have been a sticky situation, but we worked it out."

"And what did the chief of Order of Battle do?"

Colonel Gains Hawkins gave us a one-week lesson in five minutes. He raced through the purpose of Order of Battle, the importance of Order of Battle, and all the points that the Order of Battle was responsible for without taking a breath.

We heard about the identification, dispositon, composition, logistics, tactics, and miscellaneous elements of the enemy.

He told us miscellaneous things such as personalities, names of officers, post-office-box numbers of the enemy, and on and on. We heard about NSA information on enemy and collateral information of enemy. "Like a journalist has to do research in a report is how . . ." he continued.

The judge interrupted and said, "I think you're going beyond the scope of the question."

"Okay." The colonel stopped dead in his tracks. "I'll shut up if you say so." He looked straight ahead. The audience was becoming enamored with him. He told us he'd met Sam Adams out in the field, when both of them were familiarizing themselves with the country and the field officers they were relying on to send them information.

"Adams was a competent analyst. He knew the guerrillas and irregulars better than anyone else. He taught me a lot about them. But I knew the regular forces better than he did. Sam Adams was an honest man—he was one of the most honest men I ever met. He makes me ashamed of myself.''

He was asked more questions. He gave more answers. We heard about the RITZ studies, the CORRAL study, the SD the SSD.

"Were the SD counts listed in the Order of Battle too low in your estimation, sir?'' asked Mr. Boies.

Colonel Hawkins looked up through tinted glasses. His watery eyes, the way he held his head, his gnomelike demeanor, reminded me of Yoda, from *Star Wars*. He lowered his voice; he slowed down his speech. "The figure was absolutely too low—it was ridiculous.'' He stared at the floor.

Mr. Boies continued: "Let's focus now on a briefing that you mentioned giving to General Westmoreland in May of 1967.''

I looked over at the general, who usually is sitting motionless. That nervous grimace had taken over his countenance. He kept jutting out his chin and clenching his lips. He even raised his hand and wiped it over his face. The act lasted all of fifteen seconds and then he returned to total lack of emotion.

Before Colonel Hawkins could answer, the judge gave instructions: "You may answer the question to the best of your ability and the best of your recollection. Do not stray from the answer. Do not give your opinion or your emotions about the briefing. Just simply state what happened—what you said, what General Westmoreland said.''

"Yes, sir, I will strive to do that,'' answered the colonel.

"I went in to brief General Westmoreland. I believe a young man, Kelly Robinson, was with me at the briefing. I briefed each category of the enemy. The estimates were considerably higher in each category, and when I was finished, the general said—in substance, because I can't recall each word that General Westmoreland said—but he made the statement that these higher figures are politically unacceptable.'' The colonel took a breath, lowered his voice, slowed down his words, and stared straight ahead.'' He said—'What will I tell the President? What will I tell Congress? What if the press finds out?''

"Had you ever heard words of this effect from anyone before? . . .'' Boies couldn't even get the question out: Objections rang out all over the place. All the lawyers ran to the side bar. After several of these episodes, we learned of a similar reaction from General Davidson, MACV's J2.

"Did you, Colonel Hawkins, ever ask anyone to lower his figures?''

The poor man sat frozen in his chair like he was confessing a mortal sin to the world. His hands started to shake. His voice quavered, and his eyes watered. In a hardly audible voice, he answered, "I gave orders to the men—nothing justified this—I knew it at the time." And almost in a whisper: "I ordered them to lower the figures."

The tears had already welled up in my eyes. I was trying desperately to see what I was writing and concentrating on, not letting them fall down my cheeks. In the distance I could hear Boies's voice trying hard to stay unemotional.

"When you gave these orders, were you carrying out the orders of someone else, sir?"

"Yes!" Hawkins almost yelled.

"Whose orders, sir?" Boies pressed him.

"Charlie Morris, who was under General Davidson." And then Hawkins added, "I made changes too, myself—and I ordered others to make changes."

"And when it came time to take these figures to the Langley conference in Virginia?" continued Boies. "What figures did you report?"

"The figures I took to Langley represented *crap*." I squelched a smile.

Mr. Boies tried to continue the line of questioning with, "We've heard this reference to the figures before—in reference to the broadcast and—" The judge interrupted.

"When you say the figures were *crap*, what figures are you referring to?"

They were the arbitrarily cut figures we'd been hearing about for the last few hours. Boies continued, now trying to ascertain whether Hawkins was misquoted on the broadcast. All the allegations that the plaintiff made and Ira Klein's annoyance at Crile's editing—Hawkins's complete sentence had to be rectified.

"I was interviewed by Mr. Crile ten, eleven, twelve times—I was in his apartment in that overstuffed chair with the tufts out, and then he came to my room at the hotel. I had been at CBS about two or two and a half hours and then the CBS staff gave us tickets to a Broadway show. Ironically, the name of the show was *Ain't Misbehaving*." Everyone in the courtroom roared. But Gains Hawkins continued. "I was exhausted, emotionally exhausted, and my wife called up Mr. Crile and told him we couldn't use these tickets—maybe someone else can enjoy the show tonight. Mr. Crile came to our hotel room and I had had a few martinis and I opened up more then, 'cause I was tight. I mean tight—not from the martinis. I opened up more off film than I did on. I thought the film was excellent—I mean the broadcast reflected my views."

Mr. Boies turned to the judge and asked him if this wasn't a good time for a break. The judge gave instructions for an hour lunch, and as we began to file out, counsel asked him to hold his instructions and requested a trip to the side bar.

When they came back to the center of the room, we were given a choice: We could either have lunch and continue to around three-thirty, or we could have a fifteen-minute break, go to the canteen for nourishment, and commence at two. "Acknowledge by a nod," the judge directed, "or you could discuss it among yourselves."

Apparently, we were nodding in unison for a short break because even Westmoreland was laughing.

Everyone was buzzing when we got to the jury room. The feelings for Hawkins seemed unanimous. But yet a heaviness hung in the room.

I think a few of the women have their hearts set on the general. They haven't said one word lately. A couple of the jurors went down to the canteen and brought back sodas and coffees for the others. Eileen and Linda and I dove back into the latest jigsaw puzzle that Kate brought in. This one was a dilly—the solar system. Actually, because of the words and the planets, it was really a matter of following the cover, but it was compelling. We pored over this latest challenge in spite of aching backs. One of the jurors mentioned that the end was drawing near. Thank God—and about time—was echoed all over the room.

One juror stated that he felt a letdown coming on. Every one of us agreed. "It's strange—I want it all to be over with, and yet I don't want it to be. It's become a way of life. If we had summer jobs and met each other then, we would feel a lifetime bond. Yet we've gone double beyond that time. It's been four and a half months," I said. Everyone in the room added to that statement, some saying that they never had worked so closely with a group of people outside of their job. A few people said that they never even worked this closely with a group of people in their job. A couple of sobering voices reminded us that it was not over yet, and the possibility of our not speaking at all after deliberations was very strong. Everyone laughed nervously, and it was time to go back to the courtroom.

We heard more elaboration on the morning's testimony and the facts we've heard before. Hawkins said that there was a command position not to exceed 300,000 when, in effect, there were at least 500,000 enemy.

Objections and side-bar discussions were the norm. He was asked to give reasons for his 300,000 ceiling allegation. He gave a lot of examples. We heard testimony on truth, testimony on state of mind. He told about letters to his wife that verified dates. "I was dealing with highly classified information, so there wasn't much I could write home about. I wrote a lot of letters. She saved every one—she doesn't throw out any paper. So in these letters I'd write, "Hi, I'm here," and I'd tell her where I was and, "I'm thinking about you and 'bye"—so I know I had a meeting with General Westmoreland on May 28, and I got an award that I was proud of on May 29, and I met with him on 14 June 1967 for another briefing, because I checked them in the letters I sent to her. Otherwise that was almost twenty years ago—and I wouldn't remember the dates."

"You've made some serious charges, here, Colonel, about yourself and others—are they all true, sir?" Mr. Boies asked. He continued before the colonel could answer. "Do you feel any ill will toward General Westmoreland?"

"No, sir." Hawkins was most definite with his answer.

"Do you feel any ill will toward the United States Army?" Boies continued in an almost threatening voice.

"No, sir!" Colonel Hawkins's voice rang out in the courtroom. "I carried out these orders as a loyal United States Army officer."

I'd make a horrible attorney—there is no way after this last bout of questioning that I could have maintained my composure. But Boies did, and so did the plaintiff, and so did the judge. We were told there was no more testimony for the day, and then the judge gave us the schedule he'd been promising.

"We will meet tomorrow, Wednesday, February 13, at 10:00 A.M. We will be off Thursday, February 14, and Friday, February 15, and Monday, February 18, is a holiday. We will meet the following Tuesday, Wednesday, Thursday, and Friday, which is February 22.

"Now there is a possibility that we will be finished with the presentation of testimony by Friday the twenty-second. Once the summations begin, I believe, because of the interest this case has stirred, you can expect to be what we call 'sequestered.' Rather than recessing for the weekends, there is a strong possibility that we can meet right through Saturday the twenty-third and Sunday the twenty-fourth, for summations, in which case you will not be allowed to return to your homes, and you will be under the court's directions. You will be sequestered in an unknown hotel. You will not be allowed to view any television or to read any newspapers. You will not be allowed to see your families or to speak to anyone outside of your fellow jurors."

All the while he spoke, I stared straight ahead. I felt like I was being sentenced to prison. I hated the feeling. So did everyone else. We were practically in tears when we were adjourned to the jury room. A few of the jurors mumbled things, and everyone disappeared. Cheryl and I were the last to leave.

"Ask Bob if he feels like joining Bill and me for dinner Monday night. You might as well—you'll be sequestered for who knows how long." Cheryl was trying to sound cheerful. She was an alternate—I knew her letdown was worse than mine. She was Juror 17—the last possible one to replace anyone.

She hugged me before I got on my train.

February 13, 1985

Bob's first appointment was at 11:30 A.M. down on Wall Street, so he invited himself to the trial. "It's almost over. Might as well take in an hour or so of it—anyone interesting on the stand?" he asked. We looked at each other and laughed.

I bought breakfast. I left him in the downstairs foyer of the courthouse. He went up the elevators for the privileged. I went up the back stairs.

I had to laugh at his reaction in the subway. I complain each day, but he tosses it off like I'm making up the scene. He literally shoved me onto the third train. We sat in the jury room for one full hour before they called us into court (of all days!).

Colonel Hawkins was on the stand when we took our seats in the jury stand. His cross-examination was executed by Dorsen. He began in his usual way. Jumps right in: "Colonel Hawkins, you gave some letters that you had sent to your wife in 1967 to Sam Adams after the broadcast, did you not?"

I looked at the spectators who were standing in the aisles. I found Bob—he had a good seat. He flashed a big grin.

"Didn't you say you were ninety-nine percent sure that you hadn't sent the letters until after the broadcast? Here in your deposition, on page . . ."

Boies got up and asked if the statement couldn't be read aloud. Dorsen obliged. I couldn't believe what I heard.

After the entire statement was read, it was clear that Hawkins had sent the letters to Sam Adams long before the broadcast. Hawkins then said, "I would have almost sworn . . . I was ninety-nine percent sure the letters arrived after."

A few other such words were taken out of context on things and then Dorsen made the statement: "It's true, is it not, that you believed that General McChristian was an ambitious and relentless man?"

Hawkins answered that he didn't remember ever telling anyone that. If he did, he would probably like to modify that statement—it was true in a certain context: "The man *was* quick to give credit where credit was due. If you have something to that effect that I said, then I'd like to see it," said Colonel Hawkins. Dorsen quickly produced exhibit 1839.

Hawkins looked at it and looked up at Dorsen and in a dramatic way said, "Mr. Dorsen, this is the first draft, and a very rough copy, of a diary of sorts of my experiences in Vietnam. I wrote for about a month or so after I was retired and home with nothing to do. I abandoned this because of the lack of papers and statistics that I needed. These were thoughts that I never did anything with."

"Is it not true that you said McChristian was ambitious and relentless?" pressed Dorsen.

"You've taken this completely out of context, Mr. Dorsen. I'd like to be able to read the entire paragraph if I may?" Hawkins asked, almost pleadingly. He was granted permission.

I can't remember the entire passage verbatim, but the general substance of the paragraph went as follows: "General McChristian was a man who never stopped working. He was relentless—he had high expectations of his men. He was cold, he was merciless with himself. He was ambitious—he worked night and day. He had no patience with inferiority in anyone under him—or in himself. I wasn't too fond of the man."

Hawkins looked up at the courtroom at Dorsen and wistfully said, "Now, I think General McChristian would have been proud of that passage!"

The laugh monitor in the courtroom registered a 10. Even Westmoreland was shaking. When people in the courtroom finally composed themselves, Dorsen continued his questioning.

"Did you read any cables that are being used as exhibits in this trial, Colonel Hawkins?"

"Yes, sir, I did," the colonel answered.

"Did you read any depositions?" asked Dorsen.

Hawkins looked up in a pixieish way, like a child accused of doing something wrong, and answered: "Mr. Dorsen, I've read cables, I've read depositions, I've read transcripts of the trial; is this evil, sir?"

Dorsen simply stated, "I'm just asking questions, sir."

Dorsen kept asking them—most seemed to me to be grasping at straws. Most appeared to be literally taking things totally out of context, and when they weren't, as in Hawkins's diary, Hawkins wasn't the least bit tarnished by the statement.

It was a long morning, but boredom didn't plague me. There was a lively soul on the stand, in spite of outward appearances. Hawkins was a package of honest Mississippi sincerity (country boy, as he put it), and mischief. He wasn't nearly as naïvely vulnerable as he, at first glance, appeared.

When Hawkins was quizzed on documents he had intercepted—captured from the POWs—he went into an emotional monologue. It was clear from his testimony that though these things happened seventeen years ago, there was still empathy. He talked about the communists with a tinge of admiration, and I pray this last statement never gets repeated out of context—after witnessing a trial, I realize how easily this can be done. I had never in a million years gathered that Hawkins admired the Vietcong. But he had expressed a professional admiration for their record-keeping.

We've heard this type of testimony from others: They kept records; they documented all their moves; when POWs were captured, there were always papers on them—giving accurate accounts of who they were, where they were from, and what missions they were on. Aside from these official documents, we've heard more than once that the Vietcong often carried personal diaries—speaking of their wives, children, thoughts, and so forth.

Hawkins talked at length of how, as an analyst, receiving a voluminous amount of papers to analyze, he detected patterns and discrepancies. When Dorsen challenged the discrepancies, asking, "So, is it true, Colonel Hawkins, that the Vietcong lied a lot?" Hawkins answered with considerable animation: "No, not necessarily. Yes, some papers lied, but most didn't. They were just like Republicans and Democrats. Some like to lie—some don't like to lie. The communists were just like other people—most documents were authentic."

As the questioning went on—and as the objections followed and the trips to the side bar went on—I had a lot of time to think. We are only interested in the Order of Battle—the MACV Order of Battle. All acronyms. The real thing we are interested in is General Westmoreland, who was in command of the Vietnam station's Order of Battle on the enemy. It all sounds so therapeutic. Talk about initials and numbers and statistics and formulas, and one can very easily discuss the whole thing in quite intellectual terms—analyze statistics.

No wonder the military and the CIA and all these other divisions like mathematics. Mathematicians speak only in numerical terms. One hundred thirty-nine thousand SD in reality represents 139,000 people—so distraught over their position that they will pick up guns, grenades, spend hours rigging booby traps to kill an enemy, an evil force.

It's me they were after—I'm an American—I know few people who
actually were there. I wasn't aware of anyone in 1968—except perhaps a friend of a friend's oldest son was there, or a headline in the
newspaper that I just gave passing service to. I tried to picture how
many rooms 139,000 people would fill. The town I live in has a population of maybe 15,000. As suddenly as the train of thought hit me, I
blanked it out. I didn't think about it then—why am I plaguing myself
with it now? I am not to consider the Vietnam War—that is not on
trial here. *The Uncounted Enemy* is—and all I'm concerned about is
the context of the transcripts.

We were given a lunch break.

I didn't want to leave the jury room. I buried myself in a book.
Randy and Rich went down to the canteen and brought us back coffee.
The jurors filed in and out—some went to lunch, some just walked up
and down the stairs, a few of us stayed in.

In between, I studied faces—the faces of my colleagues, looking for
hints. How did they feel? What was going to happen in the next week?
I had a hard time separating the alternates from the jury. We spend all
this time together. I really have never differentiated who would be here
for the final decision and who wouldn't be.

I tried to start analyzing everyone's behavior in these terms. A couple of the alternates had been quite verbal. Was it because they felt
they wanted their feelings known? Most of them hadn't said a word,
almost acting like they were not a part of the decision. I was beginning
to get a better insight of my potential roommates.

Pat, the court clerk, came in to tell us we'd be a while longer.
Everyone jumped on him—Where will we be staying? How long? Will
you be there? Can we pick our own roommate? Will we have a roommate? Any imaginable question was asked—ones I hadn't even
thought of. All the statements were said in a jestful manner. I realized
during the questioning that the manner in which they were asked was a
coverup.

Everyone was scared.

When we got back from lunch, we had a new witness. Colonel
Hawkins will be back. This is simply a convenience matter. This witness was scheduled. We had Norman R. House.

God, how much longer can I stand this? There's nothing else to be
said. House was giving his background. He was in real estate presently, out in Arizona—he had worked in intelligence for nearly twenty
years.

Suddenly, I thought—why am I bothering writing all this stuff
down? It's unimportant. Who cares where you work, where you

worked—all we care about here is having a witness take the stand and under oath say, Yes, Westmoreland covered up numbers, no, he didn't cover up numbers.

House said Westmoreland ordered that the total numbers not be reported—in so many words. House considered General Graham completely unethical, unprofessional, and an individual he was ashamed to say the military system would believe had officer attributes. "He disregarded intelligence that had sound evidence to back it up. His actions were inexcusable. I have no respect for him to this day," House added.

Then we heard how he was transferred out of the elite division of CIIED to CICV, an organization looked upon as dealing with inferior matters.

Here we go again, I thought. Good old Westmoreland's open-door policy at work again. Sure, the door is always open—out. You can always be replaced if you complain. The list was adding up. Parkins, McArthur, House, McChristian—men with strong moral convictions got the shaft. Sam Adams was labeled a mental case. God, spare me— how much longer?

I stared at Westmoreland. He still sat like the proud general. His lawyers looked like they were attending a funeral. I wished I had a camera—the facial studies were wonderful.

Dorsen had his head in his hand in the foreground. Burt was next to him, sitting back in his chair, hands folded in his lap—for once, he looked somber. He was staring down at his notes. Murry was staring into space with a glazed look, and Westmoreland, just behind him, with his chin jutting out, looked like a proud martyr. It was a very telling study.

Finally, we were dismissed for the day. Before the judge let us leave the courtroom, we were given a lecture—a long one. He said that all indications are that the evidence the defense has to offer will be completed by Friday the twenty-second. Then summations will begin. Due to the nature of this trial and the public interest that it has received, he warned us at length about reading the newspaper or watching TV. He practically asked us not to watch TV—at least not the news or anything that might influence us. Also, because of the nature of this trial, he continued, the possibility of our being sequestered during summations was very strong. That would include the alternates. He told us that while being sequestered, we would be housed in an unknown hotel with no access to anyone but the court marshals. We would not be allowed to watch TV or to read any newspapers.

As he continued speaking, my heart sank lower and lower. He was talking about the end! Shortly, this would be all over. This whole other life that was thrust upon me—at first rather unwillingly, but as the months progressed, this was my new family. My new job. The surroundings had become old friends.

As he spoke about the magnitude of our duty being a juror, I felt the weight of the world pressing down on my shoulders. As he spoke about being sequestered, I felt like a prisoner being sentenced. I felt perhaps like the soldier who had been given months of desk training and now was told that next week he would be handed his weapon and would go off to combat. I felt like I was going to cry. But I didn't, and we filed out of the courtroom.

The moment we got into the jury room, all hell broke loose. Everyone spoke at once—everyone had a comment to add. The alternates were in a state of shock. One by one, everyone left. Cheryl and I locked the door after us, and we quietly walked down the back stairs. Have a nice weekend—thanks, you too—and we got on our separate trains.

February 14, 1985

Valentine's Day. I was back in school. The reactions from the kids were varied: Hi! Are you back for good? Are you finished? So you're finally back! I only got two Valentine's cards. Mrs. Jensen, who was out sick, had a box of them waiting for her return.

I had a good session with my reading group. We mostly talked. I told them about a book I read. They told me about theirs. I had made it mandatory that in addition to their regular reading lesson, they had to be reading a book of their choice for their pleasure. The two children who had finished their books were excited about them.

"Was there a main idea, Brian, in your book? What was the book really about? Did it tell a story? Was it exciting? Did you learn anything from the book? I wanted him to *think*.

Brian gave us a synopsis on the story and talked about the main characters, who were three foster children being taken care of by two old sisters who became ill, so the children had to go back to either their old homes or another foster home. One was a Vietnamese girl who acted bossy and angry a lot but whose feelings were hurt deeply when she overheard the other two talking about her and the fact that they didn't like her.

We talked a lot about feelings, and then I asked them if they knew of anyone that was ever a foster child. None of them had. I explained what a foster child was and told them that my parents had taken in two foster children when I was growing up. I told them that Frankie lived with us for seven years and had been reunited with his real family—that I haven't seen him since. And I told them Maryann was still my sister. They couldn't stop asking questions—we were already ten minutes into their lunch period. Finally, I walked down to the lunch room with them, still trying to answer their curiosity.

February 15, 1985

I only taught for a half day. I had an appointment with the insurance agent to investigate the damage from our radio robbery. I can hardly get in the driver's seat—the lock is jammed, not to mention I have no radio. The heat is jerry-rigged so the temperature is at least above freezing. I love this car so much—a Saab turbo. It's better than any advertisement. I love the drive, the feel of the wheel, the comfort of the seats, the heating system—especially the seats that warm up in cold weather—and the sound system—when I have it. Goddamn thieves. I'm not alone, I guess. Two friends also had radios stolen—one in Queens, one on West End Avenue. But mine was in a garage—goddamnit!!

I kept thinking about the two sixth-grade girls who came into my classroom this morning. They said they were from the *Increase Miller News,* our school newspaper, and they wanted to interview me about my experience as a juror on the Westmoreland/CBS case. I apologized to them and said, "I'm not allowed to speak to anyone from the press. I will be glad to give you an interview when this is all over."

They thanked me and apologized, said they hadn't realized that, and promised me they would come back after the trial was over.

February 17, 1985

I was working in my studio. I was upset at the fact school was on vacation this coming week and I was still dealing with this trial. Suddenly, Bob yelled from the living room. It was so uncharacteristic—I went running in to see what happened. "Westmoreland has dropped his libel suit against CBS—they just announced it on NBC."

Cheryl called. "Did you hear the news? CBS is dropping the lawsuit—I just heard it on ABC."

My father-in-law called.

The feelings I felt were ambivalent—nothing had sunk in yet.

The reports were teasers—a full statement was to be given jointly on TV tomorrow morning. Tomorrow morning took a long time to come.

February 18, 1985

Tomorrow came, and yesterday seemed like a long time ago, and we were dealing with today. The news came on TV. The newspaper had unmistakable headlines—WESTMORELAND CALLS HALT. We had to take Leslie back up to college. We talked, we speculated a little, but mostly it was quiet—no radio, no tape deck.

It was a gorgeous day for a country ride. I had taken the camera— got a few good shots. We stopped at a couple of antique stores on the way home. It was fun. There were a few messages on the answering machine when I came home. A reporter from *Newsday* and one from the *New York Post*. "What are you going to tell them?" Bob asked.

"Nothing. I'm not calling them back. Officially, I haven't been released from jury duty," I answered.

A few minutes later, the judge's secretary called with that same order. "You are to report as expected at ten. Speak to no reporters."

The TV was filled with Westmoreland. We saw George Crile and Mike Wallace playing tennis. They gave a few words of relief. We saw David Boies, all smiles in front of twenty microphones.

"When a plaintiff in a libel suit for 120 million dollars wants to drop his charges and forget the whole thing, I think"—and he paused—"we should let him."

Dan Rather talked about it. Peter Jennings talked about it. Michelle Marsh, Ernie Anastos—even Ted Koppel had a special on *Nightline*. His guest was General William Westmoreland. It was pathetic: Westmoreland was claiming a victory. "I got what I wanted—a statement saying that I was patriotic, that I dealt with my job the way I saw it . . ." He referred back to the statement several times. I found it difficult to watch.

Everyone asked why. Everyone speculated. I got ready for bed.

I woke up at four, tossed and turned for an hour or so, and finally got up to write in my diary. Here I am. The words that we heard over and over again during the trial attributed to General Westmoreland— "what am I going to tell the press?"—were now foremost in my mind.

How do I say thank God it's over? How do I say I'm angry? Yesterday, my opinion was the most important thing to all these people, and now they don't want it. How do I say I'm scared of Danny Graham, and how does such muddled thinking as we've witnessed get to such a high level of government? Do I say anything?

February 19, 1985

My father-in-law was very concerned. "You are going to be inundated with reporters. There is going to be bedlam down there. You'd better let Robert go with you. Robert, you go with her—she's going to be besieged by people." My white knight agreed.

I laughed to myself, knowing that Bob was dying to go to the courtoom today—to witness what turned out to be the most exciting day for me.

Before we could get up the steps of the courthouse, reporters were all over us. Cheryl had joined us for breakfast, so the three of us fought our way up the steps, promising the reporters that as soon as we were released from the courtroom, we would talk to them. I had to hand in my parking vouchers, so I headed down to the jury room, where our records are kept.

As I waited for Bob to make it through the detectors, George Crile appeared. This time we grinned openly at each other. He came right over and grabbed my hand. It was a strange feeling—we chatted like old friends. His wife joined him; we were introduced. He knew my name, of course—why shouldn't he? I introduced Bob. When I got upstairs, I bumped into Sam Adams. I told him how much I admired what he'd done—followed his convictions. I told him we both were born in Bridgeport, Connecticut. He introduced me to his wife, Ann, whom I had seen in the courtroom most every day. She was lovely. We chatted.

Finally, I was in the jury room. I got a shopping bag to gather the accumulated notes and puzzles. All the jurors wrote down their phone numbers and addresses. Michael refused to give his out.

We were called into the courtroom. Mr. Burt made a statement. They handed a statement on paper to the judge. The judge read it, accepted it, then he made a statement.

It was long and moving. I had wondered how he would tell us—the jury—that after four and a half months of sitting in this courtroom, being forced through this form of Chinese torture, our services would no longer be needed.

I wish I could remember the judge's speech word for word. It was excellent. In substance, he said that this trial was not for naught. We'd all learned a lot. We had given both sides a chance to air their views, and it was most important that a jury such as ours was there for them to present their case to. He complimented us on our interest and diligence, noting that we were always alert, taking notes, and took our jobs seriously, and he thanked us. He told us that though this move is unprecedented, he would allow us back into the courtroom if we wished after he visited us in the jury room.

We filed out.

The judge came into our shabby little chamber in his flowing robes. He shook Richard's hand, thanked him for serving on jury duty. Formally, he shook Randy's hand, thanked him. As he approached me, I thought, the hell with this hand-shaking. "Judge, you were great—we all just loved you." I hugged him.

"My God, I never expected this," he said. His face turned beet-red.

Cheryl hugged him, Carmen hugged him, Myron shook his hand, Norma kissed him. It was kind of emotional—all the jurors were liberal with their thanks and praises for keeping the entire tone of the case one of an honest gentleman's debate.

Finally, we were released. If you wish, the reporters are waiting. We looked at each other—tittered nervously.

"Well! Here goes." Cheryl led the pack.

It was like a cocktail party—no food or drink was necessary. Reporters clustered around each of us.

"Who were you voting for?" "How did you feel?" "Do you think the case should have been brought to trial?"

I didn't know which question to answer first, but once I began, I didn't stop. About five months of silence pent up inside of me was unleashed. What did I tell them? The truth, as I saw it—no sidestepping main issues, no veiled comments. I told them I thought the documentary was honest and accurate. I told them I thought both sides had acted questionably at one point or another, but that on CBS's side it was mainly in judgments of how to put the presentation together.

I moved away from that group. A couple of the attorneys came up, shook my hand. I saw Bob talking to Colonel Hawkins. Mike Wallace came over and shook my hand.

"I could never read you," he said. "You had this anguished look on your face in the beginning, but then I couldn't read you." I laughed and said, "I practiced those blank expressions." (That statement made the newspapers.) He said he watched us so closely he could tell if we gained or lost weight.

General Westmoreland came over. Shook my hand and started talking about Marion, the only juror who left, saying, "It wasn't even her fault—her mother got ill." He said he liked her. "She was an intelligent woman."

I said, "Your house must be filled with needlepoint—Mrs. Westmoreland kept very busy." He enthusiastically said, "She lost one, you know. We came back here into the courthouse looking for it and couldn't find it anywhere. But I think we must have left it in a taxi-cab," he added.

"Oh no, General," I said jokingly. "I'm certain there was foul play involved. You're going to see it at auction next week at Southeby's—it'll bring in a fortune." He got a big kick out of that. Mrs. West-moreland came over and put her arm around me and started talking about her garden at home, which she can't wait to get back to.

Bob came over—I introduced him—and another group of reporters gathered around me. Now I was playing this for all it was worth. I was having a ball! I told Mr. Boies we were concerned about his wardrobe and had planned on taking up a collection for a new suit. I told him how impressed we were with his presentation.

Finally, Bob was tugging away at me—let's go to lunch. It took us another half hour to get out of the courtroom. On the way out, I told Mr. Burt he should learn not to point.

George Crile hugged me. We made our way past more reporters. A cable news team lined us up for a live interview at four o'clock on cable TV this afternoon. Finally, we sneaked out the back door. I could have gone on with this the rest of the afternoon, but Bob had to get to the office—and besides, the words of Eric Hoffer rang in my ears. Upon his retirement, he said: "Anyone can ride a train—only a wise man knows when to get off."

As we headed down the courtroom steps, another shock was in store. There was a sea of reporters, cameras, microphones—the steps were cleared down the center, and they were beckoning all of us to come straight down.

Suddenly, I felt my knees turn to rubber. I felt like I did that first day in court when my name was called and I had to walk up to the jury box in front of all the world. Actually, it felt like that had just been practice. Cameras were on me now. Microphones were in front of my mouth—a hundred questions were being asked at once.

Cheryl was already talking, and she had a lengthy statement. Then the sea of faces turned to me—"And what did you think?"

What did I think? Uhh—my mind went blank.

"Actually," I started, surprising myself at the calmness in my voice, "Cheryl has pretty much summed up my views."

"We want to hear it in your own words—who were you for?" one reporter yelled.

"The evidence in favor of CBS was overwhelming," I began. I needn't have gone any further. That cut was shown on every news channel that night. Cable TV called and cancelled our appearance. But I saw myself on Channel 2 and Channel 4. Channel 7 had Bob and

Cheryl and me walking down the steps. There were cuts to the other jurors. Michael said he wished General Westmoreland could have been his general—he liked him.

Richard was saying how exciting it was to see all those secret documents and all those famous people. Randy said something good about Sam Adams.

Then I saw myself answering a question on Channel 2—"How did it feel to not go into deliberations, to be denied the chance to give your verdict?"

Very matter-of-factly, I said, "How would you feel if you took a course for six months, studied hard, and before the final exam you were told they dropped the course?"

I hadn't even remembered saying that. In fact, I couldn't remember most of what I had said—I was still flying high.

Channel 11 said stand by at 11:00 P.M. Two jurors from the Westmoreland trial were going to speak live on the news program. At 11:00 P.M., we were tuned in. There were Richard and Randy. They asked Randy, "How did it feel to not be able to go into deliberation, be denied the opportunity to make your own judgment?" Randy answered, "How does it feel to take a course for eighteen weeks and then be told they'd dropped the course?" Bob screamed, "He stole your line—he stole your line." (I'm told imitation is the highest form of flattery.)

As soon as the news was over we were in bed. The mantel clock struck once, for eleven-thirty. It struck twelve times for midnight. My body was so wired I couldn't even relax, let alone fall asleep. I tried every trick I'd ever heard—count sheep, relax your body, picture a beautiful setting and float in it. All my mind could do was think about tomorrow.

Bob woke up. We started to rehash the day we had just completed. He told me that he had a lengthy chat with the general. Westmoreland went over the entire case with him—how it began, how he had felt. Bob had enjoyed the opportunity to talk with Colonel Hawkins—he was impressed with him as a person.

I started to tell him about a discussion I had with one of the attorneys, but before I finished, I realized he was sound asleep. I was more awake than ever.

I got up and made some tea—my grandmother's cure concoction. I didn't feel a cold coming on, but I thought it may relax me. I went back to bed.

It was over.